The Frontiers
and Catholic
Identities

American Catholic Identities
A Documentary History
Christopher J. Kauffman, General Editor

American Catholic Identities is a nine-volume series that makes available to the general reader, the student, and the scholar seminal documents in the history of American Catholicism. Subjects are wide-ranging and topically ordered within periods to encounter the richly textured experiences of American Catholics from the earliest years to the present day. The twenty-six editors of these volumes reveal a command of trends in historiography since the publication of John Tracy Ellis's three-volume work, *Documents of American Catholic History.* Hence the American Catholic Identities series shows developments in our understanding of social history — the significance of gender, race, regionalism, ethnicity, and spirituality, as well as Catholic thought and practice before and since the Second Vatican Council.

The series elucidates myriad meanings of the American Catholic experience by working with the marker of religious identity. It brings into relief the historical formations of religious self-understandings of a wide variety of Catholics in a society characterized by the principles of religious liberty, separation of church and state, religious pluralism, and voluntarism.

American Catholic Identities is united by such dominant factors in American history as waves of immigration, nativism, anti-Catholicism, racism, sexism, and several other social and ideological trends. Other aspects of unity are derived from American Catholic history: styles of episcopal leadership, multiple and various types of Catholic institutions, and the dynamic intellectual interaction between the United States and various national centers of Catholic thought. Woven into the themes of this documentary history are the protean meanings of what constitutes being American and Catholic in relation to the formations of religious identities.

Titles of books in the series are:

Public Voices: Catholics in the American Context, Steven M. Avella and Elizabeth McKeown

The Frontiers and Catholic Identities, Anne M. Butler, Michael E. Engh, S.J., and Thomas W. Spalding, C.F.X.

Creative Fidelity: U.S. Catholic Intellectual Identities, Scott Appleby, Patricia Byrne, C.S.J., and William Portier

Keeping Faith: European and Asian Immigrants, Jeffrey Burns, Ellen Skerrett, and Joseph White

Prayer and Practice in the American Catholic Community, Joseph P. Chinnici, O.F.M., and Angelyn Dries, O.S.F.

Gender Identities in American Catholicism, Paula Kane, James Kenneally, and Karen Kennelly, C.S.J.

"Stamped with the Image of God": African-Americans as God's Image in Black, Cyprian Davis, O.S.B., and Jamie Phelps, O.P.

¡Presente! Latino Catholics from Colonial Origins to the Present, Timothy Matovina and Gerald E. Poyo, in collaboration with Jaime Vidal, Cecilia González, and Steven Rodríguez

The Crossing of Two Roads: Being Catholic and Native in the United States, Marie Therese Archambault, O.S.F., Mark Thiel, and Christopher Vecsey

A workshop for the editors of these books was entirely funded by a generous grant from the Louisville Institute.

American Catholic Identities
A Documentary History
Christopher J. Kauffman, General Editor

The Frontiers and Catholic Identities

Anne M. Butler

Michael E. Engh, S.J.

Thomas W. Spalding, C.F.X.

Editors

ORBIS BOOKS

Maryknoll, New York 10545

The Catholic Foreign Mission Society of America (Maryknoll) recruits and trains people for overseas missionary service. Through Orbis Books, Maryknoll aims to foster the international dialogue that is essential to mission. The books published, however, reflect the opinions of their authors and are not meant to represent the official position of the society. To obtain more information about Maryknoll and Orbis Books, visit our website at www.maryknoll.org.

Library of Congress Cataloging-in-Publication Data

The frontiers and Catholic identities / Anne M. Butler, Michael E.
    Engh, Thomas W. Spalding, editors.
        p.   cm. – (American Catholic identities)
    Includes bibliographical references.
    ISBN 1-57075-270-2 (hardcover). – ISBN 1-57075-269-9 (pbk.)
    1. Catholics – United States – History Sources.   2. Pioneers –
Religious life – United States – History Sources.   I. Butler, Anne
M., 1938–   . II. Engh, Michael E., 1949–   .   III. Spalding,
Thomas W.   IV. Series.
BX1406.2F76   1999
282'.73 – dc21   99-41112

For Our Spiritual and Scholarly Mentors

Brother Jordan Buckley, C.F.X.
Ruth Atkins Christmas
— A. M. B.

Edmund F. Airey Sr.
Martin Ridge
— M. E. E., S.J.

John Tracy Ellis
Brother Placidus Evans, C.F.X.
— T. W. S., C.F.X.

CONTENTS

Part 1
THE BACKWOODS FRONTIER

Part 2
THE FUR-GATHERING
FRONTIER

Part 3
SACRED CONTESTS
IN THE WEST

THROUGH A CATHOLIC LENS
A Photo Essay Depicting Catholic Frontiers
by Anne M. Butler
95

Part 4
MIGRANT LIVES TO SETTLEMENT

Part 5
THE PACIFIC SLOPE—
"WHEN OTHERS RUSHED IN"

Part 6
THE SOUTHWEST

FOREWORD

Christopher J. Kauffman

In his splendid introduction to this documentary history of Catholic experiences on the frontiers, Michael E. Engh, S.J., explores the complexity of the religious-identity formations in the myriad boundary situations in the diverse regional developments in American life from the 1780s to the 1970s. Recent trends in the historiography of the West have sharpened our perspectives on the role of religion, including Catholicity, in regional studies. This wide-ranging collection of documents may be viewed as breaking through the frontiers of historiography to establish a sophisticated understanding of the sense of Catholic peoplehood within the shifting social and religious topography of American life. Hence, this volume reveals the role of the frontiers in the making of American Catholicity as well as the significance of the Catholic imprint upon the American frontiers. The Anglo/European encounters with nations of Native Americans, the competition as well as cooperation with Protestants of various traditions, and the dynamic interaction with French, Spanish, and Mexican people greatly contributed to the complex self-understandings of Catholics in settlements and towns from early nineteenth-century Kentucky to late twentieth-century Alaska. Within the cauldron of conflict and controversy, some religious identities were formed while others, at times, were distorted.

Frontier experiences were so dependent upon the various mix of peoples that Catholics were both insiders and outsiders — for example, in San Antonio in the 1850s, when Latinos, once insiders, were relegated to the margins of society while European ethnic Catholic settlers became insiders, a situation replicated in other towns in the Southwest.

Academies and hospitals, whose indentities were principally shaped by women religious, had a taming effect upon religious hostility and were significant contributions to the sacralization of the frontierscape. Nevertheless, churches, schools, and health-care facilities had a pioneer character, having taken root in regional soils distinct from the urban pavements of the Northeast, where refined Catholic institutions served the millions of immigrants who had settled in that area from 1840 to 1920. The quantitative growth of Catholics immersed in well-defined subcultures in the great archdioceses of the Northeast and Midwest engendered a qualitative difference from Catholic life on the frontiers, even in those areas previously settled by Latino and French Catholics.

Several documents in this volume testify to Catholics' consciousness of their minority status on the frontier, as if Catholic life on the periphery were in stark contrast to the strong character of immigrant Catholic life in the urban core in nineteenth-century Boston, New York, Philadelphia, St. Louis, and Chicago. The core-periphery dichotomy is my conceptual framework for clarifying the distinctive religious cultures. Baltimore's Archbishop John Carroll adapted Catholicity to American life and was open to the benefits of religious liberty, separation of church and state, and pluralism. Though there were some enclaves of Catholic separation in towns in the West, the laity, women and men religious, priests, and bishops on the several frontiers tended to extol the positive character of the processes of adaptation, acculturation, assimilation, and interfaith cooperation (also fostered by Carroll) within the cultural pluralism on the American frontiers. In contrast to the emphasis upon authority, tradition, and religious separation in the urban core areas, with their well-developed ethnic and devotional subcultures, the Catholic community of John Carroll and the frontier missions, parishes, and dioceses were on the periphery, where there was relatively expansive interaction with the larger cultures. The pilgrim experience of movement, the settlements, and the missions represent boundary situations that are laden with religious meanings: people tended to reflect on the importance of ultimate values as they experienced the refounding of religious traditions on shifting culture landscapes in the United States.

The editors' decision to publish documents related to particular identities explored in other volumes in this series — those on Latinos and Native Americans — was fruitful and necessary because those identities were in part framed by frontier themes. These documents also represent a vital sense of collaboration so significant to a community of scholars engaged in a common enterprise, a well-textured documentary history of Catholicity in the United States. Collaboration was also facilitated by the overabundance of documents for each of these volumes. The topical framework within chronological periods generates the principles of selection of the documents of each book and conveys an originality free from redundancy.

Anne M. Butler, Michael E. Engh, S.J., and Thomas W. Spalding, C.F.X., are historians identified with scholarly explorations of the various and vital spheres of frontier life. Butler's two books on women in the justice system in the West and her other publications are significant contributions so congenial with her editorship of the *Western Historical Quarterly.* Engh's *Frontier Faiths,* with its focus on religions and cultures in Los Angeles during the second half of the nineteenth century, establishes him as a prominent scholar of the region. Spalding's biography of Martin John Spalding, his history of the Archdiocese of Baltimore, and his publications on the Maryland Catholic diaspora and on the theoretical framework of frontier Catholicism mark him as a seasoned scholar of regionalism. Spalding's afterword clearly illustrates his familiarity with rural and small-town Catholicism. Each of these historians has selected documents and composed introductions with a sophisticated grasp of pertinent theoretical structures, and their work has been buttressed by their commitments to render Catholic life on several frontiers accessible to general readers, students, and scholars alike.

ACKNOWLEDGMENTS

One begins a project with the mistaken impression that it will be easy. Its dependence on the expertise of others is soon apparent. Although all intellectual responsibility remains mine, my academic debts are grand and cannot be adequately repaid to the many who aided me. At my own institution, Utah State University, I thank Carolyn Doyle, who coordinated and prepared this manuscript for its three editors. Without her knowledge, cheerfulness, and confidence there would be no finished volume. I also thank two extraordinary graduate students. They brought enthusiasm, dedication, intelligence, and joy to this project. My experience would have been woefully the less without them. My deepest thanks go to Mary Gilbert Palmer for her engaged approach, spirited persistence, and constant good humor. To Heather Block, who sustained me while contributing insight, industry, balance, and a love of Catholic history, I extend that appreciation and affection that can only exist between adviser and student. We three depended on the generosity of archivists, curators, religious, and laypersons around the nation. We offer thanks to those with whom we corresponded and conversed. They include, along with their many helpful assistants, but are not limited to the following:

Archdiocese of Chicago, John J. Treanor; Archdiocese of Denver, Michael Scott Woodward; Archdiocese of Dubuque, Rev. Loras C. Otting; Archdiocese of Kansas City, Sister Ann Albrecht, C.S.J.; Archdiocese of Milwaukee, Timothy D. Cary; Archdiocese of Omaha, Rev. Michael F. Gutgsell; Archdiocese of St. Louis, Office of Catholic Deaf Ministry, Ann Pudlowski; Archdiocese of St. Paul and Minneapolis, Steven T. Granger; Archdiocese of Seattle, J. Norman Dizon; Baker City, Oregon, Public Library, Gary Dealman; Catholic Archives of Texas, Susan Eason; Catholic Church Extension Society, Brad Collins; Catholic University of America, Mary Beth Fraser; Creighton University, Marjorie B. Wannarka; Denver Public Library, Eleanor M. Gehres; Diocese of Bismarck, Kenneth Small; Diocese of Corpus Christi, Office for Persons with Disabilities, David Walsh, C.S.S.R.; Diocese of Fargo, Sister Mary James Merrick, O.S.F., and Lisa Thompson; Diocese of Lincoln, Sister Loretta Gosen, C.PP.S.; Diocese of Salt Lake City, Bernice M. Mooney; Diocese of Tulsa, Mary Jones; Gonzaga University of Spokane, David Kingma; Interpretive Center for the Oregon Trail, Virginia Bloom; Jesuit Provincial Office, Portland, Wilfred Schoenberg, S.J.; Loyola University of Chicago, Brother Michael Grace, S.J.; Marquette University, Mark Thiel; Morristown, Indiana,

Norman and Wilma Taylor; Nebo, Illinois, Rose F. Flock; Nevada State Historic Preservation Office, Ronald M. James; Redemptorist Fathers, Denver, Lisa Gibbons; St. Benedict's Center, Middleton, Wisconsin, Nancy Sandleback; University of Wisconsin, Milwaukee, Archives and Special Collections, Timothy L. Ericson; University of Missouri–Columbia, Western Historical Manuscript Collection, Sharon E. Brock; Utah State University, Special Collections and Archives, Peter Schmidt. Eleventh-hour thanks for help with details or photographs are due to Oblate Sisters of Providence, Baltimore, Sister M. Reparata, O.S.P; Sisters of the Blessed Sacrament, Bensalem, Pennsylvania, Sister Maria E. McCall, S.B.S.; Sisters of Mary of the Presentation, Valley City, North Dakota, Sister Marlyss Dionne, S.M.P.; Society of the Sacred Heart, St. Louis, Sister Margaret Phelan, R.S.C.J.; and the Franciscan Friars — St. John the Baptist Province, Cincinnati, Brother Don Rewers, O.F.M., and Our Lady of Guadalupe Province, Los Lunas, New Mexico, Brother Gerald Grantner, O.F.M.

As always, I thank my family, especially Jay, who supported this project from start to finish.

ANNE M. BUTLER

•

It was a privilege for me to team-teach with Dr. Timothy Matovina in a seminar, "American Catholic Identities," in spring 1998 at Loyola Marymount University. Students in that course who assisted with the research and preparation of documents for this volume include Laura Costello, Brandon Miles, Claudia Mineo, Gailyn Munford, Christopher Polityka, Michael Schodorf, and Clint Tanner. Also providing invaluable aid at Loyola Marymount University were my research assistants, Denis Delja and Brandon Miles, as well as Steve Thacker at the Charles Von der Ahe Library and José Ignacio Badenes, S.J., in the Modern Languages Department.

Individuals at archives and libraries who were unfailingly helpful include Charlene Alipio, Archives, Diocese of Honolulu; Virgilio Baisiol, O.F.M., Santa Barbara Mission Archive-Library, Santa Barbara, California; Jeffrey Burns, Archives, Archdiocese of San Francisco; Rose Byrne, Arizona Historical Society Library, Tucson; Kevin Feeney, Archives, Archdiocese of Los Angeles; Angelo Mercado, University of California–Los Angeles; Kate McGinn, Huntington Library, San Marino, California; Gerald McKevitt, S.J., Santa Clara University, Santa Clara, California; Anne McMahon, Archives, Santa Clara University, Santa Clara, California; Louis L. Renner, S.J., Archives, Diocese of Fairbanks; Martin Ridge, Huntington Library, San Marino, California; Julianne Ruby, Ursuline Center, Great Falls, Montana; Mary Ellen Sproufske, C.S.J., Archives, Sisters of St. Joseph of Carondelet, Los Angeles; Dace Taub, Regional History Center, University of Southern California, Los Angeles; Mary William Vinet, D.C., Archives, Seton Provincialate,

Los Altos Hills, California; Francis J. Weber, Archives, Archdiocese of Los Angeles; and Catherine Wong, Chancellor's Office, Diocese of Honolulu; as well as the staffs at the Bishop Museum Archives and Library, Honolulu; the Hawaiiana Room, Livingston Library, University of Hawaii, Manoa; and the Seaver Center for Western History, Los Angeles County Museum of Natural History, Los Angeles.

I also wish to acknowledge the financial assistance from the estate of Gilbert E. Shirack, received courtesy of Mrs. John Owens of Los Angeles.

MICHAEL E. ENGH, S.J.

•

This project took me to archives and libraries around the country. I appreciate the time and effort of all who aided me, especially the following: my colleagues at Spalding University; Rev. Paul K. Thomas of the Archives of the Archdiocese of Baltimore; Wendy C. Schlereth and staff, especially Sharon K. Sumpter, of the Archives of the University of Notre Dame; William Barnaby Faherty, S.J., and staff, especially Nancy Merz, of the Midwest Jesuit Archives; Teresa Maria Egan, C.S.J., of the Archives of the Archdiocese of St. Louis; Charles Elston, Philip Runkel, and Mark Thiel of the Archives of Marquette University; David Klingman, O.S.B., archivist, and Vincent Tegeder, O.S.B., of St. John's Abbey, Collegeville, Minnesota; Denis Fournier, O.S.B., archivist, and Terrence Kardong, O.S.B., of Assumption Abbey, Richardton, North Dakota; David Andrews, C.S.C., executive secretary, and Sandra LaBlanc of the National Catholic Rural Life Conference of Des Moines, Iowa; the Holy Cross priests and brothers of Corby Hall at the University of Notre Dame; Rev. Steven M. Avella of Marquette University; and Declan Kane, C.F.X., and Louis M. Mercorella of Baltimore.

THOMAS W. SPALDING, C.F.X.

GENERAL
INTRODUCTION

Michael E. Engh, S.J.

On a muddy prairie in southeastern Montana in April 1888, three chilled and bone-weary women beheld the decrepit and apparently abandoned log house in which they were expected to live and to establish a school. These German- and Irish-American women, members of the Order of St. Ursula, the Ursuline Sisters, had left Toledo, Ohio, in response to an appeal for women missionaries to serve in the West. Their invitation, issued by the Belgian-born bishop John B. Blondel, scarcely prepared them for the remarkable world they entered. The priests who ministered to the nuns were Belgian, Italian, and Mexican, and the students whom they had volunteered to instruct were the Northern Cheyenne.[1] These pioneer women and their successors struggled to teach their Native American charges English language skills, housekeeping, and the tenets of the Roman Catholic faith.

The poverty, isolation, and hard labor these nuns experienced, along with the ethnic diversity and the presence of both women and men in this mission, are significant characteristics of Catholicism in differing western regions between 1785 and 1920, the era that this volume treats. These traits constitute major themes that emerge in the documents in this collection. As the editors, we structured this collection of documents to encompass a variety of topics pertinent to the emergence of an identifiable American expression of Roman Catholicism in several locations viewed as "frontiers." To place this study in context, we have included an overview of pertinent secondary literature and an afterword, which focuses on the continuing frontier.

In planning this book, we drew upon our respective understandings of the frontier experience, which reflect in microcosm the present diversity among historians of the American West. Our approaches range from the classic interpretation of Frederick Jackson Turner to the concerns of contemporary New Western historians. Accordingly, the traditionalist sees a frontier in terms of time and place, while for others the word suggests shifting concentric circles

---

1. See Sister St. Angela Louise Abair, "A Mustard Seed in Montana: Recollections of the First Indian Mission in Montana," ed. Orlan J. Svingen, *Montana: The Magazine of Western History* 34 (spring 1984): 16–31.

of human contact. While this variety of perspectives enriches this volume, it also warrants explanation. We situated the American Catholic experiences of identity formation within the larger historiography of frontier and western history. The documents we selected reveal the interaction of Catholics, both lay and ordained, with their neighbors, with the environment, and with the international institutional church in those regions where Catholics and others entered (or invaded), settled, and formed communities.

These experiences in different areas of the continent followed similar paths of social change. While such developments were not "universal" or identical in every area, they were sufficiently similar to warrant attention as parallel frontier developments. Furthermore, these processes of change were essential to the formation of the nation and its distinct regions.[2] Among those people active on these frontiers were Roman Catholics from the states on the eastern seaboard, Europe, Latin America, and territories which the United States conquered or purchased, from the Louisiana Territory to Hawai'i and Alaska.

Roman Catholic participation in movements crisscrossing the continent furthered the closer identification of these peoples with their fellow citizens and with the nation to which they claimed allegiance. Long suspected of loyalty to a foreign ruler because of the spiritual leadership of the Pope, Roman Catholics struggled to find acceptance, to prove their patriotism, and to adjust to American society. This was equally as true in western fledgling towns as in eastern ethnic ghettos. In addition, Catholics faced the tumultuous social conditions, lack of established institutions, and the threat of violence typical of frontier societies.

The documents in this volume focus on topics important for understanding how these activities on the different frontiers contributed to the formation of an American Catholic identity. While many studies have examined urban Catholicism in the East and Midwest, this volume addresses the experience of Catholics on successive frontiers from the early national period of the late eighteenth century to persisting vestiges of the frontier today. Subjects in this collection include evangelization of indigenous people, competition with Protestant missionaries, adaptation to new circumstances, the work of the laity, fund-raising and recruitment, women's activities, folk piety, and controversies with fellow Catholics and people of other faiths. In their efforts to establish communities and to set down roots for their church, Catholics contended with challenges from the physical environment, such as landscapes and climates previously unknown to them, as well as the isolation due to vast distances and poor transportation, an isolation that helped to define the distinctive regions of the nation.

We structured the volume by geographic regions and included a photo es-

---

2. William Cronon, George Miles, and Jay Gitlin, *Under an Open Sky: Rethinking America's Western Past* (New York: Norton, 1992), 6–7.

say revealing the material culture of the American Catholic frontiers. In parts 1 and 2 of this volume, Thomas W. Spalding, C.F.X., documents the contributions of farming families to the settlement of the Trans-Appalachian West, with an emphasis on the Maryland Catholic diaspora, and of the French-Canadian trappers and their Native American spouses to the extension of the church from the Great Lakes to the Columbia River. For both frontiers, he depicts the hardships peculiar to their economies, the often troubled relations between clergy and laity, the moral dilemmas posed by adjustments to frontier conditions, and the slender resources available to pioneer priests and bishops.

In parts 3 and 4, Anne M. Butler presents evidence of the friction that arose in various forms on all frontiers. These conflicts pitted Catholics not only against Protestants and Latter-day Saints they encountered but also against Native Americans and against one another. Ethnic disagreements arose between parishioners and pastors, as well as in the schools between nuns and parents. Priests and bishops also collided, as did bishops and the laity. Yet the records also show that out of these struggles emerged a deeply appreciated religious identity, as Catholics focused on building and maintaining their presence in western communities. Laity and clergy alike expanded the active role of the church in a changing West. Butler's accounts from the Great Basin, Overland Trail, reservations, bonanza camps, and early urban centers also reveal that frontier conditions persisted in some areas into the early twentieth century.

In parts 5 and 6, I review California, the Southwest, and Texas and the established folk Catholicism that long predated American conquest (1846–48). Both Hispanic and Native American Catholics contended not only with arriving Protestants but also with bishops, priests, and nuns intent on Americanizing local Catholicism. The arriving French clergy in New Mexico, for example, precipitated sharp clashes with the Spanish-speaking populace, which left scars lasting until recent years. Different dynamics developed in Hawai'i, where French and Belgian religious introduced Catholicism to the island kingdom long before American annexation in 1898. Alaska's paucity of clergy continues a frontier condition, which the recent development of a Native Alaskan diaconate acknowledges and seeks to remedy.

To understand further the significance of these experiences captured within the documents, one needs to draw on the secondary literature for frontier Catholicism and for the American West. Much of this scholarship has been deeply influenced by the legacy of the most noted historian of the frontier experience, Frederick Jackson Turner. In 1893, Turner penned his famous essay, "The Significance of the Frontier in American History," which, along with later writings, captured the imagination of students, scholars, and the reading public. His attention to the impact of the frontier experience initiated a tradition of scholarly examination of the exploration and settlement of the continent. While describing the elements of the westering experience, he argued for its impact on the formation of the "American" character. Turner helped articulate the image of the West, one of the most cherished and recognizable icons for the United States.[3]

It is pertinent to this volume that Turner gave scant attention to the roles of religion in the dynamics of frontier life. Further, aside from consideration of colonial missionaries, camp meetings, and circuit riders, few of his early disciples examined the significant social impact religion exerted in every region. Historian John B. Boles noted these shortcomings, though commenting that the work on frontier religion in recent years has made important interpretive connections.[4] Areas worthy of investigation include community formation, conflict resolution, and material culture because they offer examples of the power of religious faith to sustain and to influence women and men on prairie farms and in mountain settlements. This need for further study includes Roman Catholics on and across the frontiers of the continent.[5]

Standard texts, such as Ray Allen Billington's *Westward Expansion* or the recently published work of Gregory H. Nobles, *American Frontiers,* mention Catholics only in reference to missionary work among Native Americans, as in California and in the Oregon country.[6] Robert V. Hine first sought to dispel lingering assumptions that nineteenth-century Catholicism was essentially an urban phenomenon and argued for a broader inclusion of religion, as well as Catholicism, in western scholarship. Noting one of the recurring problems of religious history, Richard W. Etulain commented in 1983 that most religious studies in the West suffered from narrow denominationalism and few were "interpretive and broad based."[7] Gary Topping and Ferenc M. Szasz offered helpful bibliographic studies on westering religion, although the studies confirm the narrow focus that Etulain observed.[8]

Protestant religious historians as early as William Warren Sweet partially

3. For helpful explanations of Turner and his ideas, see Allan G. Bogue, *Frederick Jackson Turner: Strange Roads Going Down* (Norman: University of Oklahoma Press, 1998); and Martin Ridge, *Frederick Jackson Turner: Wisconsin's Historian of the Frontier* (Madison: State Historical Society of Wisconsin, 1993).

4. John B. Boles, "Turner, the Frontier, and the Study of Religion in America," *Journal of the Early Republic* 13 (summer 1993): 205–16.

5. See the comments of Ferenc M. Szasz, "The Clergy and the Myth of the American West," *Church History* 59 (December 1990): 497–506.

6. See Ray Allen Billington and Martin Ridge, *Westward Expansion: A History of the American Frontier,* 5th ed. (New York: Macmillan, 1982), 39–41, 382–84, 463, 491–92; Gregory H. Nobles, *American Frontiers: Cultural Encounters and Continental Conquest* (New York: Hill and Wang, 1997), 29, 44, 46, 47, 49, 50, 65, 140; William H. Truettner, ed., *The West as America: Reinterpreting Images of the Frontier, 1820–1920* (Washington, D.C.: National Museum of American Art by the Smithsonian Institution Press, 1991), 83, 84, 90–91, 222; Frederick Merk, *History of the Westward Movement* (New York: Knopf, 1978), 348–52; Richard A. Bartlett, *The New Country: A Social History of the American Frontier, 1776–1890* (New York: Oxford University Press, 1974), 368, 372; and Allan G. Bogue, Thomas D. Phillips, and James E. Wright, eds., *The West of the American People* (Itasca, Ill.: F. E. Pecock, 1970), 487–95.

7. Robert V. Hine, *The American West: An Interpretive History* (Boston: Little, Brown, 1973), 234–35; Richard W. Etulain, "Shifting Interpretations of Western Cultural History," in *Historians and the American West,* ed. Michael P. Malone (Lincoln: University of Nebraska Press, 1983), 423.

8. Gary Topping, "Religion in the West," *Journal of American Culture* 3 (summer 1980): 330–

remedied Turner's omissions and published substantive accounts about the mainline Protestant churches on the frontier.[9] Herbert Eugene Bolton, at the University of California–Berkeley, and Peter Guilday and John Tracy Ellis, at the Catholic University of America in Washington, D.C., rendered similar service for Roman Catholic history. The graduate students they directed produced dissertations and other scholarly works, with Bolton's students focusing on the Spanish colonial era and the borderlands. The students of Guilday and Ellis largely concentrated on institutional and diocesan histories, biographies of ecclesiastical leaders, and the works of religious orders.[10]

The institutional orientation that emerged among Catholic scholars of the West has persisted to the present. Authors have struggled to maintain a balance between writing detailed local accounts and providing a broader context in which to situate their analysis. The best of these works offer comparative analysis and examine the Catholic experience from broader perspectives, such as race, class, gender, and region. Valuable recent examples include Virgilio P. Elizondo and Timothy M. Matovina's history of San Fernando Cathedral in San Antonio, Texas; Steven L. Baker's review of the early years of the Loretto Sisters on the Kentucky frontier; and Leslie Woodcock Tentler's overview for a proposed study of the diocesan clergy of the United States.[11] Such efforts assist American historians to understand better the ongoing dynamics of religion in the United States, as well as to study Catholicism on the frontier in particular.[12]

With the appearance in the late 1980s of the "New Western history" came efforts to expand Turner's scope to include overlooked subjects — such as racial and ethnic groups, women, the environment, community formation,

---

50; Ferenc M. Szasz, "Religion in the American West: A Preliminary Bibliography," in *Religion in the West*, ed. Ferenc M. Szasz (Manhattan, Kans.: Sunflower University Press, 1984), 99–106.

9. William Warren Sweet, ed., *Religion on the American Frontier*, 4 vols. (New York: Henry Holt, 1931; New York: Harper and Brothers, 1936; Chicago: University of Chicago Press, 1939, 1946).

10. For examples of important Catholic scholarship pertaining to the frontier, see Thomas W. Spalding, C.F.X., "Frontier Catholicism," *Catholic Historical Review* 77 (July 1991): 470–84; Francis J. Weber, *Century of Fulfillment: The Roman Catholic Church in Southern California, 1840–1947* (Mission Hills, Calif.: Archival Center, 1990); Marvin R. O'Connell, *John Ireland and the American Catholic Church* (St. Paul: Minnesota Historical Society Press, 1988); Patricia Lynch, S.B.S., *Sharing the Bread in Service: Sisters of the Blessed Sacrament, 1891–1991* (Bensalem, Pa.: privately printed, 1998); M. Jane Coogan, B.V.M., *The Price of Our Heritage: History of the Sisters of Charity of the Blessed Virgin Mary*, 2 vols. (Dubuque, Iowa: Mount Carmel Press, 1977, 1978); and Ronald E. Isetti, *Called to the Pacific: A History of the Christian Brothers of the San Francisco District, 1868–1944* (Moraga, Calif.: St. Mary's College, 1979).

11. Virgilio P. Elizondo and Timothy M. Matovina, *San Fernando Cathedral: Soul of the City* (Maryknoll, N.Y.: Orbis Books, 1998); Steven L. Baker, "Improvising on the Borderlands of Gender: The Friends of Mary at the Foot of the Cross, 1812–1834," *Filson Club History Quarterly* 71 (April 1997): 202–27; and Leslie Woodcock Tentler, " 'God's Representatives in Our Midst': Towards a History of the Catholic Diocesan Clergy in the United States," *Church History* 67 (June 1998): 326–49.

12. See John T. McGreevy, "Faith and Morals in the United States, 1865–Present," *Reviews in American History* 26 (March 1998): 239–54.

popular culture, and Native Americans — and candid discussions of the tragic consequences of conquest and expansion.[13] Debates raged about the nature of the frontier: Was it a "process," or was it a specific "region" of the country? Amid this vigorous reevaluation of western history, historians also utilized new methods to assess the dynamics associated with westering populations. Interdisciplinary approaches reveal, for example, that in boundary setting, various peoples among themselves established limits, which included the ways in which they worshiped. Further, by "self-shaping," frontier peoples made decisions that articulated local and regional identities. In both of these processes, religion played significant roles in frontier social interactions, roles that require additional assessment.[14]

Continuing along this path, D. Michael Quinn suggested that studies of religion on the frontier should be broadened to include neglected believers and sects, ethnic forms of Catholicism, and a time frame expanded through the twentieth century.[15] Quinn argued that religion played significant varied roles in the frontier experience and that the frontier in turn affected religious expression in western regions. Studies pursuing these avenues are found in several important bibliographies of the American West that include Catholicism.[16] Bibliographies that treat solely of American Catholicism have appeared, though not all are readily available.[17] Several periodicals have also

---

13. The extensive literature regarding the "New Western history" includes Patricia Nelson Limerick, *Legacy of Conquest: The Unbroken Past of the American West* (New York: Norton, 1987); William G. Robbins, "Western History: A Dialectic on the Modern Condition," *Western Historical Quarterly* 20 (November 1989): 429–49; Richard W. Etulain, ed., *Writing Western History: Essays on Major Western Historians* (Albuquerque: University of New Mexico Press, 1991); Patricia Nelson Limerick, Clyde A. Milner III, and Charles E. Rankin, eds., *Trails: Toward a New Western History* (Lawrence: University Press of Kansas, 1991); Richard White, *"It's Your Misfortune and None of My Own": A New History of the American West* (Norman: University of Oklahoma Press, 1991); John Mack Faragher, "The Frontier Trail: Rethinking Turner and Reimagining the West," *American Historical Review* 98 (February 1993): 106–17; Patricia Nelson Limerick, "Turnerians All: The Dream of a Helpful History in an Intelligible World," *American Historical Review* 100 (June 1995): 697–716; Kerwin Lee Klein, "Reclaiming the 'F' Word, or Being and Becoming Postwestern," *Pacific Historical Review* 65 (May 1996): 79–215; and David M. Wrobel and Michael C. Steiner, eds., *Many Wests: Place, Culture, and Regional Identity* (Lawrence: University Press of Kansas, 1997).

14. Cronon, Miles, and Gitlin, *Under an Open Sky*, 15–16, 18–22; Jon Gjerde, *The Minds of the Midwest: Ethnocultural Revolution in the Rural Midwest, 1830–1870* (Chapel Hill: University of North Carolina Press, 1997).

15. D. Michael Quinn in Cronon, Miles, and Gitlin, *Under an Open Sky*, 145–66. See also Patricia Nelson Limerick, "Believing in the American West," in *The West: An Illustrated History*, ed. Geoffrey C. Ward (Boston: Little, Brown, 1996), 207–13.

16. Richard W. Etulain, comp., *Religion in the Twentieth-Century American West: A Bibliography* (Albuquerque: Center for the American West, University of New Mexico, 1991), 15–19; Dwight L. Duncan, ed., *The American and Canadian West: A Bibliography* (Santa Barbara, Calif.: ABC-Clio, 1979), 183–98; and the listings for Roman Catholic history in the *America: History and Life* bibliography available from ABC-Clio in Santa Barbara on CD-ROM for volumes 19 to 35 (1982–98).

17. Richard R. Duncan, comp., "Master's Theses and Doctoral Dissertations on Roman Catholic History in the United States: A Select Bibliography," *U.S. Catholic Historian* 6 (winter 1987): 51–114; John Tracy Ellis and Robert Trisco, *A Guide to American Catholic History*, 2d ed.

published special issues dealing with Catholicism in the West, such as the *U.S. Catholic Historian* in 1994 and the *Oregon Historical Quarterly* in 1996.[18] Other important articles on Catholic frontier history appear in the *Catholic Historical Review* (1915–present), the *Records* of the American Catholic Historical Society of Philadelphia (1884–present), and the *U.S. Catholic Historian* (1982–present). The *Western Historical Quarterly*, the *Journal of American History*, and the *Catholic Historical Review* also publish in each issue a list of recent articles on the history of religion and of the West.

Catalogues published in conjunction with exhibitions offer another approach to studying frontier Catholicism through their review of material culture in various regions of the West. Jacqueline Peterson, for example, assembled the widely acclaimed *Sacred Encounters: Father De Smet and the Indians of the Rocky Mountain West*. Peterson presented a comparative approach to the spiritual traditions that met when European Jesuit missionaries encountered Native Americans, such as the Flathead and Kalispel peoples in Montana. In the Southwest, Thomas J. Steele, S.J., contributed significantly to another traveling exhibition, *Our Saints among Us: Nuestros santos entre nosotros: 400 Years of New Mexican Devotional Art*.[19] This volume concerned the local adaptation of Catholicism that New Mexican artisans, known as *santeros*, crafted to express their understanding of the faith first brought from Spain.

Other perspectives yielded further important new understandings of the frontier experience of Catholicism. Peter W. Williams provided an example of the multiple insights that emanate from the study of cultural artifacts in *Houses of God: Region, Religion, and Architecture in the United States*.[20] He demonstrated that regional identity often endured in religious architecture even after congregations moved or dispersed. Local architects and builders concretized a region's aesthetic traditions in the style and form of the religious structures they erected. An interdisciplinary approach enriched this work so that themes in religious history melded with regional design of churches and

---

(Santa Barbara, Calif.: ABC-Clio, 1982); James Hennesey, S.J., *American Catholic Bibliography, 1970–1982*, Working Paper Series, no. 12 (Notre Dame, Ind.: Cushwa Center for the Study of American Catholicism, University of Notre Dame, fall 1982); idem, *Supplement to American Catholic Bibliography, 1970–1982*, Working Paper Series, no. 14 (Notre Dame, Ind.: Cushwa Center for the Study of American Catholicism, University of Notre Dame, fall 1983); and Patrick Carey, *Roman Catholics*, Denominations in America, ed. Henry Warner Bowden, no. 6 (Westport, Conn.: Greenwood Press, 1993), 353–63.

18. See the *U.S. Catholic Historian* 12 (fall 1994) on frontier Catholicism and the *Oregon Historical Quarterly* 97 (spring 1996) on Catholic missionizing in the West.

19. Jacqueline Peterson, *Sacred Encounters: Father De Smet and the Indians of the Rocky Mountain West* (Norman: De Smet Project of Washington State University in association with the University of Oklahoma Press, 1993); and Barbe Awalt and Paul Rhetts, eds., *Our Saints among Us: Nuestros santos entre nosotros: 400 Years of New Mexican Devotional Art* (Albuquerque: LPD Press, 1998). See also Thomas J. Steele, S.J., Barbe Awalt, and Paul Rhetts, *The Regis Santos: Thirty Years of Collecting, 1966–1996* (Albuquerque: LPD Press, 1997).

20. Peter W. Williams, *Houses of God: Region, Religion, and Architecture in the United States* (Urbana: University of Illinois Press, 1997).

synagogues, national trends in architecture, and broader movements in social history. The model in this study illuminated how new methods of examination through material culture enhance our understanding of religion's roles in history.

Studies of rhetoric offer another form for comprehending the mentality of peoples. Thomas J. Steele, S.J., used linguistic analysis to trace evolving Catholic thought in New Mexico in the nineteenth century. He investigated Spanish language sermons and commencement addresses by Spanish, New Mexican, and French clerics and laymen to demonstrate the shifting self-understanding among Catholics before and after American conquest.[21] The differences in Catholic self-understanding emerge strikingly when Steele contrasts the oratory of native New Mexican speakers with the sermons of French-born clerics.

One of the most studied activities of Catholics on the frontiers, that of missionaries, receives groundbreaking new consideration in works ranging from individual biographies and the accounts of religious orders, to the consequences of clerical labors and teaching strategies. Two recent studies highlighted the famed Pierre De Smet, priest to mid-American Indians, and Blessed Damien De Veuster, priest to the stricken on Moloka'i, who continues to fascinate readers.[22] Important for the full gendering of frontier evangelization is the growing number of publications analyzing the many and different works of lay and religious women.[23] Gerald McKevitt, S.J., followed the Italian Jesuits on the frontiers of the Southwest and the Pacific Northwest, documenting the interethnic contacts that characterized both regions. His study underscored the broad appeal that the West had for numerous Europeans in the nineteenth century, the idealism which motivated clerical volunteers, and the presence

---

21. Thomas J. Steele, S.J., ed., *New Mexican Spanish Religious Oratory* (Albuquerque: University of New Mexico Press, 1997).

22. Robert C. Carriker, *Father Peter John De Smet: Jesuit in the West* (Norman: University of Oklahoma Press, 1995); and John J. Killoren, *"Come, Blackrobe": De Smet and the Indian Tragedy* (Norman: University of Oklahoma Press, 1994). Among the numerous biographies of Blessed Damien the best is still Gavan Daws, *Holy Man: Father Damien of Molokai* (New York: Harper and Row, 1973; Honolulu: University of Hawaii Press, 1984). For an alternative view, see Pennie Moblo, "Blessed Damien of Moloka'i: The Critical Analysis of Contemporary Myth," *Ethnohistory* 44 (fall 1997): 691–726.

23. See, for example, Kathy Smith Franklin, "A Spirit of Mercy: The Sisters of Mercy and the Founding of St. Joseph's Hospital in Phoenix, 1892–1912," *Journal of Arizona History* 39 (fall 1998): 263–88; Anne M. Butler, "Mother Katharine Drexel: Spiritual Visionary for the West," in *By Grit and Grace: Eleven Women Who Shaped the American West*, ed. Glenda Riley and Richard W. Etulain (Golden, Colo.: Fulcrum Publishing, 1997), 198–220; Virginia Glenn Crane, "History and Family Values, a Good Wife's Tale: Mary Elizabeth Meade Grignon of Kaukauna, 1837–1898," *Wisconsin Magazine of History* 80 (summer 1997): 179–200; Carol K. Coburn and Martha Smith, "'Pray for Your Wanderers': Women Religious on the Colorado Frontier, 1877–1917," *Frontiers* 15 (summer 1995): 27–52; and Nikola Baumgarten, "Education and Democracy in Frontier St. Louis: The Society of the Sacred Heart," *History of Education Quarterly* 34, no. 2 (summer 1994): 171–92.

among the missionaries of many political exiles, particularly from France and Germany.[24]

With the development of ethnohistory, scholars also examined how Native Americans for their own ends reacted to Roman Catholicism. Michael F. Steltenkamp, S.J., authored a valuable study detailing the conversion to Catholicism and subsequent catechetical work of the famed Sioux holy man Black Elk. Philip M. Hanley examined one of the teaching devices missionaries employed in the Oregon country, the "Catholic ladder," which depicted salvation history in terms of the origins and growth of Catholicism. Extending these topics, Christopher Vecsey explained how Native Americans identified spiritual value in Catholicism, while also using their faith to mediate imposed Euro-American culture. He found a living tradition of creative theological blending in which Catholicism coexisted with older forms of spirituality and worship. This syncretism troubled bishops for years, yet it provided catechized tribes with meaningful beliefs and rituals that persist to this day.[25]

These new studies rest upon the availability of scholarly tools that enable research into the vast array of manuscripts and other records. Standard sources in western history include encyclopedias and an atlas intended for the general public — these contain valuable entries on the Catholic Church of the frontier.[26] Guides to collections about Catholics in the West range from the four slim volumes edited by Robert Carriker and Eleanor Carriker for the microfilm edition of the Oregon Province Archives of the Society of Jesus, to the eleven-volume guide to archives of the Archdiocese of Los Angeles.

The Carrikers' compilations remind the historian of the rich ethnographic and historical materials found in the repositories of religious orders, such as the immense holdings of Indian language and mission papers which Jesuits assembled over 150 years among the tribes of the Pacific Northwest and Alaska. Records in diocesan archives, such as Los Angeles, touch upon a wide array of frontier persons who dealt with the Catholic hierarchy on matters of education, finance, social mores, construction, health care, and federal Indian policy. Further information on these matters can be found in the Roman correspondence of bishops and laity, as described in *United States Documents in*

---

24. Gerald McKevitt, S.J., "'The Jump That Saved the Rocky Mountain Mission': Jesuit Recruitment and the Pacific Northwest," *Pacific Historical Review* 55 (August 1986): 427–53.

25. Michael F. Steltenkamp, S.J., *Black Elk: Holy Man of the Oglala* (Norman: University of Oklahoma Press, 1993); Philip M. Hanley, *History of the Catholic Ladder*, ed. Edward J. Kowrach (Fairfield, Wash.: Ye Galleon Press, 1993); Christopher Vecsey, *On the Padres' Trail* (Notre Dame, Ind.: University of Notre Dame Press, 1996); and idem, *The Paths of Kateri's Kin* (Notre Dame, Ind.: University of Notre Dame Press, 1997).

26. Dan L. Thrapp, *Encyclopedia of Frontier Biography*, 4 vols. (Spokane: Arthur H. Clark, 1990); Charles Phillips and Alan Axelrod, eds., *Encyclopedia of the American West*, 4 vols. (New York: Macmillan, 1996); and Howard R. Lamar, ed., *New Encyclopedia of the American West* (New Haven: Yale University Press, 1998). See also Edwin Scott Gaustad, *Historical Atlas of Religion in America*, rev. ed. (New York: Harper and Row, 1976).

the Propaganda Fide Archives: A Calendar.[27] Not to be overlooked are the vast
holdings of the Hesburgh Library of the University of Notre Dame, as well
as the records of the Catholic Bureau of Indian Missions, now housed at Marquette University, along with those of the missions of the Society of Jesus
in the upper Midwest. Sister M. Evangeline Thomas, C.S.J., working with
others, compiled a guide to the manuscript repositories of women religious
in the United States. Many of these archives contain holdings pertaining to pioneer convents, such as those of the Sisters of Loretto, Sisters of Saint Joseph
of Carondelet, Daughters of Charity of St. Vincent de Paul, School Sisters of
Notre Dame, and Sisters of the Blessed Sacrament.[28]

Four final important resources for the frontier church include the *Official
Catholic Directory,* published by different presses and under different titles,
almost continuously since 1817. Though statistics reported for each diocese
ought to be used with caution, these annual volumes provide rich data. More
readily accessible is Michael Glazier and Thomas J. Shelley's one-volume *Encyclopedia of American Catholic History.* Finally, two newsletters also lead the
scholar to information on the Catholic experience in the West. The Cushwa
Center for the Study of American Catholicism at the University of Notre
Dame offers a complete report on studies underway or recently released. The
News and Notes of the History of Women Religious Network creates a link —
past and present — to a particularly important group in the Catholic Church.[29]

This array of academic interest and scholarship points to the history of
frontier Catholicism that is still emerging from documents, oral histories,
historic sites, and material culture. These records require a close reading,
comparative analysis, and broader contextualization, so that the patterns and
nuances of American Catholic activities emerge with greater clarity and full-

---

27. Robert C. Carriker, Eleanor Carriker, et al., eds., *Guide to the Microfilm Edition of the
Oregon Province Archives of the Society of Jesus Indian Language Collection: The Pacific Northwest
Tribes, the Alaskan Native Languages, and the Alaska Mission Collection,* and the *Pacific Northwest
Tribes Mission Collection* (Spokane: Gonzaga University Press, 1976, 1980; and Wilmington, Del.:
Scholarly Resources, 1987); Mary Rose Cunningham, C.S.C., comp., *Calendar of Documents and
Related Historical Materials in the Archival Center Archdiocese of Los Angeles,* 11 vols. (Mission
Hills, Calif.: Saint Francis Historical Society, 1990–1997); Finbar Kennealy, O.F.M., ed., *United
States Documents in the Propaganda Fide Archives: A Calendar,* 1st series, 7 vols. (Washington, D.C.:
Academy of American Franciscan History, 1966–77); Anton Debevec, comp., Mathias C. Kieman,
O.F.M., Alexander Wyse, O.F.M., and James McManamon, O.F.M., eds., *United States Documents
in the Propaganda Fide Archives: A Calendar,* 2d series, 4 vols. (Washington, D.C.: Academy of
American Franciscan History, 1980–87).
28. Evangeline Thomas, C.S.J., Joyce L. White, and Lois Wachtel, eds., *Religious Women History
Sources: A Guide to Repositories* (New York: R. R. Bowker, 1983).
29. *Official Catholic Directory* (New York: P. J. Kenedy): the work has had various titles, ed-
itors, and publishers since 1817 (except for 1818–21, 1823–32, and 1863); Michael Glazier and
Thomas J. Shelley, eds., *Encyclopedia of American Catholic History* (Collegeville, Minn.: Liturgical
Press, 1997); *American Catholic Studies Newsletter* of the Cushwa Center for the Study of Ameri-
can Catholicism, published semiannually at the University of Notre Dame since April 1975; and
News and Notes of the History of Women Religious Network, published three times a year since
February 1988 and presently edited at Mount St. Mary's College, Los Angeles.

ness. Only with such study can modern Catholics find precedents and parallels for contemporary challenges, such as the shortage of clergy and religious, clashes with authority, creative forms of lay leadership, and interethnic disagreements. Then, as now, Catholics sought to adapt to the surrounding culture while at the same time remaining in allegiance with the international church. The history of westering Catholics repeatedly offers examples of their loyalty to the nation and devotion to the faith.

Further, much like today, Catholics struggled with the realities of a multiethnic membership. The expansion of the nation's boundaries brought Louisiana French, the Spanish speakers of the Southwest, Native American converts, and immigrants from Europe into a national church linked to the earliest Anglo-Catholic families of colonial Maryland. The conflicts of the past spawned opportunities for a national religious body to learn how to incorporate culturally diverse populations. The failures in these efforts were always painful and acrimonious, and yet remain instructive. The study of these interactions enables modern Catholics to attain a sense of proportion and balance when conflicts emerge in present circumstances. This communion of believers has encountered similar challenges in the past, and this past is well worth study and reflection if there is to be improvement and growth for the future.

As editors, we believe that this volume can serve as a valuable tool for classroom use because of the range of experiences documented in these excerpts. This text provides a useful sourcebook for courses dealing with the history of the Catholic Church, both in the United States and in the international context. The issues treated here provide rich opportunities for discussion, particularly the controversies presented. Further, this volume is a needed supplementary text for history courses on the American West, religion in the United States, and American social history. Finally, the documents gathered here afford scholars immediate access to a representative sample of an immense body of widely scattered manuscript material, much of which appears here in translation.

It is the hope of the editors that students, teachers, scholars, and the reading public find this an enlightening and stimulating text. We selected the entries for this book with the intention of reaching several readerships, extending from historians of the West to Catholics seeking a deeper understanding of the American experience of their church. May this volume serve as a beacon, guiding our readers to the many thousands of records that further illustrate the meaning of frontier Catholicism. Whether we reach a reader from the general public or from the academy, we believe that these documents are important for comprehending how the frontier contributed to the formation of an American Catholic identity. Since 1785, the adjustments Catholics made as they moved across and through the continent redefined the church in its attitudes toward democratic government, leadership by the laity, roles of women, and ethnic religious expressions. From Anglo Catholics settling in Kentucky to Ursulines opening schools in Montana, the choices of these believers produced a church which is a distinctive national body. Their history on these various frontiers deeply affected how this church contributes to the nation where it set down deep roots and to the ancient church from which it has grown.

Part 1

THE BACKWOODS FRONTIER

Introduction

With but a touch of hyperbole Reverend John Carroll, then superior of the American mission, wrote of the Kentucky backwoods in 1785, "Thousands of Roman Catholics are rushing to remove thither, and nothing withholds them but the dread of wanting the ministrations of religion."[1] "Some twenty poor Catholic families," Reverend Stephen Theodore Badin would later recall, "descendants of the English colonists, came to settle there in 1785, because they could secure good lands then for almost nothing."[2] This was the first of the annual treks from southern Maryland, initiated by a league whose members pledged themselves to settle together, that would continue until the War of 1812.

The broadleaf and coniferous forests rooted in rich black soil that stretched from the Appalachians to the Mississippi and beyond beckoned irresistibly the yeomen farming families of the seaboard.[3] In Tidewater Maryland the soil had been exhausted by generations of tobacco planting, and the existing acreage could not, in any event, support the growing number of families. By the time Benedict Joseph Flaget, bishop of Bardstown, arrived at his see in 1811, there were over a thousand Catholic families in Kentucky, almost all from Maryland.

The Maryland Catholic diaspora, in fact, constituted, in many parts, the most vibrant and visible populations of the Catholic Church throughout the backwoods. From Maryland, Kentucky, and Pennsylvania (with a number of Germans), Catholics of Maryland ancestry would play important roles in the planting of the church in Georgia and Ohio and would help rejuvenate

---

1. John Carroll to [Francis Neale], n.p., 17 June 1785, in Thomas O'Brien Hanley, S.J., ed., *John Carroll Papers*, 3 vols. (Notre Dame, Ind.: University of Notre Dame Press, 1976), 1:189.
2. Stephen Theodore Badin, "Origine et progrès de la Mission du Kentucky," *Annales de l'Association de la Propagation de la Foi*, vol. 1, pt. 2, p. 24.
3. See Malcolm J. Rohrbough, *The Trans-Appalachian Frontier: Peoples, Societies, and Institutions, 1775–1850* (Belmont, Calif.: Wadsworth Publishing, 1990).

the nearly moribund residual populations of the French and Spanish efforts at empire building in Indiana, Illinois, Missouri, Mississippi, Louisiana, and Texas.[4] In Missouri, Indiana, and Illinois the first English-speaking parishes were founded by Kentuckians of Maryland descent.

There were, of course, other ethnic groups that contributed to the spread of the church in the backwoods. In significant numbers German-speaking residents of Pennsylvania and later immigrant Germans were drawn west, the latter playing an important role in the closing of the backwoods frontier of the Northwest and Missouri. Into the backlands would also plunge the ubiquitous Irish in undeterminable numbers because of their solitary penetrations. But they would also contribute to the closing of the frontier by their labors on toll roads and canals. And a small army of nondescript, many convert, Catholics, especially in the Old South, defy any attempt at identification.

Adaptation to a new environment was never easy, but Catholic pioneers, contrary to conventional wisdom, adjusted as readily as any to unaccustomed ecological, economic, social, and political conditions: to strange neighbors, new methods of cultivation, new crops, new markets, and different political arrangements and procedures. The initial adjustment to churchless and priestless areas was particularly trying, but almost as quickly as the laity pushed into new lands, the clergy followed, often as a result of the urgent, even imperious, demands of the former.

On the backwoods frontier, however, Catholic clergymen were mostly foreigners, newly arrived, and a good many of them members of religious orders. Beginning with Carroll's assignment of Benedict Flaget to Vincennes in 1792, nine French Sulpician seminary professors served as missionaries on the frontier.[5] English Dominicans went to Kentucky in 1805 and to Ohio in 1814. Italian Vincentians went to Missouri in 1818 and an American and French-born Vincentian to Texas in 1838. Belgian Jesuits went to Missouri in 1823.

Two religious sisterhoods came from France to Missouri, the Religious of the Sacred Heart in 1819 and the Sisters of St. Joseph of Carondelet in 1836. Also from France would come two sisterhoods to Indiana near the close of the frontier period, the Sisters of Providence in 1840 and the Sisters of the Holy Cross in 1843. But in Kentucky in 1812 were founded the indigenous Sisters of Loretto and Sisters of Charity of Nazareth and in 1822 the first order of Dominican sisters in the United States. Mother Seton's Sisters of Charity opened a hospital in St. Louis in 1829.

The nucleus of the parish was the mission station in a private home. By 1812 there were twenty-eight parochial congregations in Kentucky, only sixteen with

4. Thomas W. Spalding, "The Maryland Catholic Diaspora," *U.S. Catholic Historian* (hereafter *USCH*) 8 (fall 1989): 163–69; and idem, "The Catholic Frontiers," *USCH* 12 (fall 1994): 1–5.

5. Christopher J. Kauffman, *Tradition and Transformation in Catholic Culture: The Priests of Saint Sulpice in the United States from 1791 to the Present* (New York: Macmillan, 1988), chap. 3.

churches.[6] But these twenty-eight represented more than twice the number that could be found in all the other Trans-Appalachian states and territories, most of which were the remaining outposts of the former French empire.

Well into the 1830s the orientation of the Catholic Church in the United States was southern and rural.[7] Between 1820 and 1840 more dioceses would be created in the South (Richmond, Charleston, St. Louis, Mobile, Nashville, and Natchez) than in the North (Cincinnati, Detroit, Vincennes, and Dubuque). Most of the dioceses in the South, however, would remain embryonic while those in the North, as a result of immigration, would experience rapid but often unmanageable growth. The belief that the bestowal of a miter on the frontier would stimulate growth was belied in the slave states. Catholic newcomers bypassed the cotton-growing commonwealths, where the first bishops remained, for the most part, poverty-stricken, roving pastors who had few occasions to don their miters.

The reports of hard-pressed bishops of the West to the mission-aid societies of Europe, one of the most informative sources for the development of the church on the frontier, displayed a sometimes exaggerated concern about the lack of personnel and other resources but at the same time a buoyant optimism that, with a little help, the triumph of the church in the West was assured. Only in the Old Northwest was such optimism justified.

Conditions on the frontier presented the American church with fresh challenges. On the frontier, where restraints were few and the need for social diversions greater, a moral battle would be waged between clergy and laity, especially in Kentucky, where the pioneering priests were tinged with Jansenism. On the frontier the Catholic laity and often the clergy were more disposed to accept a pluralistic culture. The frontier demanded a flexibility that often discomfited an authoritarian church. The frontier, nevertheless, provided a fertile environment for the perpetuation of many of those characteristics of the Carroll church that fell victim to the development of the immigrant, or ghetto, church: an unqualified acceptance of such American principles as religious toleration and the separation of church and state and an ecumenism born largely of public service. Catholics on the frontier, the historian Thomas T. McAvoy, C.S.C., claimed, "manifested great poise and sense of security in the face of a non-Catholic majority."[8] Catholics on the frontier, the historian James Hennesey, S.J., observed, "were part of the milieu and developed their religious style in interaction with it."[9]

---

6. Mary Ramona Mattingly, S.C.N., *The Catholic Church on the Kentucky Frontier (1785–1812)* (Washington, D.C.: Catholic University of America Press, 1936), especially map before p. 1.

7. Randall M. Miller and Jon L. Wakelyn, eds., *Catholics in the Old South: Essays on Church and Culture* (Macon, Ga.: Mercer University Press, 1983).

8. Thomas T. McAvoy, C.S.C., *The Catholic Church in Indiana, 1789–1834* (New York: Columbia University Press, 1940), 19–20.

9. James Hennesey, S.J., *American Catholics: A History of the Roman Catholic Community in the United States* (New York: Oxford University Press, 1981), 129.

Kentucky

The first wedge in the Trans-Appalachian wilderness, Kentucky was the testing ground for the ability of the Catholic Church to follow the western progression of the nation. There the hopes and hardships and the patterns of adaptation and creation that would characterize all subsequent frontiers were first played out. There clergy and laity fashioned the first institutions that lent solidity and permanence to the church at the western edges of its corporate existence.

Among the first settlers in Kentucky, in 1775, were the families of William Coomes and Dr. George Hart, who (after giving the future state its first teacher and probably first physician) settled on land they had acquired in 1780 at the edge of a village established at the same time that soon came to be called Bardstown. In 1785 they were joined by the first families of the Maryland league. In a remarkably short time (on 8 April 1808) Bardstown was chosen as the episcopal see for these transplanted Marylanders.

1. Early Catholic Emigrants as Depicted by Martin John Spalding, 1785–95

In a chapter of the same name, "Early Catholic Emigrants," the future bishop of Louisville and archbishop of Baltimore, Martin John Spalding (1810–72), drawing upon the recollections of pioneers still living, including members of his own family, graphically describes the truly primitive regression required by migration to the backwoods.

... The first Catholic colony which emigrated to Kentucky, after those already named [William Coomes and Dr. George Hart], was the one which accompanied the Haydens and Lancasters.[1] They reached the new country some time in the year 1785; and located themselves chiefly on Pottinger's Creek, at the distance of from ten to fifteen miles from Bardstown. A few of them, however, settled in the more immediate vicinity of Bardstown. The selection of Pottinger's Creek as the location of the new Catholic colony, was unfortunate. The land was poor, and the situation uninviting. Yet the nucleus of the new colony having been formed, these disadvantages were subsequently disregarded. The new Catholic emigrants from Maryland, continued to flock to the same neighbourhood. They preferred being near their brethren, and enjoying with them the advantages of their holy religion, to all other mere worldly considerations. They could not brook the idea of straggling off in different directions, where, though they might better their earthly condition, they and their children would, in all probability, be deprived of the consolations of religion ... [Subsequent colonies were led in 1786 by Captain James Rapier, in

---

1. William and Basil Hayden, brothers, and Raphael and John Lancaster, father and son.

1787 by Philip Miles and Thomas Hill, in 1788 by Robert Abell, in 1790 by Benedict Spalding, and in 1791 by Leonard Hamilton, the last three settling on the Rolling Fork. After the Treaty of Greenville in 1795, which brought an end to Indian hostilities, emigration "proportionably increased."]

The early Catholic emigrants to Kentucky, in common with their brethren of other denominations, had to endure many privations and hardships. As we may well conceive, there were few luxuries to be found in the wilderness, in the midst of which they had fixed their new habitations. They often suffered even the most indispensable necessaries of life. To obtain salt, they had to travel for many miles to the licks, through a country infested with savages; and they were often obliged to remain there for several days, until they could procure a supply.

There were then no regular roads in Kentucky. The forests were filled with a luxuriant undergrowth, thickly interspersed with the cane, and the whole closely interlaced with the wild pea-vine. These circumstances rendered them nearly impassable; and almost the only chance of effecting a passage through this vegetable wilderness, was by following the paths, or *traces,* made by the herds of buffalo and other wild beasts. Luckily, these *traces* were numerous, especially in the vicinity of the licks, which the buffalo were in the habit of frequenting, to drink the salt water, or *lick* the earth impregnated with salt.

The new colonists resided in log cabins, rudely constructed, with no glass in the windows, with floors of dirt, or, in the better sort of dwellings, of puncheons of split timber, roughly hewn with the ax. After they had worn out the clothing brought with them from the old settlements, both men and women were under the necessity of wearing buckskin or homespun apparel. Such a thing as a store was not known in Kentucky for many years: and the names of broadcloth, ginghams and calicoes, were never even so much as breathed. Moccasins made of buckskin, supplied the place of our modern shoes; blankets thrown over the shoulder answered the purpose of our present fashionable coats and cloaks; and handkerchiefs tied around the head served instead of hats and bonnets. A modern fashionable bonnet would have been a matter of real wonderment in those days of unaffected simplicity.

The furniture of the cabins was of the same primitive character. Stools were used instead of chairs; the table was made of slabs of timber, rudely put together; wooden vessels and platters supplied the place of our modern plates and chinaware; and "a tin cup was an article of delicate furniture, almost as rare as an iron fork."[2] The beds were either placed on the floor, or on bedsteads of puncheons, supported by forked pieces of timber, driven into the ground, or resting on pins let into *augur* holes in the sides of the cabin. Blankets, and bear and buffalo skins, constituted often the principal bed covering.

---

2. Here Spalding is quoting from Humphrey Marshall, *The History of Kentucky,* 2 vols. (Frankfort, Ky.: G. S. Robinson, 1824), 1:123.

One of the chief resources for food was the chase. All kinds of game were then very abundant; and when the hunter chanced to have a goodly supply of ammunition, his fortune was made for the year. The game was plainly dressed, and served on wooden platters, with corn bread, and the Indian dish — the well known *homeny* [hominy]. The corn was ground with great difficulty, on the laborious hand-mills; for mills of other descriptions were then, and for many years afterwards, unknown in Kentucky.

Such was the simple manner of life led by *our* "pilgrim fathers." They had fewer luxuries, but perhaps were, withal, more happy than their more fastidious descendants. Hospitality was not then an empty name; every log cabin was freely thrown open to all who chose to share in the best cheer its inmates could afford. The early settlers of Kentucky were bound together by the strong ties of common hardships and dangers — to say nothing of other bonds of union — and they clung together with great tenacity. On the lightest alarm of Indian invasion, they all made common cause, and flew together to the rescue. There was less selfishness, and more generous chivalry; less bickering, and more cordial charity, then, than at present; notwithstanding all our boasted refinement...

> Martin John Spalding, *Sketches of the Early Catholic Missions of Kentucky from Their Commencement in 1787 to the Jubilee in 1826* (Louisville: B. J. Webb, 1844), 25–27, 31–33.

2. A Pioneer Reports Back to Maryland, ca. 1791

Leonard Hamilton, leader of one of the migrations to Kentucky and ancestor of a number of priests and religious, including Martin John Spalding, in a letter of possibly 1791 from "Washington County, Rolling Fork of the Salt River, near the Indian Licks," encourages his sister Elizabeth Hamilton McAtee to join him.

I received yours of the first of April, by the hand of Cousin Benny Green, which you may be sure gave me a singular satisfaction... You say you could wish yourself, at times, in this country, but the reflections on moving extricates all notions of the kind. I must confess to you that it is a great undertaking, but not so bad as you imagine. If you was to see the luxurious soil of Kentucky I think it would raise an ambition in your mind that would surmount all difficulties of that kind, and as I think it would be for the benefit of yourself and children in particular. I could sincerely wish you were here and happily settled a near neighbor of mine. You must expect that when your children marry and go from you, which will be the way, they must come to this country or go to some other part of the new world, and then you will be unhappy because you will be separated from your children. These are reasons that nature dictates to every feeling mind, and was one of the principal reason[s] that induced me to come to this country. I have purchased six hundred acres of land that is good. I have divided it in three Plantations, one for George, and the other two for Clem and myself. I begin now, though I have had exceeding bad luck in horses since I came to this country[.] I have lost five valuable ones, to recover my settling in the woods, which has been one of the greatest difficulties I have had to encounter with. I have 36 acres of land opened and in cultivation this year. I have next to build a house and then if please God we have [a] Church. I hope to enjoy the fruits of the fertile land of Kentucky in peace and happiness the remainder of my days, with the additional blessing of having my children settled about me...

> Maria Louise Kelley and Inez Bateman Cherault, *Hamilton Family of Charles County, Maryland* (Houston: published by the authors, 1930), 71–72.

3. Reverend Stephen Badin Informs Bishop John Carroll of Affairs in Kentucky, 1796–1810

Stephen Theodore Badin (1768–1854), the first priest ordained by Bishop Carroll and the first priest with staying power in Kentucky, in the following extracts keeps Carroll posted, as his vicar general, on the problems of frontier Catholicism, including, as he perceives them, contentious laymen and loose morals, but speaks also of his friendship with Protestants.

Priestland, Hardin's Creek, Washington County, April 11, 1796

...Last fall and winter I wrote you several letters which you have not answered doubtless for the reason that they were lost or intercepted during the journey, which frequently happens. In them I proposed some cases of conscience and asked for several dispensations; I therein exposed to you the needs of my congregations and especially my own; would that you could know them, Monseigneur, as I know them — although even I know them imperfectly; — you would be deeply afflicted, your charity for the people and priests of whom you are the pastor would rend your fatherly heart, because there is no pasturage in Kentucky for the souls that, as you assured me when I was leaving Baltimore, you tenderly love. Probably there is not in all your diocese as large congregations as are those of Kentucky, and they are increasing from day to day; there is not a Catholic here that does not bitterly lament at finding himself deprived of those means of salvation that were to be had in Maryland &c. I can assure you, Monseigneur, and you will be touched to hear it, that some among them are so afflicted as to lose their mind[s]...

Washington County, October 9, 1799

...I have been sued, warranted & executed several times by Catholics for church affairs, many Catholic people complying not with the payments they have engaged to make to the congregation. Being myself indebted to merchants for my clothing &c. I began this year to ask a salary of £60. My yearly expenses, besides the produce of the plantation amount to nearly 40£ and I have engaged myself also to furnish the altars with the necessaries for divine

Rev. Stephen Theodore Badin (right) labored in Kentucky from 1793 to 1819. In 1811 he welcomed Benedict Joseph Flaget (left), who was named bishop of Bardstown in 1808, the first frontier bishop. When they quarreled over land titles, Badin left Kentucky.

Credit: Ben J. Webb, *The Centenary of Catholicity in Kentucky* (Louisville: Charles A. Rogers, 1884).

worship . . . The demand of a salary has given great offence to Mr. John Lancaster the Kentuckian Robespierre who has been elected to the Assembly by the influence of Priests as well as [to] Robt Abell who would fainly associate themselves to rob the church of Kentucky of its land as the Jacobins have plundered the Gallican church. But I fear not their malice . . .

Washington County, June 2, 1802

. . . As to the practice of the clergy in France, I am conscious with Your Reverence that it certainly was more rigid than it is in America, & still it appears to me that America is not less corrupted than France was, so far as I know both countries, & probably I am not the only man of that opinion. I attribute the pullulation of sins & vicious habits among the American Catholics, especially in Kentucky, to their intermixture in life and connection in marriage with Protestants, Latitudinarians, Deists, Libertines &c — to the want of education, to their supine ignorance & to the scarcity of Clergymen & spiritual books — to their distance from places of worship — To the dangers, temptations & many opportunities of sin occurring during the time of their emigrations — To nocturnal promiscuous assemblies of pleasure and immodesty of dress — To the profanation, very common & almost general, of the Sundays and Holydays — To the various scandals given in the Church — To Idleness & the Luxuriancy of the country, two fruitful Parents of iniquity — To the warmth of the Climate — To the blindness of Parents & Heads of families in allowing dangerous liberties or familiarities in their very presence; to their neglect in keeping a watchful eye, & Religious as well as civil discipline — in fine to the pride, abuse or excess of liberty and an ungovernable spirit of indepedency [*sic*] &c. All which abuses cannot be effectually checked without contradiction & opposition. These & other particular causes, besides those which are common to the sinful posterity of man, have produced very sad effects in Kentucky, where we hardly witness anything else but impiety & irreligion or deceit & Hypocrisy, triumphant vice[,] public immoralities & incessant scandals of every description. I must make an exception in favor of a certain number of virtuous Christians: but indeed it is very common to find among Catholics lamentable & public disorders especially profane curses *addito S. nomine Dei* [including the Holy Name of God], the Youth & Blacks are miserably depraved, and to be short *ferè omnis caro corrupit viam suam* [generally all flesh corrupts its way]. I have incessantly before my eyes the miseries of mankind to gain some little experience, & considering how the doctrines & practices of the world are diametrically opposed to those of the Gospel, I know not after much reflection how to mollify my general principles in the application thereof to particular cases. I wish in theory, but I wish in vain to widen the road which leads to life and to enlarge the door, I do still find in practice the one and the other to be narrow, and that all those who say Lord, Lord, shall not enter the kingdom of Heaven...

Bardstown, 3 October 1810
...I received this day a letter of Mr. Fairbairn giving his assent that the church of St. Louis be built on his lots [in Louisville]: but some of the Trustees who are Protestants (mirabile dictu) want to procure a five-Acres-lot, that a Priest also be accommodated. If all the Catholics are not my friends, I am amply compensated by the friendship of many non-Catholics of respectability...

Carroll Papers, 1-E-1, 1-E-16, SpA-J-2, 1-J-10, Archives of the Archdiocese of Baltimore. Printed by permission.

4. Reverend Charles Nerinckx Describes the Hard Life of a Missionary, 1805

From "Holy Mary's at the Rolling Fork" Charles Nerinckx (1761–1824) tells his parents in Belgium how he has adjusted to the arduous duties assigned him,

revealing in the process that uncompromising zeal responsible for the remark-
able piety and regularity of Kentucky's pioneering Catholics (Badin's opinion
notwithstanding).

We [I] have some twenty-four missions to attend to. The most remote church
is sixty miles from here, but we are sometimes called as far as one hundred
and eighty miles in either direction. This does not happen often; but, thank
God, when it does happen, I do not suffer from riding on horseback as I used
to. Three hours in the saddle fatigued me very much; now, I have traveled one
hundred and fifty miles on horseback in two nights and one day, through bad
roads and all kinds of weather, and I stood it better than I expected.

My usual occupations during the week are as follows: On Sunday morning I am in the saddle about four o'clock A.M. so as to reach one of my
mission churches about half-past six. I there find a crowd of people awaiting
my coming to go to confession. We first say the morning prayers, followed
by meditation; I then give them my instruction on the sacrament of penance and prepare them for it. At intervals of half an hour, marked by my
ringing a bell from the sacristy where I am hearing confessions, one of the
congregation, whom I designate myself, says the beads at a determined intention, until about eleven o'clock, when I vest for Mass. Before beginning
the Holy Sacrifice I deliver a short address, and I preach after the reading of
the Gospel. After Mass, during which the people usually sing some English
hymns, I have the children pray for special intentions as I did in Meerbeke
[Belgium]. The congregation is dismissed between one and two P.M., when
I baptize infants and bury the dead. Seldom do I eat anything before four
o'clock except some water and milk; and it happens that some one is ready
to take me out on a sick call of twenty or more miles by the time I have
had a bite.

This is my order of the day for Sundays and four of the six week days. I
hear confessions every afternoon until seven, in Summer until eight or nine
o'clock P.M.; so I have to figure closely to find time to say my office. Today,
November 8, 1805, I am still giving Holy Communion at five P.M., and that
happens almost daily. I spend the other two days at St. Stephen's with Father
Badin; and as soon as the people know that the priests are at home, we need
not think of rest.

I also undertook five weeks ago a very hard work, viz., to prepare the
young ladies above fourteen years of age for their first communion; they number ninety in my three congregations. The exercises last seven weeks, and a
few days each week are set apart for spiritual exercises. To attend a dance, or
to be unbecomingly dressed, is punished by refusal of admission to first communion, and I succeed wonderfully well in abolishing these abuses. Those of
the first class in *St. Charles,* who were sufficiently instructed, made their first
communion on the name's day of their holy Patron Saint. I now call up a

new class of those who are from twelve to fourteen years old. It is the hardest work I ever undertook.

Camillus P. Maes, *The Life of Rev. Charles Nerinckx* (Cincinnati: Robert Clarke, 1880), 161–63.

5. A Dominican Complains of the Severity of Pastors Badin and Nerinckx, 1806

Samuel Thomas Wilson, O.P. (1761–1824), superior of the first religious order of priests on the frontier, in a letter to Bishop Carroll, indicts Badin and Nerinckx for their rigorism, exposing a contention over morals between the secular and religious clergy as well as between the people and pastors.

...No place in the world, Dr Sir, is more in want of a prudent Bishop than Kentucky where thousands are living in constant neglect of the Sacraments, through the too great zeal I fear of [Badin and Nerinckx]. Young people are not admitted without a solemn promise of not dancing *on any occasion whatever*, which few will promise & fewer still can keep. All priests that allow of any dancing are publicly condemned to Hell! People taught to believe that every kiss lip to lip between married persons, is a mortal sin. Old men not allowed the marriage act more than once a week. People publicly warned on our [the Dominicans'] arrival, that there are all sorts of Priests good & bad. &c. Women refused absolution for their husband[']s permitting a decent dance in their house, not to mention a thousand things far more ridiculously severe...

Carroll Papers, 8B-L-6, Archives of the Archdiocese of Baltimore.

6. Bishop Flaget's Report to the Pope, 1815

Benedict Joseph Flaget, S.S. (1763–1850), tells of his creation of the first seminary in the West soon after his arrival in 1811 as bishop and his authorization of the foundation of two sisterhoods. He also describes the remote parts of his extensive diocese and tells of a visit to Missouri, making clear that Kentucky was the hub of Catholic expansion in the West.

...Destitute of almost every hope of obtaining co-laborers from Europe, I decided at the beginning of my episcopate to establish a Seminary. I had already brought with me some young men from France, and, as I have already said, they accompanied me to Kentucky. After six months, on the fifth day of December, 1811, the Seminary was begun in the house which the above-mentioned pious layman [Thomas Howard] had bequeathed and which his good widow, who had the right according to the will of her husband of retaining it till her death, was generously willing to bestow on me. The beginnings were small and the progress slow, for at first very many of the pupils had to be instructed not only in Latin and grammar, but also in the very elements of reading and writing, such is the great and almost barbaric ignorance of this district. However, the Seminary, like the grain of mustard seed, is increasing by divine mercy and gives hope of harvest. But, alas, how few for so great a harvest! Many of our pupils are maintained at our own expense. The property on which we live is far from sufficient for our many expenses; but, so far, by the charity of some pious friends, the boys, who are of good character and fine talent, are drawn towards piety and daily advance in knowledge and virtue. We are careful to imbue their minds with great veneration for the Holy Apostolic See and with filial love for the Father of all the faithful . . .

For the religious education of girls, two communities of women have been established by my authority. One is dedicated to the Blessed Virgin at the Foot of the Cross of Jesus [Sisters of Loretto], and its members after a sufficient time of probation bind themselves by the simple vows of religion. This community now consists of twelve young women who are diffusing the good odor of Christ on all sides. The author and founder of the order is Rev. Charles Nerinckx, the bearer of this letter, who leaves his young charges desolate and afflicted with deep sorrow, for surely they are losing a beloved Father and they have no one to take his place. And that this may be done they cease not to ask from God with anxious prayers. The other community I founded myself not far from the Seminary, under the rule of the Daughters of Charity of St. Vincent de Paul.[1] It consists of ten young women, already spoken well of for their piety, humility, obedience, and other religious virtues. They are engaged in the education of girls, the care of orphans, of the poor and sick, and in other works of mercy. The greatest help, if God favors us, is expected from them for the salvation of our neighbors.

Such are the facts which I desired to set before Your Holiness about the Church of Kentucky.

To come now to the other States and Territories. In the neighboring State of Tennessee there are about twenty-five Catholic families, who are destitute of every help of the Church. Once or twice, many years ago, they were visited by a priest from Kentucky; at length it was possible for me to go to them. On my journey to Baltimore I found fifty Catholic families in the State of Ohio. I heard that there are many others scattered in various parts of the same State, but those who have migrated from that State to these regions have never seen a priest. Hence many of those I met have almost forgotten their religion and they are bringing up their children in complete ignorance. And this neglected portion of the flock committed to me, I am compelled to leave on account of workers, for I can scarcely send a missionary to them even once a year.

In the Territory of Indiana is a town known as *Poste Vincennes*, and its inhabitants are for the most part French who formerly migrated thither from the borders of Canada. There is a parish called *St. Francis Xavier*, and it is

---

1. Bishop John Baptist David, coadjutor of Bishop Flaget, and Mother Catherine Spalding are considered the cofounders of the Sisters of Charity of Nazareth.

indeed very dear to me as I had charge of it for three years immediately after my coming to the Province of the United States. I visited this parish lately with the greatest consolation and confirmed over 230 persons there. It consists of 130 families whose number would soon be greatly increased if I could send a priest there. Until the Lord makes this possible to me, in order that the faith may not be wholly extinguished there, I decided to send a priest from Kentucky to them twice in the year. There will be sufficient there for the support of two missionaries.

In the Territory of Illinois there are three parishes which I also visited the past autumn [Cahokia, Kaskaskia, and Prairie du Rocher]. There are two priests there, one of whom [Donatien Olivier] was forced to flee on account of the persecution of France into Spain, whence he afterwards crossed to America. He is very much enfeebled by his years. The other [Francis Savine] is a Canadian priest who came to these parts with his bishop's permission. In these three parishes there are about 120 families, mostly French. The Americans who inhabit these regions are for the most part heretics, and are generally without ministers of their own sects and could be brought into the Catholic faith with little difficulty if there were missionaries who joined to their zeal and doctrines a knowledge of the language of these people. There are no fixed revenues in these parishes. Stipends are paid by the faithful to their pastors.

On the opposite bank of the Mississippi River, which is called Upper Louisiana, I visited since they are close to my Diocese, six parishes which belong to the Diocese of New Orleans; and indeed with great consolation and not a little harvest of souls. For the spark of faith, not yet thoroughly extinct, was revived by the new and unusual presence of a Bishop. Five of the parishes are made up of French [St. Louis, St. Charles, St. Genevieve, Florissant, and Portage des Sioux], one of Americans [Tucker's Settlement]. In these parishes and in the three above mentioned on the left bank, I administered the sacrament of Confirmation to 1200 persons. In that region I found only one priest [Marie Joseph Dunand], of the Order of St. Bernard (Congregation of Trappists), who is being recalled by his superiors with great loss to those parishes and much against my will. For the result will surely be that the American congregation will be deprived of all spiritual aid and the five parishes of French will receive no help, unless it be what these two missionaries established on the left bank can do for them.

In the territory of Michigan there is a parish called *St. Anne's,* in a town known as *Detroit.* It is so large that it seems necessary to divide it into two parts. One contains 1500 souls. The other is a place called *La Rivière aux Raisins,* the name of which I do not know [St. Anthony of Padua], which consists of about 500 souls. They are in charge of a Sulpician [Gabriel Richard]. The parishioners pay their tithes to him. I could not visit these places on account of the War which was raging in those places at the time of my visitation.

Besides these, on my journey, I heard of four French congregations settled in the midst of the Indians, who belong to my diocese, one on the upper part of the Mississippi [Prairie du Chien], one in the place commonly called *Chicago,* another on the shore of Lake Michigan [Green Bay], a fourth near the head of the Illinois River [uncertain]. But neither the time nor the war would permit me to visit them...

What shall I say about the numerous tribes of Indians who inhabit these vast regions on both sides of the Mississippi River or on each side up to the sources of that stream, and many of whom never heard of the Gospel!...Mr. [William] Clark, who ascended the Missouri River for a distance of 3000 miles with a large body of companions and crossed over the mountains in which it takes its rise, and then along the Columbia River on the other side of the mountains to the Pacific Ocean, told me that he found many Indian nations on each side of the mountains who had never seen white men before and whom he testified to be of a very mild and gentle nature, who, therefore, would bend their heads easily to the yoke of the Gospel. Whom shall I send and who will go for us? When I ponder over these and similar things in my mind, great joy is brought to my heart by the news of the restoration of that remarkable Society of apostolic men [the Jesuits] who brought the light of the Gospel in years gone by to so many barbarous nations...

> "Bishop Flaget's Report of the Diocese of Bardstown to Pius VII, April 10, 1815," ed. and trans. Victor F. O'Daniel, O.P., *Catholic Historical Review* 1 (1915): 315–19.

The Old Southwest

When Bishop Louis William DuBourg (1766–1833) of the Diocese of Louisiana decided to build his cathedral in St. Louis in 1818, that city, not New Orleans, became a center for the expansion of the church in the Old South and its extensions into Texas and Arkansas. From his clergy was eventually chosen the first bishop in Alabama in 1826 (Michael Portier) and from the seminary he founded the first bishop in Texas in 1841 (John Mary Odin). Though the Diocese of St. Louis would experience rapid growth, no other sees south of Kentucky and Missouri would outgrow their frontier condition in the antebellum years.

7. Indian Attacks as Described by Father Marie Joseph Dunand, ca. 1817

Before the coming of Bishop DuBourg the upper Mississippi Valley was a dangerous place to live, as Father Dunand, a Trappist, revealed in his reminiscences,

*incorrectly called a diary. He was asked by Bishop Flaget to stay behind when
his community returned to France because of the scarcity of priests in the area
of St. Louis.*

... Constantly the people came to tell me that the Indians had attacked such
and such a place; one was killed working in the fields; another on a voyage; others again were slain in their beds. One scarcely speaks of anything
except such misfortunes. One day they killed five of my parishioners during vespers. Amidst these dangers the French were less exposed than the
Americans; for the Indians were at war with the latter only, on account
of taking their land. Consequently they said to the French: "Live always
as you have been accustomed to live in order that we can distinguish you
from the great Couteaux["] (as they call the Americans). When they captured
Americans they treated them very cruelly; and if they spared them for the
moment it was to put them to death by slow torture and to feed upon their
flesh.

One day two Americans fell into their hands, and lest they might escape
they brought them to a savage village. While their fate was being decided
they were laid on their backs on the earth; then their four extremities were
stretched out fastened to four pegs driven very deep into the ground. One
was condemned to be boiled in a large kettle and afterwards eaten; the other
was to be roasted alive before the fire over which the pot was boiling which
contained his companion. The first, having been disembowelled was pulled to
pieces and crammed into the kettle; the other was stripped of his clothes and
led before the fire from which the flames rose more than six feet. The Indians,
weapons in hand, formed a circle round him that he might not escape. The
women were in front, each holding in her hand a pointed stick with which
to prod the unfortunate man and to oblige him to turn towards the fire. It is
worthy of note that under such circumstances the women are far more cruel
than the men. One of these women had her child in her arms. She was the
most vicious of all. The poor creature who was thus roasting, unable to bear
such cruel torture conceived the idea of making them kill him at once; and
for this purpose grabbed her child and flung it in the pot with his companion. Seeing this, the savages, clapping their hands to their mouths, cried out:
"He is a hero! He is a hero!" and the mother of the child coming forward
adopted him as her son; in this way he was spared; but on condition that he
recognize as his mother her whose child he had thrown into the pot. One
need not be astonished at this, for it is the custom among these people for
the woman to adopt as her husband or son him who has been the murderer,
if he is caught...

"Diary of the Reverend Father Marie Joseph Durand [*sic*], Translated from the
French by Ella M. E. Flick," *Records of the American Catholic Historical Society
of Philadelphia* 27 (1916): 54–55.

8. Bishop Louis William DuBourg's Arrival at St. Louis, 1818

To Didier Petit Bishop DuBourg describes three days after his arrival the primi-
tive state of St. Louis, where he had decided to build his cathedral rather than
in the troubled city of New Orleans. He tells of his plans to establish a seminary
and college at a settlement of Catholics from Kentucky.

...Here I am at St. Louis, and it is no dream...I visited several parishes en
route. Everywhere the people came in crowds to meet us, showing me the
most sincere affection and respect. My house is not magnificent, but it will be
comfortable when they have made some necessary repairs. I will have a parlor,
a sleeping room, a very nice study, besides a dining room, and four rooms for
the ecclesiastics, and an immense garden. My cathedral, which looks like a
poor stable, is falling into ruins, so that a new church is an absolute necessity.
It will be one hundred and fifty feet long by seventy wide, but its construction
will take time, especially in a country where everything is just beginning. The
country, the most beautiful in the world, is healthy and fertile, and emigrants
pour in. But everything is very dear. The question of my episcopal revenue has
not yet been decided, but there is immense good feeling, and I am not troubled
about it. The people are most anxious that I should erect a college. I shall
found a small seminary, with as little delay as possible, upon a piece of ground
given me by the people of a new parish composed entirely of very zealous
Catholics. Bishop Flaget is their idol. They have known him for twenty-four
years, which is a much longer time than is needed by him to win their hearts.
He has found a way of interesting them in the new bishop, who can never
be grateful enough to him. His friendship for me has doubtless inspired all his
preparations for my installation, but his zeal for religion is his chief motive...

Annales de l'Association de la Propagation de la Foi 2 (1828): 338–39.

9. Bishop Joseph Rosati's Report on the Progress of the Church in St. Louis, 1830

Joseph Rosati, C.M. (1789–1843), after being made coadjutor-bishop to Bishop
DuBourg, became the first bishop of St. Louis in 1827. In 1830 he was able to
boast of the several institutions that brought its pioneering period to an end
to Reverend Frederic Résé, a founder of the Leopoldine Society in Vienna and
future bishop of Detroit.

I hope you will not forget the Diocese of St. Louis in the report you send
the Association you have established in Germany. The Diocese contains 1°
The state of Missouri 2° The Territory of Arkansas 3° half of the state of Illinois 4°. All of the territories beyond these states to the Pacific ocean. It has
for borders Mexico and Canada. The expanse is immense. We have Catholics
who speak French, of which the number is very great, others who speak English, and some savages...The number of Catholics of this diocese has never

been calculated exactly, it being impossible to take an exact census; but one can conjecture approximately forty thousand. The episcopal see is in the city of St. Louis twelve miles below the mouth of the Missouri; this city contains presently about eight thousand inhabitants, of which at least three thousand are Catholics; it prospers and grows continually. More than three quarters of the Catholic inhabitants speak French. We have here the following establishments: 1° The Cathedral begun about eleven or twelve years ago on a fairly grand plan, but so badly executed by the workers that it is threatened by ruin. I have been obliged to pay the debts for this building of more than six thousand dollars to prevent the sale of the land and the houses in which I live with my clergy and at present make every effort in my power to make the repairs and necessary additions which I estimate will grow to ten thousand dollars. You know that as with also nearly all the bishops of the United States I have no fixed revenues. It is necessary then to count on providence. I have with me only two priests who serve other parishes in the countryside where there are no curates. 2° We have in St. Louis a House of the Religious of the Sacred Heart; they raise a certain number of orphans, conduct a boarding school for young ladies, a day school, and a free school. About a hundred girls profit from the advantages this establishment offers. 3° We have also begun a hospital which has been entrusted to the Sisters of Charity of the Congregation of Emmitsburg. It is the means by which providence cares for a good number of laborers, sailors, and blacks, who are received there gratis, and with a charity that astonishes protestants and Catholics alike ... The buildings of the hospital are still poor old wooden houses. Here everything is still *in fieri* [just beginning]. 4° St. Louis has also a beautiful Catholic College that belongs to the Jesuits. They opened it last November and they have already more than 80 students of whom a score are boarders, the rest externs, these last instructed free of charge. This establishment will do much good.

The Seminary of the Diocese of St. Louis is at the Barrens near Perryville, in Perry County, Missouri, 80 miles south of St. Louis and six miles from the Mississippi river. It belongs to the Priests of the Congregation of the Mission of St. Vincent de Paul; it was founded about twelve years ago; it has prospered through the country; it has presently 28 seminarians and 72 boarders in the College, four priests of the Congregation of the Mission, and nine brothers of the same Congregation. The parish counts about two hundred families, all American. There are two churches: one 15 miles from the Seminary, where one of the Priests of that establishment goes once a month to hold church, and another near the Seminary where every Sunday and feast day services are held with great pomp and majesty. Mass is still said in the old church, which is a *log house;* but a new one has begun 120 feet long and 72 wide; it is [only] 3 feet high even though it was begun nearly five years ago; lack of means in a parish composed entirely of poor people caused the work to languish, and it is only through the help of strangers on whom they depend that they hope to finish it...

[Rosati then provides information on the other parishes of the diocese: in Missouri at Ste. Genevieve (with Little Canada), Fredericktown, Carondelet, Florissant, St. Charles, Portage aux Sioux, La Dardenne, Côte sans Dessein, New Madrid, Mines de Plomb (and Potosi); in Arkansas at Poste; in Illinois at Cahokia, Prairie du Rocher, O'Hara Settlement (with dependent missions), Kaskaskia, and Sangamon. Fever River and Prairie du Chien are also listed but as too far away to be served. In all but Potosi and O'Hara Settlement and dependencies the populations are described as being predominantly French-speaking.]

Leopoldine Society of Vienna, Bishop Joseph Rosati, 10 March 1830 (MLEO7/158), Archives of the University of Notre Dame, Notre Dame, Ind. Printed by permission.

10. Reverend Mathias Loras Tells His Mother of His Missionary Life in Alabama, 1830

Mathias Loras (1792–1858), whose father was guillotined in the Reign of Terror, left a promising career in France to serve a fellow Lyonnais, Bishop Michael Portier, in Alabama in 1828. Labors that carried him long distances were typical of missionaries in the South. He would in 1837 be named bishop of Dubuque, Iowa.

You may now say truly indeed that you have a son who is a missionary. Here I am at the extreme end of Alabama, more than a 100 leagues from Mobile, with Mr. [Gabriel] Chalon, a young priest, cousin of our bishop. During the past month we have been traveling about our vast diocese, in order to visit and encourage the Catholics to take measures accordingly to procure for them the aids of religion which they lack entirely. How heartbreaking is the spectacle constantly before our eyes! Villages and whole cities where one can count no more than one or two or three Catholic families, and others still where Catholicism is unknown save as a thing to be despised. These poor, unfortunate people are nearly all Protestants, but are divided as usual into a multitude of sects, the chief ones being the Episcopalians, the Presbyterians, the Methodists, and the Anabaptists. However, this is not an irreligious people, as so many others are. Many of them seem to me to be indeed in good faith. And, according to their principle that all religions are good, they willingly listen to preaching, even to that of Catholic priests. This is a disposition which, I hope, will lead many of them to a knowledge of the truth. Mr. Chalon, who knows English well, preached at Montgomery, at Tuscaloosa and at Huntsville, not in churches, which are all Protestant, but in town halls. Catholics and Protestants all gathered there and appeared very well satisfied. Some, I believe, have had good reflections, and very likely these first casts of the net will not be without effect. It was something new indeed for the residents of Tuscaloosa, which is the seat of government, and where no Catholic priest had ever yet penetrated, the sight of the ceremonies of the Mass which we celebrated, and of Baptism, which we administered in a particular house, the home of a zealous Catholic.

However, Divine Providence arranged a few consolations for us at Moulton, a little village near Florence, on the left bank of the Tennessee, celebrated by Chateaubriand. We were expected there. Mr. O'Neil, an excellent Catholic, informed of our coming, received us with all the eagerness that sincere attachment to the true religion can inspire. We were visited at once by others who were similarly minded as he, and who contended for the honor of offering hospitality to the messengers of God. We said Mass in his parlor, baptized several infants there, and on the following Sunday Mr. Chalon preached at the Town Hall, where a large audience, for that region, listened with the greatest attention, and one can say with a kind of veneration... What will it be if ever I have the consolation of being able to preach in English! Oh! this I desire, I assure you, with keenest ardor. The apostle should not think he is sent just to baptize, but rather to preach. We will continue on our course for several weeks. I shall give you the detail of other successes which the Good God doubtless has in store for us, and then I shall go and plunge myself into the midst of an American family, so that I may devote myself during several months to the study of English.

However, our Bishop, is alone at Mobile, to direct the Seminary, to administer the parish, and to superintend our large building operations at Spring Hill. And why? because we lack priests. The good ecclesiastics of the Diocese of Lyons, and of other parts of France, so well supplied with ministers of the altar should therefore give a thought to our poor diocese! What abundant harvest offers itself!...

"Documents," *Acta et Dicta* 4 (1916): 291–93 (translation modified by a reading of the original in the *Annales de l'Association de la Propagation de la Foi* 4 [1830–31]: 684–87).

11. Bishop Richard Pius Miles's Report to the Leopoldine Society, 1840

Maryland-born Richard Pius Miles, O.P. (1791–1860), was provincial of the American Dominicans when chosen to be the first bishop of Nashville, Tennessee, in 1837. Chosen largely to relieve the aging Bishop Flaget of this distant charge, Miles began his episcopal career with fewer resources than any other American bishop.

The Diocess of Nashville, to which I was appointed two years since, was, prior to that time, a part of the Diocess of Bardstown. From want of Priests this portion of the Diocess had been almost entirely neglected, receiving only an occasional visit from a Clergyman living at the distance of fifty leagues.

When named bishop of Nashville just after being chosen by his fellow Dominicans as their provincial in 1837, Richard Pius Miles had no clergy in Tennessee and only one unfinished church in his see city.

Credit: John Gilmary Shea, *History of the Catholic Church in the United States,* vol. 4 (New York: J. G. Shea, 1892).

Many Catholics for want of instruction had lost their faith; whole families reared in ignorance of their duties, deprived of the sacraments & consoling advice & admonition of a spiritual guide, had either become infidels, or had joined the different sectarians among whom they lived; most of those in whom a glimmering of faith was yet visible, were luke-warm & indifferent; the more pious portion despairing of ever having a Priest stationed in Nashville had long since left there, to seek the consolations of Religion elsewhere.

I found in Nashville a small church unfinished & the only one in the Diocess & this in a place so inaccessible as to render it very difficult to get to it in bad weather; we need greatly at present two other churches.

I was one year alone without a Priest to assist me, & was obliged during that time to traverse a region of country entirely unknown to me, in search of the scattered catholics who had been wandering for many years, as sheep without a shepherd; some of them had not seen a Priest for thirty years! My journeys were made on horseback, without a companion, carrying with me from house to house the necessary ornaments for the celebration of the Holy Sacrifice; at length from excessive fatigue of body & anxiety of mind, I fell sick of a malignant fever, & in a few days my case was considered hopeless; at this moment of my greatest distress Divine Providence sent to my assistance a Pious Priest [Joseph Stokes], who came and administered to me the last sacraments; this priest is yet in my Diocess & will continue.

During the first year of my Episcopacy I had no means of subsistence but the voluntary contributions of my poor flock, many of whom had but little more than the mere necessaries of life; this was my only resource until I received assistance from the Leopoldine Society who were the first to relieve my distress, from whom I acknowledge with gratitude I have received on two occasions the aggregate amount of twelve thousand florins.

Having been taken from a religious order, I came to my Diocess with my hands empty; having not even a book; I have one plain mitre, no crozier nor any ornaments proper for a Pontifical Mass; these I must procure in Europe as they cannot be had in America.

I have purchased a lot of ground on which to build a church a seminary & a dwelling house; I hope by the united assistance of the Societies of Vienna and Lyons to begin my church next year.

The only means of spreading catholicity in our diocess is to build churches and to place clergymen in them to explain our doctrines to the Protestants who usually frequent our churches in great numbers & attend well to the instructions when delivered with mildness; I have hopes of making many converts by this means; it is also an inducement for catholics who always settle where there is a church.

For the want of churches we are now frequently obliged to preach in protestant places of worship or in the town house [court house], or wherever we can collect an audience, not infrequently under the shades of the trees in the woods.

I have now five priests actually engaged in my Diocess & two others learning the language of the country to fit them for the mission; two students of theology whom I am obliged to feed, clothe, & educate gratis.

Leopoldine Society of Vienna, Bishop Richard Pius Miles, 1840 (MLEO 1/64c), Archives of the University of Notre Dame, Notre Dame, Ind. Printed by permission.

12. Father John Odin's Early Efforts in Texas, 1842

French-born John Mary Odin, C.M. (1800–1870), was professor of theology at the Vincentian seminary and missionary in Missouri when sent to Texas in 1840. There he ministered to many of his former parishioners from Missouri. When he wrote the following to the procurator general of the Vincentians in Rome, he was unaware he had been named vicar apostolic of Texas.

... My intention was to spend the summer in Galveston, but after three weeks preparing for their Easter duties those who had still not fulfilled them, I was told that the house that served as a chapel was going to be occupied by a family newly arrived in these parts. Not knowing where to set up my portable altar, after carrying it painfully from place to place, I thought that while I was waiting for the completion of the small church I had begun my time would be better spent visiting the Catholics scattered on both sides. I left then for Houston.

It was the time the fevers broke out in that town; all those stricken by it hurried to reconcile themselves with God, and many other people presented themselves at the tribunal of penance and the holy table. However, at the end of two weeks the quarters where I assembled the faithful was converted into a tavern, and it was necessary for me to think of moving still farther. On the banks of the Brazos thirty miles from Houston live about twenty Catholic families, who came some years ago from Kentucky and Missouri; as I had not been able to visit them up to then, I went to them and was quite edified by the zeal and the eagerness with which those neophytes welcomed me. Everyone, young and old, went to confession. There was sickness in all the families: so I offered the holy sacrifice in each house to give everybody the consolation of attending holy Mass. Sunday I celebrated in the most central dwelling, where a great number of non-Catholics came to assist at the instructions. This little flock, who wished eagerly to erect a humble chapel to the Good Shepherd, did not have the means: I hope one day to be able to fulfill their wishes! A protestant who was ill a long time begged me to come see him; we spent a long time together conversing about Religion, following which he embraced our holy Faith: when I thought him sufficiently instructed I administered the sacraments, and I have learned since that he died a most edifying death.

I left these good catholics to go to Mills Creek and Cummings Creek between the Brazos and the Colorado, but on the second day of the journey I was attacked by a violent fever, accompanied by almost continual vomiting. Finding myself in a part of the country little inhabited, alone and without any acquaintance, I determined to push to the Lavaca River, where lived some settlers who resided formerly in Missouri. Though scarcely sixty-five miles away, it took me three days to make this short distance. You cannot imagine all I suffered from the rays of a scorching sun, from want of water, and from a burning fever. The second day especially I thought I had reached my last hour. I stopped often to lie on the grass but soon the violence of the illness made me get back on my horse.

I did not know exactly where I was going when two or three miles along I discovered a forest. The hope of finding relief in its shade made me go to the first woods I saw. The improvement I wanted was not realized. As soon as I stretched under a tree the illness always got worse. Consumed by thirst, I got back on my horse, wandering about, when Providence made me spy in the distance a column of smoke that seemed to indicate a dwelling. I hurried in that direction and had the good fortune of finding, in the bosom of a family newly arrived from Michigan, all of the help the most tender charity suggested. I drank deeply and spent the night in their tent. The next day, feeling a little better, I continued my journey, and reached finally the homes of my old friends of Missouri. The fever did not leave me for twenty-four days; there

was neither doctor nor medicine; so I abandoned myself entirely to the good
care of Providence...

Annales de l'Association de la Propagation de la Foi 15 (1842): 433–35.

The Old Northwest

The Old Northwest was the product of two frontiers: one an extension of
the farmers' backwoods frontier from Pennsylvania, Maryland, and Kentucky;
the other an extension of the fur-gathering frontier of the Great Lakes from
Canada. The second will be documented in part 2. Ohio's first Catholics
were actually German-speaking farmers from Conewago, the starting point
also for Latrobe and Loretto in western Pennsylvania, which in turn were
springboards for the wooded lands above the Ohio River.

13. Reverend Demetrius Gallitzin on the Founding of Loretto and His Contention with Thomas Elder, 1800

*Demetrius Gallitzin (1770–1840), a convert from the Russian nobility ordained
by Bishop Carroll in 1795, writing from Conewago, tells him of the beginning
of his backwoods community later called Loretto but also of a Marylander who
chose Kentucky instead of Pennsylvania.*

Being just now arrived from the Backwoods, and hearing of James Driscolls
going to Baltimore, I cannot let this favourable opportunity slip, to give your
Lordship some brief account of the state of that part of the Spiritual Vineyard
entrusted to my care. I am sorry that I cannot be as diffuse as the importance of the subject seems to require; but the shortness of the time does not
allow of it.

Our Church which was only begun in harvest, got finished, fit for service
the night before Christmas. It is about 44 foot long by 25, built of White
Pine Logs, with a very good Shingle roof. I kept Service in it at Christmas
for the first time, to the very great satisfaction of the whole Congregation,
who seemed very much moved, at a sight which they never beheld before.
There is also a house built for me 16 foot by 14 besides a little kitchen and
a stable. I have now, thanks be to God a little home of my own, for the first
time since I came to this country, and God grant that I may be able to keep
it; the prospect of forming a lasting establishment for promoting the cause
of Religion, is very great; the Country is amazing fertile, most entirely inhabited by Roman Catholicks, and so advantageously situated with regard to
Market that there is no doubt but it will be a place of refuge for a great many
Catholicks. A great many have bought property there, in the course of these
three months passed, and a good many more are expected. The Congregation

consists at present of about forty families, but there is no end to the Roman Catholicks in all the Settlements round about me. What will become of them all, if we do not soon receive a new supply of Priests I do not know. I try as much as I can to persuade them to settle around me...

Mr Elder went out with me to the Backwoods last September was a year, in order to hunt for Land as he was reduced so low near Taney-town that he could hardly raise the necessary subsistence for his family.[1] He liked my land so well that after considering a few days on the subject, he resolved to buy it; and in the presence of five witnesses, whose depositions I took down in writing, very lately, bound himself by a promise to buy my land after selling his own and to pay me four dollars an acre, 50 pounds down and 50 pounds a year, and to move to the said place, provided I would promise, after obtaining the Bishops consent to live there myself...[There follows a lengthy account of Elder's failure to live up to the bargain by moving instead to Kentucky after Gallitzin had cultivated the land for him.]

One of Mr Elders daughters, the only one that never wished to go to the backwoods, was at Conewago last Summer, and met Yr Lordship there. She told her parents on her return that you advised them not to go to the backwoods, but to Kentucky. This seemed to have influenced them a good deal. However I am very well convinced that yr Lordship never was acquainted with any of the above circumstances...

Carroll Papers, 8A-N-2, Archives of the Archdiocese of Baltimore. Printed by permission.

14. Bishop Edward Fenwick Begs Reverend Stephen Badin for Help [1827]

Maryland-born Edward Dominic Fenwick, O.P. (1768–1832), after founding the first Dominican house in the United States, served as a simple missionary until named bishop of Cincinnati in 1821. Unlike later bishops in the South he is able to report progress within his first few years.

...I am hardly equal to the work and worry of the exercise of the holy ministry, the administration of the diocese, and the necessary arrangements of providing for the subsistence of the clergy. Rome, in creating the bishopric, did not endow it. When they made me a bishop, I had not a penny to my name, having employed all my patrimony in founding the convent of St. Rose [in Kentucky], and they have forgotten to provide for the subsistence of the bishop.

I found in Cincinnati neither a house prepared for my lodging nor a church in which to pray and assemble the congregation. When I established myself

---

1. Thomas H. Elder (1748–1832) was the grandfather of Archbishop William Henry Elder of Cincinnati.

In this painting preserved in St. Joseph's Church, Somerset, Ohio, Father (later Bishop) Edward Dominic Fenwick, O.P., blesses in 1808, when passing through, the first permanent Catholic settlers in Ohio, Germans from Pennsylvania.

Credit: OPUS, the Dominican History Project, Chicago. Reproduced by permission.

eight or nine years ago in Ohio, there was only one poor little chapel twenty-two feet by eighteen erected [in Somerset] by the zeal of our good Germans, who, few and very poor, have not been able to finish it. Upon becoming bishop, it was necessary for me to leave (as at St. Rose) that chapel, the cabin next to it, and the farm, to take up lodging in Cincinnati and earn there my daily bread as best I could. There were only three or four Irish Catholic families and six or seven German ones, all poor and incapable of providing for my existence. In 1822 there were here only five communions at Easter; it was the first year of my episcopacy and of my residence in my episcopal city: at Easter this year I counted at least three hundred. Then I had only one priest with me, to traverse that immense country and administer the sacraments to the catholics scattered here and there. Today I have nine (not counting four missionaries in Michigan). I ought to have twelve, but three left me. The others seem content with their poor state, which obliges them to wear coarse and much used clothing.

We have eleven churches, if I dare call them that. Five are brick and only partly constructed because we lack the means. These buildings are erected on such a simple scale that 3,000 dollars would be enough for me to complete them. We need also an annual sum of a hundred dollars for the support of a priest who would do nothing else than travel over the countryside to baptize, instruct, and gather the stray sheep. Two hundred dollars, just once, would be needed for new equipment, the purchase of a horse, etc.; I flatter myself that, some way or other, you will find me the means to do this good work. To that end I place my confidence in divine Providence, *in te, Domine, speravi* [in you, O Lord, I hope].

Annales de l'Association de la Propagation de la Foi 3 (1828): 291–92.

15. Bishop Simon Bruté's Report to Rome, 1836

The scholarly Simon Felix Bruté de Remur (1779–1839), a founder of Mount St. Mary's College and Seminary in Emmitsburg, Maryland, was ill-suited to the tasks of a frontier bishop but responded well to the demands of the changing Catholic populations of Indiana when chosen first bishop of Vincennes in 1834.

I. In and about Vincennes I had to care for 1,500 impoverished Catholics, primitive and illiterate, souls long neglected, amiably, however, and reverently enough disposed, but struggling under a decline of piety and religious instruction. [Having] no companion priest with me, I lived entirely alone.

I gave two instructions every Sunday and feast day, one in French the language of the greater number, the other in English.

During Advent and Lent I catechized the younger people, six and some eighteen and even twenty years old, who had not received Communion. I received 20 at Christmas and 60 at Easter at First Communion, later 90 at Confirmation.

I had sick people to visit, often at a great distance, of whom I attended 23 to the grave...Only 10 marriages — 68 baptisms, indeed some of adults and of Protestants 4 or 5; others of children of Protestants.

As a new guest in this place, received humanely even by Protestants, I have had to visit many and to win them to myself — I have had to inquire of sects (6 there) and of the newspapers of the sects for our Catholics; and much also had to be written very accurately, that is, for submitting to the press...Thus in the beginning of my new condition in a higher state [my] correspondence was extensive and even oppressive to a bishop living alone, and without a secretary or companion.

To this must be added the arrangement and collection of registers and papers and the fresh charge, as something new, to get acquainted with the church, the surrounding lands, the caretaker and the magistrates of the place; yet I am little competent, as I am sorry to confess, in temporal matters. I found in Vincennes, for example, a new church erected a few years ago, from wall to wall of the building 115 feet long, 60 feet wide, entirely bare, decorated with not even one picture of any kind — the cost of the building not yet paid...[Bruté wished to give some of its land to the Jesuits for a college. He obtained four Sisters of Charity of Nazareth for a girls school in Vincennes. He had little success with seminarians.]

II. Thus I was pastor of Vincennes. — In the diocese I accomplished what I could. In the vicinity I was pastor likewise at places 3, 4, 5 leagues distant in Lawrenceville, Cheese, Au Chat, &c. I was likewise pastor farther away in Terre Haute & Paris (for I have villages by the name of Paris, Rome, Carthage, &c.) in so far as to celebrate mass in them, administer the sacraments to many on several occasions, &c. And in the form of visitations I was often in the parishes of Mr. [Simon] Lalumiere, which are 6 or 7 leagues (25 and 28 Italian miles) distant. Also I have blessed (the first by me) a kind of church built of rough logs in the name of St. Mary the Mother of God. This is near St. Peter's.[1]

Then, before I left for Europe, I decided to visit the places further distant, from 80 to more than 100 leagues. — First, Chicago (225 miles on a direct line but more indeed by way of the missions) where I administered confirmation to some and consoled the fine young priest [Irenaeus St. Cyr], who for several months is not able to see a fellow priest. Then I went to Pokagon, a village in the diocese of Monseigneur [Frederic] Rese [of Detroit] but inhabited by many of my subjects also, savages or men of the forests. Also I visited another within the limits of my own diocese, the village of Chicakos, the residence of other savages — I administered confirmation to 16 of them. — But the missions of Mr. [Louis] Deseille from Belgium who has lived among them for a long time had prepared more than 50 of the best of them for baptism and prepared 30 for first communion; thus increasing his flock of forest men (or savages) which already consisted of more than 600 in Pokagon and 200 in Chicakos.

Meanwhile, after travelling 600 miles or 200 French leagues on horseback for 23 days, passing through many towns where I found a few Catholic families and, as occasion offered, ministering by words or by sacraments, I returned to Vincennes, my see . . .

Thomas T. McAvoy, C.S.C., trans. and ed., "Bishop Bruté's Report to Rome in 1836," *Catholic Historical Review* 29 (1943): 188–91.

16. Reverend Joseph Kundek's Report on German Settlements, 1839

Joseph Kundek (1810–57), a Croatian priest newly arrived, was sent in 1838 to the German Catholics of Jasper, Indiana, who had settled there in 1834. In this report to the archbishop of Vienna he tells also of visiting workers on the canals that would bring a close to the frontier period. In 1840 Kundek would found the town of Ferdinand, another German Catholic stronghold in southern Indiana.

---

1. The first English-speaking parish in Indiana, St. Peter's was founded in 1818 by Catholics from Kentucky.

With a sad heart I must inform you that God called our good Bishop [Bruté] to Himself on the 26th of June, a little after midnight, and has bestowed upon him the crown of an apostle...I am the proud possessor of several letters written by him, letters that never fail to console me in my arduous work as missionary. Since he asked me to write a detailed account of my activities here to your Grace, I now hasten to do so. As soon as I could get away from my home station at Jasper, I decided to pay a visit to various other points. First I went to Vincennes to consult with my Bishop regarding this matter. Here I had occasion to preach in German, to give instruction to the German Catholics, and to hear their confessions. General [William Henry] Harrison had given these Germans, some sixty all told, a plot of ground free of cost; however, as they have no German priest to take care of them, the Bishop could not as yet agree to carry out the project.

From Vincennes I journeyed over wide prairies towards Lake Michigan in the state of Illinois and also visited Picquet's Settlement. These prairies are immense level tracts of land, without hills or valleys or streams: all you see is the heaven and the sea of waving grass. In winter, if one is caught upon such an immense prairie, there is danger of being frozen to death. Many travelers have thus been lost. In summer, if the dry grass happens to catch fire, the scene is remarkable at night, something like the Aurora borealis. I have witnessed it several times.

This settlement of Mr. [Joseph] Picquet in Jasper county [Illinois], north of these prairies, contains some 18,000 acres of land. This good man, who hails from Strassburg, Alsace, has in mind to gradually turn it over to worthy Catholic emigrants from the country of Alsace. He has also erected a priest's house and a church, which is completely furnished. The Redemptorist Fathers are thinking of founding a house there so that they can take charge of the local parish and of the surrounding country. As this settlement stretches out from nine to twelve miles on all sides, there is plenty of room for the spreading of the word of God.

From there I went by way of Princeton to Evansville some sixty miles away. Upon arriving there I learned to my sorrow that I would not be able to say Mass, since the pastor, Father [Anthony] Deydier, a truly apostolic man, had taken the missal and the church vestments with him, as he was gone on a collecting tour for the building of a church. However, since there are more than thirty German families here or in the immediate vicinity of the town, I could not refrain from conducting services for them, and as there were English speaking Catholics there too, I spoke in both English and German. I closed the services with the Litany of the Blessed Virgin and other prayers. Several had gone to confession but they could not receive Holy Communion, as there were no particles. Still these services, conducted in the room in which the good priest lives, and where he dines on a poor diet, consisting mainly of potatoes, proved to be of a consoling nature to the assembled faithful. The Germans here have been anxiously awaiting a German priest for years...

Hardly had I returned to Jasper when I was sent to visit the workers who are engaged in digging the canal that is to connect the Ohio with Lake Michigan, a distance equivalent to that between Vienna and Munich. Upon arriving there I found many Protestant preachers present. As they used to attend my sermons, I made it a point to dwell often on those subjects in which they differ from the Catholic teachings. My purpose was twofold, for not only did I seek to strengthen the faith of the Catholics, but at the same time I sought to convince the non-Catholics of the truths of Catholicity. On the 4th of May I spoke to a mixed gathering on the bank of the White River. We were grouped together under a mighty tree; perhaps at the same spot the Indians formerly offered up sacrifice to their gods...

Francis S. Holweck, "Two Pioneer Indiana Priests," *Mid-America* 1 (1929): 64–66.

17. Bishop William Quarter Writes of the Early Years of the Diocese of Chicago, 1845

Irish-born William Quarter (1806–48) was chosen first bishop of Chicago in 1843. In the following letter to the Leopoldine Society he describes the still-primitive state of a diocese nearing the end of its frontier era with an emphasis on the Germans for the benefit of the mission-aid society to which he was making his appeal.

... I cheerfully fulfill your request for information regarding my new diocese, so that you may become fully acquainted with its temporal and spiritual needs. But how can I present an exhaustive report on the latter, since our wants are so manifold and numerous that a European can scarcely form an adequate conception of them. This is true of all western dioceses in these States, but it applies to mine in a special manner... [Quarter gives a history of the state going back to the original natives and the French-Canadian settlements.] An immense area of the state is still covered by impenetrable forests, which at intervals alternate between meadows and marshes. Of particular note are the so-called prairies or immense meadows, perfectly level, which are found here in Illinois. The soil, as a general rule, is good and its cultivation advances from day to day. The State is being populated by immigration, which is also a great boon to this community from a religious standpoint, and would be moreso if America would favor the only true and holy faith.

The Catholic population of this state consists mostly of immigrants, of whom a great percentage are Germans. If, as customary, these people settle on farms, far distant from a church, they soon lose that love and devotion they [once] entertained toward the Catholic religion... We have no means of saving such for the Church, since we have no priests in these western districts who might prevent it, and consequently in recent years the number which has thus been lost to the Church is by no means small ... Truly we stand in great need of priests and churches in this new diocese. These churches need not be costly edifices, but mere simple low chapels of frame construction, i.e., houses built of logs which are cut and laid crosswise upon each other and then clamped or nailed firmly to each other, the spaces between being filled out with earth and plastered up with clay. In Europe people would scarcely use such houses for barns, and here they serve as dwellings for the Lord God of Hosts!

The immigrants to this state are on the average extremely poor. If they purchase farms immediately they find it very difficult to raise the purchase price and to procure the necessary house furniture, the farm implements, the wagons, the requisite live-stock, horses, cows, oxen, etc. During this long period of purchases and equipment they give little heed to their religion and leave it altogether to the priest to find ways and means to build a small and shabby-looking church. If at such times the priest would appeal to them for help and support, he could rest assured he would be turned down on the plea that they are not able to assume such burdens ...

During the past two years my band of missionaries has been increased by sixteen, which is indeed a source of much consolation to me. A new clerical seminary has also been erected, at which one professor especially teaches the German language in order that the students on entering the holy priesthood may be enabled to preach and hear confessions in this language. The new cathedral is likewise completed and was dedicated on the first Sunday of October, 1845. German priests are administering to the Catholics in their own language both here in Chicago and vicinity, as well as in other parishes of this diocese. But as yet the Germans have no church of their own, which is indeed a great drawback. The faithful of every nationality gather in one and the same church; this condition does not permit of special religious instructions for the German children and people in their own language, and consequently no German priest can exercise a direct wholesome influence over them, which would be possible if they had their own church, in which the sermons and instructions could be conducted in the German language.

I therefore urgently beg you to provide me with means to ameliorate these conditions and to build a church for the German Catholics of this city.

Francis J. Epstein, "Illinois and the Leopoldine Association," *Illinois Catholic Historical Review* 1 (1918): 229–33.

Part 2

THE FUR-GATHERING
FRONTIER

Introduction

"I am then, my reverend father," the young Jean-Pierre Aulneau wrote to a fellow Jesuit in 1735, "about to set out on a journey of twelve hundred leagues, to go among savages who have never yet met a frenchman or a missionary." He was to accompany the expedition of Pierre Gaultier de Varennes, Sieur de la Vérendrye, to find an Indian people who lived on a great river that led to the Sea of the West, "the great river," Aulneau conjectured, "which father [Eusebio] Kino, a German Jesuit, mentions in the map which he traced to the regions lying to the north of california."[1] Another Jesuit remarked with less enthusiasm that the Canadian officials were "looking not for the western sea but for the sea of beaver."[2] Father Aulneau never made the journey; he was slain by Sioux at the Lake of the Woods. La Vérendrye and his sons, however, would be the first Europeans to set foot on the northern plains of what would become the United States, this well before English colonists crossed the Appalachian Mountains.[3]

The economy of the fur-gathering frontier determined its far-ranging character. While the Spaniards had been lured by gold and the English by land, the French were drawn ever westward in their pursuit of fur. English penetration into the backwoods of the middle tier of North America was, by comparison, slow and deliberate. The French were given to great leaps into the unknown. They were by temperament explorers, and their natural routes of exploration were waterways — the St. Lawrence River to the Great Lakes, then down the Mississippi River. West of the Mississippi, French-Canadian voyageurs (canoe paddlers) would come to know every twist and turn of every watercourse from the Red River of the North to the Red River of the South well before the Americans arrived. French-Canadian trappers initiated

---

1. Reuben Gold Thwaites, *Jesuit Relations and Allied Documents*, 73 vols. (Cleveland: Burrows, 1896, 1901), 68:249–55.
2. Ibid., 68:283.
3. G. Hubert Smith, *The Explorations of the La Vérendryes in the Northern Plains, 1738–43* (Lincoln: University of Nebraska Press, 1980).

31

the American mountain men into the intricacies of the career that made them famous.

The Great Lakes, however, was the first region in which the two civilizations met and mingled. Although land-seeking Americans would eventually replace fur-seeking *Canadiens* south of the American border, it was one of the contributions of the latter to determine the centers of American Catholic growth. Detroit, Chicago, Milwaukee, St. Paul, and a considerable number of other cities on the Great Lakes and upper Mississippi River Valley had their beginnings in the attempts of ordinary French-Canadian trappers to stake out their claims with Native American traders in furs.

The first clergy on this frontier of the American church were those priests, for the most part foreign-born, who were compelled by a desire to win the souls of the pagan Indians. Those of the Great Lakes were the last to evade the American Indian removal policy. The great majority of French-Canadian trappers had, according to the custom of the country, taken Indian wives.

Beyond the Mississippi, Canadian trappers and traders to a remarkable degree laid out the roads of Manifest Destiny. The important role of the *Canadiens* in New Mexico has rarely been acknowledged.[4] Their not insignificant role in demonstrating the farming potential of the Willamette River Valley in Oregon has been largely ignored. Their indispensable role in the success of the fur companies of American foundation in the upper Missouri River Valley has excited few historians. While such self-proclaimed mountain men as Kit Carson, Jim Bridger, Tom Fitzpatrick, and Jedediah Smith were never wanting for popularizers, their mentors, Etienne Provost, Lucien Fontenelle, Antoine Leroux, and the Robidoux brothers, were content with obscurity.[5]

Also unchronicled were a number of other contributions of the insouciant *Canadiens*. They served as a socioeconomic bridge between Anglo, Hispanic, and Native American cultures, in the process delaying an inevitable conflict between red and white men for a generation or more. These unlettered trappers acted as instructors, interpreters, and guides for explorers, writers, artists, and scientists, and especially for the priests who came to convert the savages of those parts, only secondarily to serve the trappers themselves. The fur-trappers' fraternity was almost totally devoid of religious prejudices on the part of those members both of Catholic and of Calvinist background.

Wealthy creole families of St. Louis, particularly the powerful Chouteau clan, were the sole organizers of trading and trapping expeditions until newly arrived Americans perceived in the 1820s the tremendous profits to be made

---

4. But see David J. Weber, *The Taos Trappers: The Fur Trade in the Southwest, 1540–1846* (Norman: University of Oklahoma Press, 1971), chap. 6.

5. See Janet Lecompte's introduction to LeRoy R. Hafen, ed., *French Fur Traders and Voyageurs in the American West* (Lincoln: University of Nebraska Press, 1993).

in fur. The creole families were generous benefactors, particularly of the missionaries who went west from St. Louis.

The fur-gathering frontier in the United States was ephemeral, the 1820s and 1830s being the decades of most intense pursuit of the lowly beaver. After its depletion, some of the *Canadiens* continued to chase the buffalo. Others settled down to farming, others to servicing western migrants. Still others acted as scouts and interpreters for the army. They remained a part of western society.

Because of the transient character of the fur-gathering frontier, the contributions of the French Canadians to American Catholicism are less obvious than those of English or German farmers and Irish miners. The church, however, would never have advanced so rapidly nor anchored itself so well geographically were it not for the westering propensities of these simple voyageurs, as the many French place-names throughout the areas they traversed bear witness. Their presence, moreover, was not unrelated to the fact that the third largest group of Catholic farmers in 1900 were of French-Canadian ancestry.

The Great Lakes

French-Canadian activities south of the national boundary that ran through the Great Lakes were monopolized by the Northern Department of the American Fur Company founded by John Jacob Astor in 1808 and headquartered at Michilimackinac, on the Straits of Mackinac, between Lakes Huron and Michigan. Its trading posts became in the 1820s and 1830s the chief centers of the Catholic Church in that part of the United States.

18. Gabriel Richard's Account of the Church in the Michigan Territory, 1826

French-born Gabriel Richard, S.S. (1767–1832), intended originally for the Sulpi-cian seminary in Baltimore, was sent instead by Bishop Carroll to the Illinois country in 1792 and to Detroit in 1798. There he would see his French-Canadian flock overwhelmed by Americans, as the following statistical report to the Society for the Propagation of the Faith reveals.

The land where I have exercised the ministry from June 3, 1798, is called the Michigan Territory...[Richard describes the limits stretching from Lake Erie to the Lake of the Woods.] In this immense extent of land there is at this time a Catholic population of approximately:

	Catholic Families	Individuals	Churches and chapels
At Prairie-du-Chien, at Fort Crawford, near the mouth of the Wisconsin at the Mississippi	120	720	0
At Green Bay, at Fort Brown, the old mission of St. Francis Xavier	84	504	1
At Michilimackinac, mission of St. Anne	80	480	in ruins
At Drumond Island	40	240	0
At Sault Ste. Marie	40	120	0
At Clinton River (St. Francis de Sales) and environs	70	420	1
At St. Clair River and environs	55	330	0
At Detroit, along the river, fifteen miles above and twenty miles below Detroit (that is, on Lake Erie)	300	1800	2
At River Raisin (St. Anthony)	150	900	1
At Miami Bay (St. Joseph)	90	540	1
At Miami River and environs	40	240	0
From May 1 until October 1 to Michilimackinac came more than six hundred Canadian voyageurs to exchange furs for merchandise		600	
Total	1849	6894	6

Mr. [Vincent] Badin arrived March 7 from a mission tour he had made the first three weeks of Lent, to the ends of St. Anne's parish of Detroit, a distance of thirty-six miles (twelve leagues), where he confessed a very great number of people at six different stations. One very important thing is that at four of the stations, without holding meetings, he called all the residents who soon cut and squared all the wood necessary to build chapels.

If to these 6,894 Frenchmen originally from Canada, you add three hundred and six Catholics who speak English scattered here and there (nearly all poor Irish), hardly a score born in America, you would have seven thousand for a total population of white Catholics: there is also a hundred people of color.

The American Protestant population is up to about thirteen thousand. It is probable that as many will come from the states of the East during the next season by the great [Erie] canal of three hundred sixty-five miles from Buffalo to Albany. In the month of May we saw arrive at Detroit each week, six steamboats, of which four were built this winter.

One of those that came last summer has brought several times more than three hundred persons. There is a continual movement from the east to the west, and especially to the superb lands of Michigan, which the government sells at a dollar and a quarter an acre, which is about five francs and five sous for a French arpent.

Detroit is already a considerable city, where in the course of the summer one saw more than a hundred and fifty merchant vessels. Seventy-two new houses were built last summer, and it is certain there will be more than a hundred in the course of this one. You can judge by this the importance of one city where must pass all the vessels which travel on three immense lakes, altogether a navigation of three hundred and fifty leagues, from Buffalo or Niagara to Chicago.

What hope for religion!

Although it is eight hundred miles from Detroit to New York, we can go there in six days for twenty-four dollars. When the steam boat that Perkins constructed in England on a new plan will be achieved, I think I could go to Europe from Detroit in fifteen or eighteen days.

Mr. Badin left April 18 to visit his missions of Sault Ste. Marie, Drummond Island, Mackinac, Arbre Croche, and Green Bay. He intends to make an apostolic excursion as far as Prairie du Chien, at the mouth of the Wisconsin at the Mississippi. Since the Jesuits of old, this place has seen only one priest, Father [Marie Joseph] Dunand, Trappist. I hope Mr. Badin succeeds in building a chapel there...

Annales de l'Association de la Propagation de la Foi 3 (1828): 325–29.

19. Account of Samuel Mazzuchelli, O.P., of the Mission of Green Bay, 1831

Samuel Charles Mazzuchelli (1806–64) as a Dominican seminarian in Rome volunteered for the American wilderness and would serve many cultures on the frontiers of the Old Northwest and Middle West. In his memoirs he recalled his earliest efforts to rekindle the faith of French-Canadian fur trappers on Lake Michigan.

The gentle breezes tempered by the rays of the April sun, messenger of a new life to nature, were beginning to melt and disperse the solid ice which in winter covers Lake Huron and Michigan for many miles in that strait dominated by Mackinac Island. Already the sight of a few sails gladdened the islanders and led the priest [Mazzuchelli himself] to hope that he could go again where, in the preceding autumn, he had sown a few seeds of the divine word upon a soil promising abundant harvest. At the beginning of May he left his little flock and went in a trading vessel to Green Bay in Wisconsin Territory.

The village consisted of a considerable number of houses scattered on both banks of the Fox River, where it empties into that inlet of Lake Michigan called, because of the color of its waters, Green Bay. There was a tradition among the old settlers that the Jesuits had begun a mission there in the seventeenth century; no traces of it remain however. At this time the people numbered approximately one thousand; almost all were of Canadian descent and married to the Indians. Left for many years without religious instruction, even though they had not abandoned their faith, they had at least forgotten all its practices. Many persons, though of mature age, who called themselves Catholics had not yet been baptized; a very small number had received the Eucharist only once; not a few were ignorant of the sacrament of matrimony.

The vice of drunkenness with all its detestable results prevailed without a single voice being raised to stop this ruinous, deep-seated habit.

The trade carried on with the Indians was extensive, since the country had an abundance of animals whose furs brought considerable profit. The poor Indians, in their dealings with the Canadians and with various traders who went there to exchange merchandise for pelts, had learned many vices — theft, vengeance, and an insatiable craving for strong drink. In fact, brandy was the universal medium of exchange; it could buy everything from the Indians including morality, and was the cause of unspeakable excesses...

[But] it must not be supposed that the Lord has no faithful adorers even in the midst of widespread corruption. Thus the Missionary found in this place several devout persons in whose houses he celebrated the Holy Sacrifice. On account of the distances between dwellings, however, he often had to change the place which was to serve as a church in order to make it easier for the people to get to divine service. Sometimes the altar was in an attic, sometimes in a deserted house; then again it would be moved to a large hall. In this way the presence of Christ sanctified the places in which the powers of darkness had ruled. Not a day passed without either public or private instructions. Some persons were guilty of drunkenness, others of theft, revenge, or unlawful transactions. Some scorned religion, others presumed to associate it with their vices; all, in short, needed the help of that holy teaching which prepares the saving remedy for all men, in all evils, and in all the circumstances of life. Needless to say, with such wayward people, the priest found abundant reasons for eloquence without ever having studied that noble and elevated art...

The venerable and humble Bishop Edward Fenwick arrived at Mackinac about the beginning of July [actually June 3] accompanied by the Reverend F[rederic]. Baraga, who was destined for the missions among the Indian tribes in the northern part of the state of Michigan. The bishop, who had heard of the good results in the western region, set out without delay to help in the work of conversion. Having obtained the use of a large room for several days, he began spiritual exercises for the French in Green Bay. It would not be easy to describe how earnestly and zealously the Bishop and his priest tried, with divine help, to bring about the desired improvement. A proof of this is the tireless application which kept both of them in the confessional throughout the week; the day not being long enough, it was necessary to use part of the night as well. Almost all the confessions covered a number of years — some included ten, twenty, or thirty. The holy day of Pentecost found many coming to the most Blessed Sacrament who had almost forgotten it; more than forty Indians were regenerated in the waters of baptism. The sevenfold grace of the Holy Spirit by the imposition of the Bishop's hand in the sacrament of confirmation descended upon many, among them not a few poor Indians. To these apostolic labors the outpouring of celestial grace corresponded. As the

With the help of French-Canadian residents, Rev. Irenaeus St. Cyr erected Chicago's first church in 1833.

Credit: Francis P. Clark Collection, Archives of the University of Notre Dame, Notre Dame, Ind. Reproduced by permission.

number of sins visibly diminished, scandals were less frequent, and the service of God was more whole-hearted . . .

Maria Michele Armato, O.P., and Mary Jeremy Finnegan, O.P., trans. and ed., *The Memoirs of Father Samuel Mazzuchelli, O.P.* (Chicago: Priory Press, 1967), 40–43. Printed by permission.

20. Reverend John Mary Irenaeus St. Cyr on the Beginning of the Catholic Church in Chicago, 1833

In April 1833 Bishop Rosati of St. Louis received a petition from 122 citizens of Chicago, most of them French Canadians, some mixed-blood Potawatomis, for a priest. Immediately he sent the young Irenaeus St. Cyr (1803–83), who would address also the Protestant citizens of the growing town.

If I have delayed so long to send you news you may be sure that this is not owing to negligence or much less to any lack of good will on my part. The fact is that as I have no acquaintance as yet with the people of Chicago and do not know how they stand as to the establishment of religion in their town, I have wished to sound them a little to the end that I may be less uncertain as to what to say to you about conditions here in the matter of religion.

While the number of Catholics is large, almost all of them are entirely without knowledge of the duties of religion. Still, the regularity with which they are present at Mass every Sunday and the attention and respect with which they assist thereat, give reason to hope that with patience and some Sunday instructions, we shall be able, with God's help, to organize a congregation of good Catholics. Many Protestants, even of the most distinguished of Chicago, appear to be much in favor of the Catholic religion, in particular Mr. [Thomas J. V.] Owen, the Indian agent, as also the doctor and several other respectable families who come to Mass every Sunday to assist at it with much respect.

The people of Chicago have taken up a subscription amounting to 261 dollars, and they hope to go even somewhat beyond that. Mr. Baptiste Beaubien gives a site on which to build the church...[1] As to what the Indian chiefs are reported to have promised for a church, nothing certain is known up to this. We must wait and see what the outcome will be of the treaty that is to take place next fall.

The eagerness shown by the people of Chicago, the Protestants even, to have a Catholic church, allows us to place great hopes in the future. Every Sunday so far, I have given an instruction alternately in English and French. I aim particularly to remove prejudices by showing as clearly as possible in what the teaching of the Church consists. In my first instruction I explained the meaning of the invocation of the saints, the difference there is between praying to God and praying to the saints, the meaning of the veneration paid to images and relics and the doctrine of the Catholic church regarding Purgatory. The second Sunday I preached in English on the unity of the Church of Jesus Christ. I showed its necessity, bringing out also how this unity is found in the Catholic Church. On Ascension day I preached in French on the real presence and afterwards explained in English the ceremony of the Mass. Pentecost day I set forth the rapid progress of the gospel throughout the world and the great results it accomplished in reforming morals (this in English). On Trinity day I explained in French the symbol of St. Ambrose on the Holy Trinity and then the Apostles' Creed, as also what we must absolutely know and believe in to be saved. I tell you all this, Monseigneur, not to show you what I have done, but that you may see whether what I have done is right or wrong and that I may learn how to proceed in the future. A number of persons have approached the tribunal of penance. I presume, Monseigneur, that you put some books in my trunk, as you gave me to understand at my departure. Up to the present I have been left to my own resources. I should like exceedingly to have some instructions in English and French, some French catechisms and two or three mission hymns.

To give you some idea of Chicago, I will tell you that since my arrival more then twenty houses have been built, while materials for new ones may

---

1. Jean Baptiste Beaubien was perhaps the first white person to settle in Chicago after the Fort Dearborn massacre of 1812. See "The Beaubiens of Chicago," *Illinois Catholic Historical Review* 2 (1919): 96–102.

be seen coming in from all sides. The situation of Chicago is the finest I have ever seen. Work is now proceeding on a harbor that will enable lake vessels to enter the town. Three arrived lately crowded with passengers who came to visit these parts and in most cases to settle down here. Everything proclaims that Chicago will one day become a great town and one of commercial importance...

Gilbert J. Garraghan, S.J., *The Catholic Church in Chicago, 1673–1841* (Chicago: Loyola University Press, 1921), 49–51 (translation modified by a reading of the original in the Archives of the Archdiocese of St. Louis).

21. Vincent Roy's Recollections of La Pointe, 1840

Son of a mixed-blood father and full-blooded Chippewa mother, Vincent Roy became a wealthy and respected merchant of Superior, Wisconsin. In 1839 he went with his family to La Pointe on Lake Superior, where the missionary and future bishop Frederic Baraga (1797–1868) was laboring. Here Roy recalls not only the missionary's habits but life at the trading post itself.

He [Baraga] said but one mass on Sundays. I do not recollect his teaching catechism on Sundays. Several times during the week he taught catechism regularly in the afternoon. In his visits he would hastily gather the adults and children of the neighborhood and teach his impromptu class the truths of faith. Vespers on Sundays without sermon. No stations on Fridays, but during Lent (he had stations) on Fridays and other days of the week. Benediction was given, I think, only on the first Sunday of each month; not oftener than once a month. The singing for mass was in Gregorian chant, vocal only, only male voices allowed. Vespers were sung in Chippewa, vocal only. Christmas singing was vocal, accompanied by violins and flutes. The choir was composed as follows: Alexis Charpentier, Antoine Gaudin and a Mr. McGillis. On Christmas day the instrumentalists were: Violin, Mr. Agnew, a clerk of the American Fur Company, flute, Charles La Rose, government interpreter...

There were no pure European families in La Pointe at that time. European males married into mixed-blood families, with the exception of the families of the Presbyterian mission — Rev. Sherman Hale and teacher Sprote (two families). The population varied very much according to the season. In the winter they would number about thirty or forty mixed-blood families, besides a very few Pagan Indian families. In the summer the population would about double in all shades. It must be borne in mind that La Pointe was pre-eminently the Indian depot for the distribution of goods to the different minor posts; and it was necessarily the headquarters for all engaged in the fur traffic. Fishing was also a branch of the American Fur Company's business.

There was but one store and that was the fur company's. They carried in stock everything that was necessary — groceries, dry goods, hardware, etc. The grocery department occupied a two-story building about the same size as the dry goods department building, one standing on each side of the street leading from a dock about the same place where the present dock now is. There was also a baking department, which was situated about 200 feet east of the other buildings. *There was no saloon* [emphasis is Roy's]. There were two carpenter shops, one operated by Mr. Perinier and the other by Dufault; also one large cooper shop maintained by the company, one blacksmith shop, etc. There was also one very large warehouse for repacking fish; it was about 200 feet long and was situated on the dock. In the rear of these buildings the company also maintained a very extensive garden and orchard, in which were raised all kinds of garden vegetables, grapes, cherries, crab-apples, currants, strawberries, etc. This was enclosed by a high board fence and was in charge of Old Man Oakes, father of Charles H. Oakes, lately of St. Paul, who was an expert gardener. Antoine Gaudin assisted him one or two years...

Borup and Oakes were headmen for the fur company (John Jacob Astor). All voyageurs, "runners," as they were called, were employed by said company. They would leave La Pointe about the beginning of September, stay away all fall and winter among the Indians in their respective districts, collect furs, and return about the beginning of June. They would take along blankets, clothes, guns, etc., to trade with the Indians for their furs. They took along very little provisions, as they depended mostly on hunting, fishing, wild rice, and trade with the Indians for their support. There were several depots for depositing goods and collecting furs; for instance, at Fond du Lac, Minn., Sand Lake, Courtes Oreilles, Lac du Flambeau, mouth of Yellow River, etc. The vessels used on Lake Superior for the fur trade were the "John Jacob Astor," a three-mast schooner; the "Brewster," and the "Siskowit," built by old man Perinier...

P. Chrysostomus Verwyst, O.F.M., *Life and Labors of Rt. Rev. Frederic Baraga, First Bishop of Marquette, Mich.* (Milwaukee: M. H. Wiltzius, 1900), 197–99.

Beyond the Mississippi

Fur trapping and trading beyond the Mississippi River were still centered at trading posts instead of on rivers, most of which had their source in the Rocky Mountains. The posts on the Red and Columbia Rivers were established by Canadian fur companies, the rest by companies founded by St. Louis families. To the latter John Jacob Astor's Western Division of the American Fur Company would become a rival in 1822 but later a partner. West of the Mississippi, French Canadians shared the stage with American mountain men. Most of the latter were independent trappers who sold their pelts to the companies at the annual rendezvous.[1]

22. A Missionary at Pembina Presents His Bishop with Cases of Conscience, 1819

Reverend Sévère Dumoulin at a post of the Hudson's Bay Company on the Red River of the North presented Bishop Joseph-Octave Plessis of Quebec with moral dilemmas connected with the fur trade. The extension of the American boundary about the time he wrote would place Pembina in the United States.

My Lord, Permit me to appeal to you for a decision of the following cases, first in order to be more sure, and second, to set my conscience at rest, because it cannot always be satisfied with the decisions of a theologian twenty-five years old with only two and one-half years of theology.

1. What should be exacted of an *engagé* [company man] who has traded for his *bourgeois* [superior] in the following manner, which is the one generally accepted in this country: upon going to an Indian camp the trader gives the Indians liquor gratis; after making them drunk, he trades with them, dilutes the rum with water, and ends by getting all they have for very little, so that he has paid even less for the peltries, etc., than the low price agreed upon by the *bourgeois* and the Indians. The *engagé* has done this only to please his *bourgeois,* who has not actually ordered him to add so much water, but who will reproach him for having wasted his goods if he does not trade in this manner; furthermore, the *engagé* knows very well that he has not done right, but he reassures himself by saying that such is the custom, and the profit is not for him.

2. What should be done if the *engagé* has robbed the Indians at the same time, for the same reasons?

3. This *engagé* is the father of a large family whom he supports by hard work.

4. To whom should restitution be made? The Indians mentioned have gone away; they are scattered here and there; perhaps several of them have died.

5. An *engagé* has robbed a company, but this company has refused to pay all his wages; can, and ought, recompense be made?

6. What should be done with *engagés* who buy rum from the *bourgeois* and who then trade it, making too great a profit thereby? Say, for instance, for a gallon of rum they obtained two horses.

7. What is it absolutely necessary to know in order to be baptized and married? N.B. It would, perhaps, be well to be able here to marry Catholics to Protestants in order not to force the people to demand Protestant priests.

---

1. David Wishart, *The Fur Trade of the American West, 1807–1840: A Geographical Synthesis* (Lincoln: University of Nebraska Press, 1979).

8. Is it necessary to teach the wives of Protestants even when it is almost certain that they will not want to be separated when they are told that they must?

9. A *brûlé* [half-breed] was very much given to drinking; he has reformed, but he still drinks occasionally, not being protected by the divine Grace. Is it necessary to wait till he has abandoned it altogether, and how many times must he resist? For it is not possible for him to drink often.

10. All the Indians here would be willing to receive instruction if the means to do so were at hand; furthermore, they realize that once their children are baptized they are obliged to have them taught, and they are even somewhat afraid to pledge themselves to do so. Can we baptize their small children now four or five years old, who probably will have the means of receiving instruction by the time they are capable of it? One thing which might militate against this course is the fact that should these children fall ill, their infidel fathers would use on them their absurd medicines. These are full of superstition, which, nevertheless, would not keep these poor little ones from going to heaven.

11. Ought one ever to baptize those whose fathers may be bigamists or inveterate drunkards?

12. Would it be right for me to make perhaps 150 people miss hearing Mass on Sundays and feast days in order that I might go to spend some days or weeks among the Indians, to begin to teach them, as well as to learn their language, seeing that it is almost impossible to learn it here? Might I do such a thing even though I knew it would be possible to visit only a very few lodges — for example, ten in two weeks?

13. Some of the Indian women have been taught, and would be ready for baptism and marriage if they were not already married, according to the custom of the land, to drunken Canadians. What shall be done with these women? Must we wait until their husbands are converted or advise them to abandon them? They can do so only at serious cost, such as leaving their children or perhaps returning to the Indians, where it would be impossible for them to receive instruction.

14. Is it better to wait till children over seven are old enough to make their first communion before conferring the sacrament of baptism on them, or would it be better to baptize them as soon as they have been made to understand something of its meaning?

15. Are we allowed, when eating with others, to partake indiscriminately of everything that is offered us, even when we are told that these meats have been received from the Indians in exchange for rum or otherwise traded in an illegal manner?

Grace Lee Nute, ed. and trans., *Documents Relating to Northwest Missions, 1815–1827* (St. Paul: Minnesota Historical Society, 1942), 170–72. Printed by permission.

23. Reverend Benedict Roux Tells of the Unpromising Beginnings of Kansas City, Missouri, 1834

Reverend Benedict Roux, sent by Bishop Joseph Rosati to a small community of French Canadians probably to please the powerful Chouteau family of St. Louis, a member of which was the founder of the future Kansas City, tells Rosati of his disheartening efforts to form a parish.

...It is time that I speak of myself: of the disappointment, the privations, the letdowns that I meet here in the course I pursue. Twelve families having at their head some old voyageurs, without guidance, always drowned in Whisky, saying nothing against the truths of religion but not fulfilling their duties, eleven or twelve poor souls like shafts of wheat, such is the French congregation you have, Monseigneur, entrusted to my care. I plant, I water as best I can, may God deign to do the watering. Every eight days I say Mass here in our little chapel two miles from my residence. I begin mass precisely at ten o'clock; it is preceded by the Rosary and by a hymn, a verse of which is sung after each decade. A French and English hymn are sung immediately before mass. Before the Credo I preach in French on the fundamentals of Christian doctrine, a familiar course of instructions I began some months ago. I preach immediately afterwards in English. Here I must make a virtue of necessity. I have the pleasure of seeing many non-Catholic Americans attending regularly our little congregation. I hope God will grant another priest their conversion; they join eagerly in the singing of the English hymns, in such wise that I see a kind of emulation between them and the French as to who will sing the better. My First Communion children in general approach the Sacraments regularly every month; some of the grownups are beginning to imitate them. This gives me a little consolation. The men are beginning to be regular in coming to mass. At last I perceive in them some rays of hope. I customarily say mass every Thursday at my residence at seven o'clock; some of the French assist at it; it is followed by morning prayer and by reading from the life of a saint...

Providence has sent three master builders to put up a house for me. It is Mr. Jean Baptiste Roy who has done me this good deed. In less than five days they cut and pointed the wood necessary to build a house 25 feet square and from twelve to fifteen in height including the roof. A similar house will be built twelve feet away from the other; next year if we are less straightened financially we shall have both of them; and if by that time I find I have a good establishment of nuns, they will be given to them. I should like to begin the church towards the end of autumn this year. If you wish it, Monseigneur, it will be done. That depends on you; and how? by sending me the 100 dollars you subscribed; and if you are willing to add to it a bell such as your generosity may wish to send me, pardon my indiscretion and too great liberty, from that moment I shall recognize my fault and never doubt again that you are interested in the mission of the Kansas river; that is the promise you made me

at St. Louis; that is the promise which determined me to make the sacrifices
I have...

Archives of the Archdiocese of St. Louis. Printed by permission. A large part of
this letter, incorrectly dated, is translated in Gilbert J. Garraghan, S.J., *Catholic
Beginnings in Kansas City, Missouri* (Chicago: Loyola University Press, 1920),
72–74.

24. Archbishop Blanchet's Later Account of His First Visit to the Settlers of the Willamette Valley in 1839

*Francis Norbert Blanchet (1795–1883) and Modeste Demers were sent in 1838
to minister to former employees of the Hudson's Bay Company. As soon as he
was able, Blanchet visited the largest group, on the Willamette River, some of
whom had not attended the sacraments in thirty or forty years.*

The Catholics of the Willamette valley were very anxious to see among them
at least one of the priests they had so earnestly asked for. On the day appointed for going, two large canoes from the [Willamette] valley, conducted
by two of the most respected citizens of the colony, Mr. Stephen Lucier and
Mr. Peter Béléque, were ready at Vancouver for departure. The vicar general
[Blanchet himself], leaving to Father Demers the charge of continuing the
mission of Vancouver, started on Thursday, Jan. 3rd, at three p.m.

THE WILLAMETTE FALL, a beautiful fall of 30 feet, across the river, which
requires a portage of canoes and baggage for a quarter of a mile, was passed
early on Friday; and on Saturday at 10 a.m. the *campement de Sable* (Champoeg) was reached. The four miles from thence to the log church (for there
was a church already) were made on horseback. And as Mr. Lucier and
Mr. Béléque were neighbors, and on his way, the vicar general stopped and
visited their families, who were so glad to be the first to see the priest and
see him in his true ecclesiastical *Robe* or *Soutane*, which the two missionaries continued to wear in traveling, at home, and in the town of Oregon City
until 1849.

That log church was built in 1836, as soon as they had any hopes of having priests. It was built 70 feet by 30, built on a prairie on the eastern side of
the river, on the road to Champoeg. The vicar general took possession of a
part of the church, at the back of the altar, measuring 12 by 30, which being
afterwards divided by an alley [corridor] of six feet, gave sufficient accommodation for two bedrooms on one side and a kitchen and dining room on the
other. Later on, in order to make room for some orphans, the alley became
the kitchen.

The afternoon of that day was spent in receiving visits, as all, especially
the women and the half-breed children, were very anxious to see the priest so
long announced and expected. That day was indeed a day of joy and tender
emotions to all.

The following day, January 6th, being Sunday and the Epiphany of our Lord, the church was blessed under the patronage of the great apostle St. Paul, after which was celebrated the first Mass ever said in the valley, in the presence of the Canadians, their wives and children. It was surely a great day for them all; for the Catholics who had not seen a priest nor heard a Mass for 10, 20, 30, and some for nearly 40 years; and for their wives who were at last beholding one of those priests their husbands had so long spoken to them about. Sweet and touching indeed were the sentiments these Canadians experienced on seeing themselves at the foot of an altar, of the cross, and before the face of a priest. These poor people were overjoyed, and the women were amazed at beholding the priest at the altar in sacerdotal vestments and prayer. The holy Sacrifice of the Immaculate Lamb of God was offered; the pastoral letter of the bishop who had heard their voice and sent them priests was read; the commandments of God and the Church were published, as well as the rules to be observed during the mission; and all terminated with reflections and advices which were very touching on both sides. All went home happy and willing to obey the Church, even in regard to separation from their wives until their unions would be blessed. And so great was their desire to have their wives and children instructed, and to lose nothing of the instructions given, that they brought them from home to live in tents around the church. The men would not do less; those living the nearest came every day to hear Mass and passed the whole day at church, returning home to attend to their business and prevent the wasting of their crops by their hired and slave Indians. Those who lived farthest away remained several days before returning home, sleeping in the large hall not yet divided by an alley. And let not one suppose that in that season the people had to suffer from the inclemency of the weather; not at all; for the weather was so extraordinary fine and mild, and so similar to the month of May in Canada, as to make the good Canadians say: "The good God has pity on us; it is for us; it is for us that He has sent this fine weather."

The exercises commenced every day by the celebration of Mass with an instruction, after which followed the recitation of prayers in French, the explanation of the Apostles' Creed and the most important truths of religion, intermixed with singing of hymns, from Mass till 12 a.m. (noon) and from 1 to 4 p.m. And as the women did not all understand French, and there were among them a variety of tongues, some being of the Chinook, others of the Colville and Flathead tribes, the difficulty was overcome by using different interpreters to convey to them the words of the priest. At dusk took place the evening prayers, the reading of pious books and singing of French hymns; after which some boys were taught to read in French and serve at Mass... The men had also to be examined and re-affirmed in their prayers, but they generally were found to have retained them in a surprising manner.

The instructions and teaching of prayers lasted three weeks. The fruits of the mission were consoling; for many of the Indian woman and a number of grown up boys and girls, and young children had learned to make the sign of the cross, the offering of the heart to God, the Lord's prayer, the Hail Mary, the Apostles' Creed and some of the Acts; 25 Indian women were baptized in excellent dispositions, and their unions with their husbands blessed by the Church; 47 other baptisms of children were made, to which, if we add those two of an old Indian man and a young Indian girl, both sick, who soon died, and were the first to be buried in the new cemetery, we will have 74 baptisms and 25 marriages; the 26th couple, being a Canadian, married in the valley by Rev. D[avid]. Leslie [one of the Methodist associates of Reverend Jason Lee], without the certificate of the death of his wife he had left in Canada, the vicar general could not bless their union, but ordered and obtained a separation until such time as her death could be ascertained ...

In fine, taking the fourth and last week of his mission to rest a little, the vicar general went and took possession of a tract of ground of 640 acres for the mission, and went around the whole establishment to visit the settlers, who received him with the greatest demonstration of joy and thanks to God for the consolations of religion they had received. Their joy, nevertheless, was greatly lessened in not being allowed to keep among themselves, at least one of those they had called for. But they expected that this would not last long, and that their good father, Dr. [John] McLaughlin, would obtain a change ...

> "Historical Sketches of the Catholic Church in Oregon during the First Forty Years (1838–1878)," in *Early Catholic Missions in Old Oregon,* ed. Clarence B. Bagley, vol. 1 (Seattle: Lowman and Hanford, 1932), 64–67.

25. Reverend Joseph Williams's Poor Opinion of Roman Catholic Trappers, 1842

Reverend Joseph Williams, a Methodist minister of Indiana, in the company of Father Peter John De Smet, S.J., whom he judged "a very fine man," went out to the Oregon Territory in 1841. On his return trip he was compelled to stay at the trading post of Antoine Robidoux, whom he judged a very immoral man, as also his companions.

... We are now on the head of the Wintey [Uintah] River, down which we pursued our journey toward Rubedeau's [Robidoux's] Fort. About two miles of our journey was almost impassable for the brush, and logs, and rocks. Then we got out of the mountains into a prairie, and reached the Fort about 2 o'clock.

We had to wait there for Mr. Rubedeau about eighteen days, till he and his company and horsedrivers were ready to start with us to the United States. This delay was very disagreeable to me, on account of the wickedness of the

Among the sketches of Nicholas Point, S.J., can be found this depiction of the primitive living conditions of the fur trappers and early Jesuit missionaries of the Rocky Mountains.

Credit: De Smetiana Collection RMS IX C9-34, Midwest Jesuit Archives, St. Louis. Reproduced by permission.

people, and the drunkenness and swearing, and the debauchery of the men among the Indian women. They would buy and sell them to one another. One morning I heard a terrible fuss, because two of their women had run away the night before. I tried several times to preach to them; but with little, if any effect.

...I was told here of a Frenchman who lived with an Indian woman, and when one of his children became burdensome, he dug a grave and buried it alive! At another time he took one of his children and tied it to a tree, and called it a "target," and shot at it and killed it!

Mr. Rubedeau had collected several of the Indian squaws and young Indians, to take to New Mexico, and kept some of them for his own use! The Spaniards would buy them for wives. This place is equal to any I ever saw for wickedness and idleness. The French and Spaniards are all Roman Catholics; but are as wicked men, I think, as ever lived. No one who has not, like me, witnessed it, can have any idea of their wickedness. Some of these people at the Fort are fat and dirty, and idle and greasy.

July 27th. We started from Rubedeau's Fort, over the Wintey River, and next crossed Green and White Rivers. Next night we lay on Sugar Creek, the water of which was so bitter we could scarcely drink it. Here two of Rube-deau's squaws ran away, and we had to wait two days till he could send back to the Fort for another squaw, for company for him . . .

Joseph Williams, *Narrative of a Tour from the State of Indiana to the Oregon Territory in the Years 1841–2* (reprint, New York: Cadmus Book Shop, 1921), 80–81.

26. Bishop Thomas Grace's Impression of the Métis of the Red River Valley, 1861

Thomas L. Grace, O.P. (1814–97), created bishop of St. Paul, Minnesota, in 1859, discovered in the Métis of Pembina and St. Joseph, descendants of French-Canadian trappers and Native American spouses, a distinct culture that represented a survival of the fur-gathering frontier.

. . . The Congregation is much scattered over an area extending six miles in all directions from Pembina. It is composed of Halfbreeds with six or eight Canadian families and numbers about 300 souls. They speak the Cree and Chippawa [*sic*] languages and also a corruption of the French. These people are simple in their habits & modes of life, are strongly attached to their religion and piously inclined. Their chief dependence for subsistence is the chase of the Buffalo & fishing. Nothing is or can be done in the way of aggriculture [*sic*] until the Indian claim to the territory is extinguished & the Government furnish some protection against the depredations of the Indians. It is doubtful whether they can be easily induced to abandon their present mode of life & the excitement of the chase notwithstanding its hardships, exposure and uncertainties. When asked they invariably reply that they are quite happy & content and doubt whether the tameness of aggricultural [*sic*] life would suit them . . .

Mass said . . . we got on our way to the village of St. Joseph at the foot of Pembina Mountain 30 miles distant west from Pembina . . . About five miles distant from the village the Bishop was met by a cavalcade of 200 of the red sashes villagers dressed in their costume of Red River hunters: forming a line on both sides of the road, they descended from their horses, and bending on one knee received the Bishop's blessing as he passed through: mounting again and firing a volley with their guns, they followed after the Bishop in full gallop into the village.

The town of St. Joseph [Leroy, North Dakota] is composed of almost 200 families numbering about one thousand souls, all Canadian Half-breeds . . . St. Joseph has more the appearance of a town than any place we have seen since leaving St. Cloud. The houses though of wood are well constructed and placed parellel [*sic*] to the streets which cross each other at right angles. The squares or blocks are much larger than usual; each house occupying one square and so having a field of several acres attached fenced in and cultivated. Several of the squares are fortified with pallicades [*sic*] to furnish a place of refuge for the villagers & their horses and cattle in cases of attack by the Sioux who make frequent incursions in the neighborhood...

The inhabitants of St. Joseph like those of Pembina are immigrants from the Hudson Bay Settlements, & their occupation chiefly that of hunting. The spring and autumn hunts occupy each about two months, the balance of the year is employed in curing & drying the meat and dressing the skins or buffalo robes for the market; these latter duties, however, are appointed chiefly for the women assisted by the boys not yet grown. It is a wild, free, bold life this and full of thrilling interest. No nobler specimens of physical proportions & manly strength can be found anywhere than among these people. Sickness is seldom known among them...

Bishop Thomas Grace, O.P., "Journal of Trip to Red River August and September 1861," *Acta et Dicta* 1 (1908): 176–79.

Part 3

SACRED CONTESTS
IN THE WEST

Introduction

The American West emerged as a volatile arena in which, across a long span of history, people of many persuasions competed for control of spiritual and temporal landscapes. The spectacular, diverse land with its grand plains and grander mountains, its lush rivers and parched deserts, proved the most obvious booty to be claimed — whether by indigenous native or newcomer migrant. But parallel to that desire, fueling the movements of clan and kin, was the zeal for belief or faith or identity — to hold to one's own, to change another's, to craft a new canon. The rush for dominance, whether over body or soul, left the West with a heritage of conflict that wounded the mind and the heart of many who set forth across the deserts and the valleys of western America.

While inspiring accounts of courage and triumph pepper the annals of western history, humanity and justice as defined within any culture seldom drove the events. People with conflicting goals jockeyed for national or tribal dominance; at the same time, personal spirituality, defined in the language of their own culture, underlay their behavior. A powerful sense of the "sacred" infused much of the interaction in a region known today as "the West." Because that sense varied so dramatically between and among cultures, the West took on the sound and fury of a contested region, one where the sacred disputes intertwined with the territory battles, where spiritual conviction mingled with material desire.

Yet, by shifting the historical lens from conflict to agency, people of all cultures seem less as hapless villains and victims and more as actors whose lives interlocked in the western saga. Certainly, the Europeans enjoyed advantages, especially of technology, in this exchange, but native people brought their own strengths to the experience.[1] From within both groups, the bold, the curious, and the perceptive stepped forward — those willing to explore the seemingly

---

1. For a discussion of this point, see Richard White, *The Middle Ground: Indians, Empires, and Republics in the Great Lakes Region, 1650–1815* (Cambridge: Cambridge University Press, 1991).

strange patterns and beliefs of another people, to risk the unknown outcomes of cultural exchange.

The 1804–5 trek of Meriwether Lewis and William Clark up the Missouri River and to the Pacific coast hardly initiated the European interest in the people and places west of the Mississippi or the corresponding economic and political objectives of native groups. Indigenous and European contact already had a long history by the time Lewis and Clark, accompanied by the slave York and the woman Sacajawea, marked new ground for the United States.[2] Nonetheless, Anglo Americans' land desires primed them to use the information of the Lewis and Clark expedition, as well as of the fur trappers and traders who followed them. By the 1830s, Americans, soon to be joined by a flood of European immigrants, were poised to head for a variety of locations in the West. As farmers tilled and filled the land east of the Mississippi River, others looked beyond its banks for new homes and profits. Stephen Austin led his colonizers into Texas; New England traders sailed along the California coast; the American Board of Commissioners for Foreign Missions sent its representatives into the Willamette Valley of Oregon.[3] In effect, by the 1830s, Anglo/European cultures surrounded the native- and Spanish-speakers of the West. The cultural stage was set for the clash, exchange, and brokering that shaped the future.

In this mid-nineteenth-century scenario, Roman Catholics wanted to expand and protect the gains their missionaries had made in earlier forays into the Southwest and California. Not only were there tribal contacts to maintain, but in the 1830s and 1840s the U.S. government's removal policy, in a move that brought new prospects for missionary work, relocated large numbers of eastern Indians onto western lands.[4] In addition, the rapidly growing white population coming into the West generally worshiped under a Protestant banner, a development that threatened to erode the gains of eighteenth-century Catholic proselytizing throughout the Southwest and California.

Small wonder that most nineteenth-century records of Catholic activity in the West came from the hand of missionaries who accepted a frontier assignment — one designed to continue a strong presence among Indian people, bring the faith to Catholic immigrants, and stem the overall influence of the advancing Protestants. The result created a jumble of contacts, many of which became part of Catholicism's written legacy in the letters, journals, and mem-

---

2. See James P. Ronda, *Lewis and Clark among the Indians* (Lincoln: University of Nebraska Press, 1984).

3. For these various events, see Richard White, *"It's Your Misfortune and None of My Own": A New History of the American West* (Norman: University of Oklahoma Press, 1991), 48–50, 64–73.

4. W. David Baird, "Cyrus Byington and the Presbyterian Choctaw Mission," and Bruce David Forbes, "John Jasper Methvin: Methodist 'Missionary to the Western Tribes' (Oklahoma)," both in *Churchmen and the Western Indians: 1820–1920*, ed. Clyde A. Milner II and Floyd A. O'Neil (Norman: University of Oklahoma Press, 1985), 5–40, 41–73.

oirs of frontier missionaries, who methodically informed their colleagues in the East and Europe about life in the West.

Catholic missionaries — sisters, priests, brothers — proved the most regular chroniclers of the frontier church. They came to the West and embarked on lives with slim connection to the seminaries and novitiates they left behind, but tempered with experiences common to pioneers. In the West, they encountered opportunity, adventure, danger, discrimination, fear, and exhilaration. They supported themselves, endured isolation, struggled alone, and died young; they recognized a beloved mother house would never be seen again, changed their ideas about humanity, and found new rhythms in the beliefs and values that sent them forth in the first place. They arrived to teach the "heathen" and save the "fallen." They learned to appreciate a western way of life and western people. Above all, the missionary persevered, not with the hope of the personal gain that inspired most migrants, but with an inner conviction that the American West called Catholics to perform "God's work."

In Native American contacts, the physical power of the western environment and the intellectual impact of the Indian cultures transformed the thinking of missionary priests and sisters. In addition, the missionary often moved between cultures, ministering to Indians one day and whites the next. Whether planned or not, missionaries bridged between communities, serving as mediators in the overlapping social dynamics.

The writings of Fathers Charles Van Quickenborne, S.J., Christian Hoecken, S.J., Joseph Cataldo, S.J., and Ignatius Panken, S.J., captured these elements. Buffeted by the vagaries of an often unfriendly terrain, each, between the 1830s and 1870s, traveled a harsh route to bring Catholic ritual to native people. Day by day, they met both receptive and reticent Indians. Written records from Native Americans remain few, but where they exist, as with the Yankton Pananniapapi and an anonymous Sioux Indian, they give voice to the perspective of those who watched these missionaries enter their world. While Father Eli W. J. Lindesmith, of Fort Keogh, Montana, labored mainly among the white community, visits from other priests kept him well informed about successes and failures in the mission fields. Collectively, these documents provide a partial description of the meeting grounds between Native Americans and white missionaries across the West.

The continuation of those meetings depended on a steady flow of donations from European and American Catholics. Perhaps the most important figure in sustaining the finances of Catholic mission work among Indians was Katharine Drexel, heir to a Philadelphia banking fortune. In 1887 and 1888, Drexel began to funnel her vast resources toward the building and staffing of Indian schools across the West. Through her direct infusion of money, Catholic mission schools sprang up in Kansas, Montana, California, Oregon, and Minnesota. Within five years, the Chippewas, Crows, Blackfeet, Cheyennes, Pueblo, Sioux, and other major tribes had schools served by Benedictine,

Charity, Franciscan, Ursuline, and Mercy sisters. The singular importance of Drexel's monetary and spiritual contributions to the American church can be seen in an 1899 letter by Monsignor J. A. Stephan that outlines a major plan for providing Catholic education to people of color. In 1902, Drexel, now known as Mother Katharine Drexel and now superior of the Sisters of the Blessed Sacrament for the Indian and Colored Missions, toured the Oklahoma Territory and, in long letters to her convent in Pennsylvania, reviewed the impact of her years of charity. Although her program did not always produce the social and economic results she envisioned, she provided Native American people with educational centers from which they launched a variety of initiatives far into the twentieth century.[5]

Not everyone saw the missionary in noble terms. While the scant population of the arid Great Basin region seemed to suggest few reasons for religious conflicts to materialize, such was not the case. As the Spanish missionary Francisco Garces noted, Great Basin Native Americans possessed a long-standing and deep knowledge of Catholic ritual, a circumstance itself that did not always lead to harmony. The 1847 arrival of the Church of Jesus Christ of Latter-day Saints, or Mormons, into the Salt Lake Valley transformed area demographics, a change that shifted again after the 1849 California Gold Rush brought thousands of miners, many of them Catholic, into the region.[6] Within this stark western environment, the potential for religious conflict between the oft-persecuted Mormons and anyone else ran high. The most strongly worded attack on Catholicism came, however, as it had for several years in America, from mainstream Protestants, who, in their opposition to the church, feared the West would become a dumping ground for immigrant Catholics.[7] As the words of two Protestant clergymen revealed, deep-seated animosity toward parochial schools and a belief that Catholics lacked loyalty to the United States inspired much of the rhetoric.

Far less animosity crackled between Utah Mormons and Catholics. Indeed, Brigham Young, Mormon leader from 1846 until 1877, enjoyed a cordial relationship with the Sisters of the Holy Cross, who came to Salt Lake City

---

5. For a full biography of Katharine Drexel, see Sister Consuela Marie Duffy, S.B.S., *Katharine Drexel: A Biography* (Bensalem, Pa.: Mother Katharine Drexel Guild, 1966), and Anne M. Butler, "Mother Katharine Drexel: Spiritual Visionary for the West," in *By Grit and Grace: Eleven Women Who Shaped the American West*, ed. Glenda Riley and Richard Etulain (Golden, Colo.: Fulcrum Publishing, 1997), 198–220.

6. There is ample literature on the Mormon frontier experience. See especially Leonard J. Arrington, *Brigham Young: American Moses* (New York: Knopf, 1985), and Leonard J. Arrington and Davis Bitton, *The Mormon Experience: A History of the Latter-day Saints* (New York: Knopf, 1979). For the national impact of the Gold Rush, see Malcolm J. Rohrbough, *Days of Gold: The California Gold Rush and the American Nation* (Berkeley: University of California Press, 1997).

7. In 1846, Edward Beecher, of the famed abolitionist family, warned in an address to the Ladies Society for the Promotion of Education in the West that Catholics were trying to proselytize the West by opening female seminaries. See Thomas Woody, *A History of Women's Education in the United States*, 2 vols. (reprint, New York: Octagon Press, 1966), 2:456–57.

in 1875, and with Father Lawrence Scanlan, the first priest permanently assigned to the Utah Territory.[8] As the reports of Father Scanlan in 1876 and
that of Father Kiely six years later demonstrated, however, religious rivalries
in Utah were multifaceted and not limited to a competition with the Mormons. Nonetheless, Catholics as a minority in Utah drew strength from their
scant numbers, as evidenced by the 1917 *Intermountain Catholic* reports that
gloried in Catholic expressions of faith.

Conflicts in the Great Basin spread to regions beyond Salt Lake. In Nevada,
the Daughters of Charity, who established a school, orphanage, and hospital in Virginia City, unintentionally became embroiled in partisan politics.
Once the territory developed sufficient infrastructure to open its own orphanage, Republican legislators accused the sisters of racial segregation in
their government-supported asylum. Sister Frederica McGrath, D.C., whose
congregation rested its mission statement on the all-encompassing charitable directives of Vincent de Paul, responded by withdrawing the orphanage
from government funding and turning to private support from Virginia City
residents.

The public controversy for the Daughters of Charity reflected the larger
problem that sometimes faced sisters summoned to small towns and left
there with little or no institutional support. While some citizens, regardless
of religious affiliation, begged for the sisters to open schools or hospitals,
others looked on nuns as purveyors of evil. The ensuing ill-will and rudeness
challenged small convents staffed by a handful of young women missionaries.[9]

This challenge emanated not only from non-Catholics on the frontier.
Catholic communities also faced disputes among themselves over a variety
of issues. Lonely missionaries vented the frustrations of their assignments, as
seen in the letters of Father John C. Perrodin and Father Fidelis Steinauer,
both writing to distant superiors. Small congregations of nuns and priests,
stressed by meager resources and poor accommodations, often clashed over
the distribution of money, the requirements of Holy Rule, or the role of the
missionary, as seen in the letter of Demetrius di Marogna, concerned about
the future of Benedictine nuns in remote Minnesota.

That remoteness, far from the centers of Catholicity, created administrative dilemmas for the church in the West.[10] How could mother superiors or

---

8. Renée Sentilles, "Forgotten Pioneers: A Comparative Study of the Sisters of the Holy Cross
of Utah and the Sisters of the Holy Family of Louisiana" (master's thesis, Utah State University,
1991), 50–76.

9. Early histories of religious congregations are often written from a pious and noncritical
perspective. Yet a careful reading can illuminate the difficult living conditions, national tensions,
and power struggles that missionaries faced in frontier communities. For examples, see Mary Cortona Gloden, O.S.F., *The Sisters of Saint Francis of the Holy Family* (St. Louis: B. Herder Book,
1928), 41–66, and Mary Ildephonse Holland, R.S.M., *Lengthened Shadows: An Illustrated History
of the Sisters of Mercy of Cedar Rapids, Iowa* (New York: Bookman, 1952), 69–87.

10. The complex administrative difficulties caused by poor communication from the frontier are well delineated in Mary Generosa Callahan, C.D.P., *The History of the Sisters of Divine*

bishops living amid centuries of church tradition in Munich or Paris, or even Philadelphia or Baltimore, grasp the reality of the mission world in the far West? What frame of reference did they have to understand the celebration of Mass inside a hut made of birch logs and pine branches? What did it mean when Catholics — lay and cleric — each holding high the cross of Jesus, looked at each other across language barriers and national competitions? In these circumstances, how could the church hierarchy keep far-flung Catholics within the embrace of the church? These questions faced many bishops, both American and European, who wanted to contain the possible schisms that arose from isolation, as seen in the 1871 response of the Dominican Bishop Thomas Grace to a maverick priest in Minnesota.

By and large, squabbles among Catholics centered on the rancor that surfaced among immigrants of differing national origins.[11] Teaching sisters and parish priests, whose national heritage rankled local Catholics, absorbed the brunt of such disputes, often abandoning a small mission and seeking a friendlier location. Lay people did not hesitate to voice their displeasure, for example, over French nuns teaching German children, as seen in a 1910 letter to the mother provincial of the Sisters of Mary of the Presentation. In part, these disagreements reflected a lack of care by priests in soliciting religious congregations for western outposts, especially when the church had not yet decided whether to retain its European flavor or to adopt the mantle of Americanization. The disputes also pointed to the force with which the frontier laity expressed its needs to the clergy, as all debated the generally contentious matters of Americanizing immigrant children, preserving national languages, and endorsing the use of English in Catholic institutions.

In a contested West, Catholics waded through disagreements with native populations, strife with Protestant opponents, and their own arguments. No region of the West and no decade in the period escaped these cultural conflicts. While quarrels and bickering appear to be unseemly components in religious history, they point to the liveliness of personal belief. Throughout the nineteenth and into the twentieth century, these abrasive forces underlay the processes that marked the emergence of the frontier church. While not always attractive, conflict infused the western Catholic experience and helped to shape its character. In recognizing the discordant features of western history, Catholics can better appreciate that they crafted a regional identity out of vibrance, spirit, commitment, and faith — elements closely identified with the American frontier.

Providence: San Antonio, Texas, Catholic Life Publications (Milwaukee: Bruce Publishing, 1955), 132–56.

11. Two works that capture the ongoing national difficulties between immigrant Catholics and religious congregations are Paul Horgan, *Lamy of Santa Fe: His Life and Times* (New York: Farrar, Straus, and Giroux, 1975), and Marvin R. O'Connell, *John Ireland and the American Catholic Church* (St. Paul: Minnesota Historical Society Press, 1988).

Native American Contacts

27. A Missionary Speaks with Keokuk, a Kickapoo Prophet, 1835

Father Charles Van Quickenborne traveled north of Fort Leavenworth to explore mission prospects. There an Indian prophet, Keokuk, after initial resistance, paved the way for the Jesuit missionary's reception. In this letter, Van Quickenborne describes his trip and his meeting, in which the Indians articulate the appeal of the bachelor missionary.

To get to the Kickapoo it was necessary to cross the Kansas River. I was not a little su[r]prised to see that the Delaware Indians had established a ferry there in imitation of the whites. We arrived at the Kickapoo village July 4, a Saturday, the day I consecrated to the Blessed Virgin. The next day I said Mass in the trader's house, where the prophet who was anxious to see me, put in an early appearance. After the first exchange of courtesies, he at once brought up the subject of religion. "What do you teach?" he asked me. "We teach," I answered, "that every man must believe in God, hope in God, love God above all things and his neighbor as himself; those who do this will go to heaven, and those who do not will go to hell." "Many of my young people believe that there are two Gods. How do you prove that there is only one and that he has proposed certain truths to us to be believed?" I said in the course of my reply: "God spoke to the Prophets and the Prophets proved by miracles that God had spoken to them." He at once interrupted me, saying: "This is the very way I got to be believed when I began to preach: I raised the dead to life. There was a woman," he continued, "who, so every one thought, could not possibly recover her health. I breathed on her and from that moment she began to improve and is now in good health. Another time I saw an infant just about to die: I took it in my arms and at the end of a few days it was cured." I said in reply that there is a great difference between a dead person and one who is believed to be at the point of death; that in the two cases alleged he had merely done what any one else might do; and that, since on his own admission those two persons were not dead, he had not as a matter of fact brought them back to life.

My answer irritated him greatly and he remarked that no one had ever dared to contradict him in this fashion or give him such an answer. Seeing him in anger, I kept silent. Then my interpreter, a friend of the prophet, told him it was wrong of him to become angry when he could not answer the remarks made by the black-robe and that this only showed that he defended a bad cause. After some moments of silence he softened and admitted himself to be worsted. "I realize," he said, "that my religion is not a good one: if my people wish to embrace yours, I will do as they." The following Sunday he repeated in assembly what he had often said before, that he should not be deceived in his hope and in the pledge he had given them that the Great Spirit would send some one to help him complete his work. God alone knows whether he spoke sincerely. On Monday I received a visit from several of the inferior chiefs; all expressed a desire to have a Catholic priest among them. I was unable on that occasion to see the head chief, who had gone on the hunt and returned only ten days later. I paid him a visit immediately on his return and explained to him that I had made this journey because I heard it said that his nation wished to have a priest and I was eager to ascertain if such was really the case; that in his absence the other chiefs had sought me out to assure me of the truth of what I heard; but that before speaking of the affair to their grandfather (the President of the United States), I desired to know how he himself regarded it. "Have you a wife?" he asked me. I answered that he ought to know that Catholic priests do not marry and that I was a black-robe. At these words he manifested surprise mingled with respect and excused himself by saying that, as he had just arrived and had not yet spoken to any of his people, no one had informed him of the fact that I was a black-robe. He then added that in a matter of such importance he wished to hear his council and would return his answer in St. Louis whither he proposed to go. He did not go there, however, but sent me his answer by a trader. It was couched in these terms: "I desire, as do all the principal men of my nation, to have a black-robe come and reside among us with a view to instruct us."

Father Charles Van Quickenborne, S.J., in *Annals of the Propagation of the Faith* 9, no. 99, quoted in William W. Graves, Gilbert J. Garraghan, S.J., and George Towle, *History of the Kickapoo Mission and Parish: The First Catholic Church in Kansas,* Graves Historical Series, no. 7 (St. Paul, Kans.: Journal Press, 1938), 3–5.

28. A Priest Describes the Hardships of Western Travel, 1850

Another Jesuit missionary, Christian Hoecken, turned his attention to the Sioux Indians. Fluent in several Indian dialects, Hoecken published a grammar and a dictionary of Kickapoo languages. A year and a half after the trip described here, Hoecken contracted cholera while nursing passengers on a Missouri River steamboat and died at age forty-three.

I set out last June for the Sioux country. The season was quite favorable when I left Kansas, but I had a pretty cold time as I crossed Missouri, Iowa and Minnesota, till I got to the post of the American Fur Company, called Post Vermillion. My inability to get a guide to lead me to Fort Pierre, the great post of the Missouri, made me lose five days of excellent weather. At last I found a companion who had crossed backward and forward for the last thirty years, every plain, mountain, forest and prairie of the west. I set out one day before the weather changed. On the third day the snow overtook us. On reaching James river we found it impassable; the water was too high and too cold for our horses to swim it. We traveled eight or nine days without finding any place to cross. A violent north wind set in so we were nearly frozen to death.

We began to descend the valley of the river, but had not made over five or six miles before night surprised us, and we had to encamp in a spot which offered scarce wood enough for one night. We had scarcely encamped before the north wind began to blow with a horrible violence; the snow fell so thick and fast that you would have said the clouds had burst. Sleep was out of the question. The next morning we struck our camp. The snow and wind raged with unabated fury for two days and two nights. In some spots there were six, fifteen and even twenty feet of snow. Conceive our position if you can, as we made our way along the valley of the James river, which runs between two chains of mountains, with deep ravines near each other.

We were almost out of provisions, entirely alone in a sad desert where we could see nothing but snow. The snow grew high around us, our horses would not proceed. The gloomy thought that we could never cross the river crushed out our courage; but I was consoled when I remembered the words of Divine Wisdom: "It is good for you to suffer temptation." To fill up my misery, rheumatism seized both my knees, so that I could scarcely set one foot before another. One of our horses fell lame and was no better than myself. Moreover, the keen northerner froze my ears, nose, and feet...I was forced by dire necessity to march against my inclinations, or rather to drag myself along as best I could. I walked along in the snow from morning until night, praying and weeping in turns, making vows and resolutions...We advanced painfully over the mountains of snow, till night summoned us to plant our tent, which consisted of a square piece of skin tent-cover. We set to work clearing away the snow, getting down a frame work and wood enough for the night. The fire kindled; we finish our night prayers; we have a morsel to eat. Now then for repose for a few hours. Impossible. Sleep has fled from our eyes; the smoke blinds and stifles us. How sleep with wolves howling and prowling around us. The snow and sometimes rain and hail fell on us all night long.

...My greatest fear every morning was that my companion would bring word that our horses were dead of cold or hunger in those bleak sterile tracts...Yet by care, pain, fatigue and patience we arrived with our two horses at Post Vermillion on the 8th of December.

Father Christian Hoecken, S.J., to Father Pierre De Smet, S.J., "Sioux Country, Post Vermillion, December 11, 1850," in William W. Graves, Gilbert J. Garraghan, S.J., and George Towle, *History of the Kickapoo Mission and Parish: The First Catholic Church in Kansas,* Graves Historical Series, no. 7 (St. Paul, Kans.: Journal Press, 1938), 48–50.

29. Indians Speak to Missionary Visitors, 1866 and 1870

Indian voice in the records of Catholicism frequently derived its tone and interpretation from a white amanuensis. Nonetheless, where such documents exist, they shift the focus of faith from the missionary to native people and illuminate the many forces that drove western religion.

[Pananniapapi, Yankton Chief, to ?]

My...sincere and conscientious duty to the Great Spirit,...I desire to discharge. I made up my mind on this subject (twenty-two years ago). I wish to put the instruction of the youth of my tribe into the hands of the Black-robes; I consider them alone the depositaries of the ancient and true faith of Jesus Christ, and we are free to hear and follow them...Since my first talk with the Black-robes I have no other thought but to embrace the ancient religion of Jesus Christ, if I can make myself worthy. My mind is made up. [Pananniapapi waited twenty-two years to be baptized by Pierre-Jean De Smet, S.J., in 1866.]

•

[The-Man-Who-Strikes-The-Ree, Little Swan, Feather in the Ear,
Medicine Cow, and Jumping Thunder, to Pierre-Jean De Smet, S.J., 1866]

There is another religious [teacher] that wants to come and remain with us. He wants to teach us the Santee language, but we do not want them. We want no other but you and your religion. The other wants to learn us how to read and sing in the Indian language and which we all know how to do in our own way. What we want is to learn the American language and their ways. We know enough of the Indian ways. I am now very old and before I die, I want to see a school and the children learn how to read and write in the American language, and if you will try and get with us, I will be very happy...

•

[Sioux Indian to Jesuit Missionary, 1870]

Blackrobe, I wish to speak to you...Blackgown we heard about your coming two moons ago. My wife was then very sick, almost at the point of death. She was anxious to see you and be blessed with the water. You did not come. She told me to have this child blessed as soon as you should come. I therefore brought this child to be blessed.

Hiram M. Chittenden and A. T. Richardson, eds., *Letters and Travels of Pierre-Jean De Smet, S.J., 1801–1873*, 4 vols. (New York: Francis P. Harper, 1905), 4:1285, 1287; Peter Rosen, *Pa-Ha-Sa-Pah, or Black Hills of South Dakota* (St. Louis: Nixon-Jones Printing, 1895), 239–42; also quoted in Sister M. Claudia Duratschek, O.S.B., "The Beginnings of Catholicism in South Dakota" (Ph.D. diss., Catholic University of America, Washington, D.C., 1943), 21, 60, 45.

30. A Jesuit Priest Recalls His Mission Days, ca. 1870s

The memoirs of a missionary offer rich insights into the spiritual and political values that fueled relationships on the frontier. This account by the Jesuit

*mission priest Joseph Cataldo encompasses the perspective of both Native
Americans and whites, as they struggled to find a common ground of religious
understanding.*

In my travels I became very much interested in the Spokanes. I heard so much
of Spokane prairie and the Spokane falls.

When I was traveling from California to the Coeur d'Alenes I passed by
where the city of Spokane is now located and saw the Indians fishing there at
the falls. They seemed to be very much alone, and I felt they should have a
missionary to bring them faith.

Selteese,... chief of the Coeur d'Alenes, was a half-breed whose father was
a Coeur d'Alene and whose mother was a Spokane. He was a Catholic, the
Coeur d'Alenes having been converted by my predecessors, and he told me
he was much interested in the Spokanes as they were his people. He said the
fathers should do something for them. That was in October, 1865.

Occasionally the Spokanes were visited by a father, but the visits were too
short and nothing serious could be done. So this man Selteese was insisting
that the fathers should go to Spokane and see what they could do.

Then I began to think of the possibility of establishing a mission among
the Spokanes. I studied the Spokane language, which is from what we call the
mother language, the Flathead, the Spokane being a closer dialect to the main
tongue than the Coeur d'Alene. I was helped by an Indian who spoke these
dialects and had an old gramar [sic] composed by Father Mengarini, S.J., who
was here 25 years ahead of me...

Next we visited the Spokane camp. But the Spokanes told me to come back
some other time. "Come some other time and we will be ready to listen to
the teachings of Christianity," they said. "Now we are too busy catching the
salmon." They were fishing for the fall, or lean, salmon.

And truly all were busy, both men and women. So I employed myself with
a few children.

Then I inquired from one, Baptiste Peone, who was a half-breed, rather
he was one-fourth white, one fourth Spokane, one-fourth Kalispel, and one
fourth — I don't know what — anyway he came in fourths. He was already
a Christian.

"You cannot expect busy people to listen to religion," he said. "You should
come when we are not so busy." I asked him when I could come and he said
"come about the first of November." So I took my guide and went back to the
mission at Cataldo...I came down again, and went to the home of Baptiste
Peone...Peone told me he would help build a log house, and he would call the
Indians...Next day I went again to Peone...and said "where are the Indians."
"They will come," he said, "just have patience." Again I came, and the same
answer, and again, until it was about a week. Then he told me that the Indians
were on a buffalo hunt. "You must wait," he said, "because you cannot build

a house until you get permission from Chief Garry when he returns..." So I asked if there was anyone else left at home from the hunt.

"Only Polotkan," he said, "and Polotkan is very old." Peone persuaded the old man, who had been a chief, that he had power to permit me to stay for at least four months. "Look here, Polotkan," I said. "Your people invited me to come for the winter, which would be about four months. I must have a little house and you have so much timber here. Why not let me put up a house for the four months and those who desire to become Christians can be baptised. When the four months are up I will go, leaving the house in your possession..."

I said mass in the new church, which was camp house, rectory, church and everything, all in one room and very rough. It was December 8, 1886...I had time for but two meals because I must give most of my time to the Indians.

Besides teaching them religion I taught them some prayers and songs. To learn was easy for the children, but hard for the old people...

So I taught the children for two hours in the morning and two hours in the afternoon, and the older people came in the evening and all were very happy. I passed those three and a half months in continual teaching prayers and catechism in the Indian language. It was very hard for them, but they finally succeeded.

There were about 100 in camp and about 20 children. About 100 were baptised and so made their first communion. After four months were up I told Baptiste I was going back to the old mission. "You must stay," he said. "You must not go away now that we are beginning to learn and appreciate so much..."

...I received a letter from my superior directing me to go to St. Ignatius mission in Montana...I was to...begin a mission among the Nez Perces at Lapwai, about 10 miles south of Lewiston, Idaho...

I decided to stop at Lewiston. There were a few Nez Perce who had been going to the missions at Colville and Cataldo and were baptised and I wished to instruct them.

There were a few Catholics among the whites and I built a little church and began to call on them. During the week I would visit two Indian camps on the Clearwater river...They were all pleased to see me but one Indian preacher by the name of Eagle, he did not like to have the priest around. When I shook hands with him and said "we are friends," he said "yes, we are friends, but you take care of the Whites and I will attend to the Indians."

...The Indians were not disposed to become practical Catholics. They wanted to take time. They were willing that the children should learn. The reason for the trouble was their dispute with the United States government over their lands...

"We want to be practical Catholics," the chief said, "but we cannot be practical Catholics on account of our difficulty with the government. What good will it be if we are now baptised, and the next day we fight the government?..."

Later I got permission to go on a long visit among the Nez Perce...I started and sent word ahead to the Indians that I would pass Sunday in Lewiston among the Whites and visit their camps later.

To my great astonishment I saw more Nez Perces in town on Sunday than I had ever seen in my three years among them..."We are ready," they said...Calling there into the church, (as many as could get in, others were left standing outside) I took out my little prayer book that I had made in their language three years before. I will try them out, I thought. "Now we will begin to say prayers," I annunciated. As soon as I began they all followed. I stopped, but they continued on to the end. Morning prayers and evening prayers. Then I began singing, and they all joined. I stopped, they continued. "That is a nice thing," I said. Then up spoke Chief Waptashamkein (Eagle Shirt) who before had told me they were not ready for baptism, and told me they were now ready. They were about 200.

"I see that you are in earnest," I said, "but I want you to tell me how all of you learned the prayers."

"Didn't you teach our children?" he asked. "Well these children have been blaming the old people and crying to have the Black Gown back..."

"Very good" I said. "I see you are in earnest. But you are too many for this little church, and anyway the Whites would not like to see so many Indians in town." You see trouble was still in the air.

...I arranged for all the Indians to bring their tents and make a camp across the river. Here I taught them for about two weeks. I wanted to be sure that they were prepared for baptism, and that not only the children, but also the old people should know the prayers and know what they were doing.

Then I selected 25 who were best fitted and took them back to the church where I baptised them. These I asked to assist in instructing the others. And again I took 26 and baptised them, and repeated until I had baptised 100 in all...

There was an old [Jesuit] brother there who at first could not believe that the Nez Perces were in real earnest. But when he heard them praying all together, and singing, he cried for joy because he saw they were serious. That was in 1872.

Laurence E. Crosby, *Kuailks Metatcopun: Black Robe Three-Times-Broken* (n.p.: Wallace Press-Times, n.d.), 3–16.

31. An Army Chaplain's View of the Indian Missions, 1883

Rev. Eli W. J. Lindesmith served as a U.S. army chaplain at Fort Keogh, Montana, for eleven years. Although in large part he dealt with military personnel and settlers, as this excerpt from his diary demonstrates, he was well informed about the cultural struggles that ensued from missionary initiatives.

June 29, 1883...this morning two Jesuit Fathers arrived at my quarters —
Peter Barcello and Peter Prando. The former has been among the Crow Indians three years, and the latter is now three years among the Piegan Indians.
Father Barcello is very quiet and retired, constantly reading and praying, and
seems to be a very learned man. He says almost nothing of his work or experience among the Indians. He is a Mexican by birth. Father Prando is a very
lively, cheerful and talkative man. His conversation is always about the Indians and his success and difficulties among them, how he did and what effect
it had on them.

He is an Italian of Piedmont. He spoke of his college life, and of his being
professor in Jesuit colleges in Italy. He spoke of how they did and what they
did, how he invented new plans to induce the boys to be good and learn fast.
He said that he desired and asked for fifteen years to go to the Indian Missions,
before he obtained leave to go. He is very much pleased and satisfied, he wants
to live and die among the Indians.

He said that one of his greatest difficulties among the Indians has been the
plurality of wives. Among the many things he did to stop this he explained
how that God created the first man and made for him but one wife, and that
Adam and his wife went to heaven, and that after a long time some of the
descendants of Adam had two or more wives, but that God was displeased
with them etc.

Then after all this teaching, he had a large painting made and put up in
the church, on which he represents hell fire devils etc. and an Indian in great
torment, and abuses from the devils, and three squaws, the wives of this Indian
also in this hell suffering the same punishment, all because the three squaws
had one man.

After this he composed a song which explains this picture, in which he
sings that God made one man and gave him one woman and that they are in
heaven and that if an Indian has only one wife and if they are good, they will
go together to heaven; but if an Indian has two or more wives it will happen
to him like it did to the Indian and his three wives in the picture. They will
all go to hell.

He then taught the Indians to sing this song altogether in the church. This
made a great impression upon them. They soon learned to sing it and they
liked to sing it, especially the young squaws who soon were much pleased
with the doctrine of one wife. He said that when an Indian who had a wife
came to see a squaw to get her for his second wife, the young squaw would
sing for him the hymn about the Indian in hell with his three wives.

So he says that at present there are only a few yet who have more than
one wife.

The two Fathers have been at my quarters until today, July 7th, awaiting a
guide and interpreter, to go with them to the Cheyenne Indians at the junction
of Tongue River and Otter Creek about 75 miles from here. This morning the

Fathers went to Miles City to work among the whites, a few days until they can go to their destination.

Diary of Rev. Eli W. J. Lindesmith, Fort Keogh chaplain, 1880–91; excerpt printed in *Miles City Star,* 25 January 1971. Copied from Eli W. J. Lindesmith Papers, Archives of the Catholic University of America, Washington, D.C. Printed by permission.

32. Thoughts about Pierre-Jean De Smet, S.J., 1887

In 1887, Ignatius Panken, S.J., wrote a detailed account of Pierre-Jean De Smet's final mission trip to the Sioux Indians during June and July of 1870. This journey in many ways captured the interactions that took place across the West between Native Americans and Catholic missionaries.

Father P. J. De Smet and myself left Sioux City, Iowa, in June, 1870, on the steamer Far West for the Grand Sioux Agency, the principal agency in Dakota. Our work commenced on the boat with giving instructions to the mates, hands and travelers. Then at every landing place the boat stopped either to wood or deliver freight, when we spoke to the Indians, settlers, and working men.

At one landing place, while the boat was wooding, an interpreter took me to a small camp of Indians who wished to see a black robe. When I got there about a dozen small children were brought to me to be baptized...

We stopped on going up the river at the Cheyenne Agency, five miles above Fort Sully. The Indians came immediately and surrounded us. Fr. De Smet made them a short speech and presented them with a box of tobacco saying that he was sorry he could not give them any more. The "Great Mandan," a powerful chief, replied: "Blackgown, we thank you; your box is small but your heart is big."

On our arrival at the Grand River Agency Indian chiefs greeted us, we smoked the calumet, though it was 4 o'clock A.M. We stayed there over three weeks and baptized over 200 children and four adults, and we held several councils with Indians. I went to the camp of the Piegi Indians of Sioux-Blackfeet, to attend a dying girl who was about 19 years old. She seemed to be a good, modest girl. I baptized her after some preliminary instructions. When I was about to leave, the mother of the girl lifted up her hands and wished me the favors and blessings of the Great Spirit and hoped that her daughter would meet me in the same happy land. The girl died the next day.

On Sundays we held service, Mass and sermon for the Indians and the whites. It was always well attended by both Indians and whites. From Grand River Agency we went on the steamer Peninah down to Fort Sully. We had to land about 3 miles below the fort. The ambulance came to get us and our baggage.

During our stay at the fort we visited the Indians at the Peoria bottom, baptized some of them and rectified marriages. Mass was said daily, confessions heard, and the sacraments administered to the whites.

We traveled by wagon from Fort Sully to the Crow Creek Agency. At night we slept on the ground. At this agency we did much good among the soldiers. Of one company 35 men went to confession, and they came in a body the next morning to Communion. Some Indians asked us to baptize their children; we did as asked, but one child dying soon after, the medicine men profited by the occasion and deterred others from having their children baptized. In this they were partially successful.

Whilst there we were the guests of Col. Ilges and Capt. Hamilton. In the meantime there arrived at the camp Gen. J. Hardie, U.S.A., Inspector-General of the Dept. of Missouri. He had the kindness to take us along to the Lower Brule Agency where we found several troops and Indian camps in the neighborhood. The Indians were several times visited and instructed. Fr. De Smet married the interpreter to an Indian woman whom he had baptized. This good man was a great help to us. Fr. De Smet knew him well, having made his acquaintance years before. A boat from the upper river arrived and we all went down the river. Father De Smet had become quite ill and determined to go to Sioux City. Gen. Hardie and myself stopped at the Whetstone Agency, some miles above Fort Randall. I said Mass, was invited to the Indian camp, baptized several children, also an Indian woman, the daughter of a hostile chief, and married her to an Irish settler. They expected me to stay longer but I could not. Then the representatives of 80 families of Indians and half-breeds came to ask me to stay with them; I told them that I could not. I was then urged to tell Fr. De Smet to send them a blackgown. I ascertained later that some of these Indians are good Catholics.

Saturday evening I went to Fort Randall. The next day I said Mass late and preached. Many officers and soldiers attended. On Monday morning at 3:30 we crossed the Missouri on a skiff. A Dakota storm overtook us whilst yet on the river. Arriving at Yankton Agency we stopped for a few hours for sleep. I found neither priest nor church there. At Vermillion we met some pioneers ready to go over to the Black Hills country in search of gold. At a settlement some twelve miles from the Big Sioux river I found a church but no priest, so I continued my journey until I reached Sioux City; here I found Fr. De Smet, who was much improved and ready to go to St. Louis. It was understood that I should with some missioners go to Dakota next spring, and I was told by my superiors to stay at Leavenworth and hold myself in readiness. But when the time came for opening the mission, Father P. J. Meester, S.J., and F. X. Kuppens were sent to Dakota. They remained but a few months, being recalled before winter set in.

Ignatius Panken, S.J., to Father Rosen, 12 October 1887, quoted in Sister M. Claudia Duratschek, O.S.B., "The Beginnings of Catholicism in South Dakota" (Ph.D. diss., Catholic University of America, Washington, D.C., 1943), 45–48.

In 1888, Katharine Drexel (left), the Philadelphia heiress and future foundress of the Sisters of the Blessed Sacrament, stopped, with her two siblings and Bishop Martin Marty (seated left), at the Thompson Ranch on their way to Red Lake, Minnesota, to inspect conditions at the Benedictine Indian mission there.

Credit: Archives of the Sisters of the Blessed Sacrament, Bensalem, Pa.

33. An Appeal to Mother Katharine Drexel, 1899

The broad goal of bringing Catholicism to people of color often took on practical, competitive, and even unattractive hues, as evidenced by this letter of Monsignor J. A. Stephan to Mother Katharine Drexel (1858–1955), who donated millions of dollars to Indian education.

Reverend dear Mother,

I thank you and your Sisterhood for the great and most liberal donation of $83,000 for the support of our Indian schools during the year just ending. It will prove their salvation for another year at least, for, without this help they would be forced to close and close forever. But mingled with this my joy very serious thoughts on the subject occur to me. I will present them to you as it is of the utmost importance to look at matters as they are, and comprehend clearly the dark future of the Indian work of the Church.

Are you prepared to, and will you in the future pay all the expenses of the Indian missions, amounting to about $170,000 annually, while the 13,000,000 Catholics in this country should furnish the needed funds?

You and your Sisters devote your lives and services to the Indian and Colored Missions. Your only recompense in this world being the satisfaction you have in serving God. Should you, in addition, be expected to provide the means to board, educate, clothe, feed and lodge the children in attendance at our Indian schools?

It is the duty of the Catholics of the United States to supply the money needed to keep up our Indian schools, and the people would cheerfully do this if they were instructed and called upon for help. Often I have been asked by the faithful to tell them something about the Indians, as they hear nothing but abuse of them, and thus grow indifferent towards them. The priests are very loathe to say a good word, as a general rule, for the Indians either in private or from the pulpit and when the annual collection for the Indian and Colored Missions is taken up, with very few exceptions you will not hear any hearty appeal in behalf of, or favorable explanation of the needs of these poor unfortunate people. Nearly everyone is afraid to raise his voice in their behalf, forgetting that Christianizing and civilizing the Indians is a sacred debt we owe that race. Even Bishops say: "The people will give nothing for Negroes and Indians." If the truth were told the people and the subject brought before the faithful forcibly and courageously, there would be plenty of money given to support all Indian and Colored Missions. Our Catholic population is at least thirteen millions of souls. Suppose four million would each pay 25 cts., we would get one million dollars annually...

At last year's meeting of the Most Reverend Archbishops, I advocated, as a matter of sacred duty, the plan of sending through the country six or eight priests, Indian missionaries — with instructions to tell our people the sufferings and needs of the Indians, from whom we have gotten our lands and riches, and what we owe this much persecuted race. But my appeal was ignored. They should tell, without fear or favor, the truth to the people, and when we have sowed the seed of truth, God will give His blessings and a good harvest.

Adverting to the future of our Indian schools, I think it would be the part of wisdom for the Rt. Rev. Bishop Horstmann [of Cleveland] to call upon the President, and...to notify him, that it is the desire of the Hierarchy that these things be done for the benefit of our Indian schools: (a) That the Government shall continue to make provision for the support of the contract schools now in operation. (b) That the objectionable Browning Ruling which denies the rights of Indian parents to select the schools where their children shall be educated and the enforcement of which is a menace to our schools, be rescinded. (c) That the right of Indians having trust or other funds belonging to them in the United States Treasury, to determine the use of such funds in the matter of the education of their children, shall be respected and recognized...

In conclusion, let me ask your consideration of what follows... You and your order have to face peculiar conditions and circumstances, unlike those to be met by any other religious community. In the first place, your subjects are

Indians and Negroes from whom you cannot receive postulants. These must be recruited from the Whites or your order will not be able to continue its work. All other communities have in charge only white children, who are trained by and brought up under the eye of the Sisters from early childhood to womanhood, and from whom they have no difficulty in procuring postulants as they are needed...[T]hose communities have means of providing for their own support by teaching and nursing, from both which they derive revenue. In addition their work appeals directly to the charity of the people at large, and generous financial help is being constantly rendered them. Your community has no such resources. Those to whom your lives are consecrated, are poor; they can give you nothing substantial in return for what you do for them. Your work being among the Indians and Negroes, receives little or no sympathy from the people, and hence you need not expect financial aid from the outside. It follows that you must not only give your time and that of your Sisters to the work of elevating the Indians and Colored races, but you must, from your own resources, provide the means of living and keeping up your order. While you are spared there will...be no difficulty about financial matters; but would this be the case if you were called away in the near future? Would your community then have a capital from which to derive an income sufficient to keep the order in operation? Is it not a certainty that it would not?...Would not this condition of affairs lead to dissatisfaction among the Sisters, the discouragement of postulants and the dissolution of the order at no distant day? Does it not, therefore, follow that your first duty is to so conduct your financial affairs as to insure, if possible, a firm permanent foundation for your community, and to make provision for the traditional "rainy day?"

Monsignor J. A. Stephan to Mother Katharine Drexel, 29 September 1899, *Annals of the Sisters of the Blessed Sacrament* (1899–1902), 11:46–51, Archives of the Sisters of the Blessed Sacrament, Bensalem, Pa. Printed by permission.

34. Observations of Mother Katharine Drexel in the Oklahoma Territory, 1902

In the following letter, written as she toured the Oklahoma Territory visiting mission schools, Mother Katharine Drexel described the many elements — religious, economic, political, social — that she perceived were involved in Native American relationships with the church and with white settlers.

My very dear daughters in the B[lessed] S[acrament],

When I last wrote you were with me in spirit under the spreading branches of elm trees in the Wichita Reservation and you all promised to pray for the girl who went to the Methodist school...I depend on your prayers — through Mary Immaculate and the Miraculous medal to bring that poor child into Holy Mother Church and St. Patrick's School.

I also introduced you to Mr. Turkey, his wife and child. It delighted the Santa Claus heart of Father Ricklin to behold these Catholic children of his seated under the shade of the elms to enjoy a water melon.

"Look at the Turkey Family," says he benevolently. An enterprising white farmer had brought in a cart load of this fruit — small specimens — and he sat in his cart and sold them to the Indians at 10cts. Apiece. It was interesting to behold Indian after Indian purchasing the same, and watch him carry it under a tree, and beckon to his friends to have a treat. There they sat in groups of five or four enjoying a water melon party. The one who purchased the melon cut it in two, they laying both halves on the ground, he and his friends put their hands into the red pulp and tore out a portion which each demurely and silently consumed. There were two groups of 8 who were not eating water melons. We stood and watched playing Monte — a gambling game. Two women were playing with the men. Each player seemed to have about $5 in dollars, halves, and quarters. Under the big square refreshment tent I espied a fine looking boy of 9 or 10. I asked Father Ricklin to ask the parents to send the child to St. Patrick's. Of course Father went and with his inimitable, cordial manner he accosted the lad. The fellow at a safe distance off pertly called out, "Oh, you won't want me, I'm too bad." "Guess you're not," says Father, glowing with benevolence. "You better come and try, you'll be all right." His mother, who was grounding the coffee, called out, "You can't do anything to that boy," at which my lad looked triumphant. But Father was not to be repulsed. He whispered to me, "That's the kind of fellow I like; he'll come all right when he gets with the others." So here, Sisters, is another soul I commend to your prayers that his parents may send him to St. Patrick's and that he many renounce the devil and all his works and pomps. You will have to pray hard for his parting words were, "You'll not get me."

We drove 8 miles farther on to another Wichita camp. I saw from a distance a girl of fourteen standing by her tent. I thought, "here is a subject for the school." On approaching her I found a baby tied to her back and her husband soon turned up from behind a tree. It seems these Indians marry very young. There was a wee boy with a broken arm in one of the tents. Its parents had bandaged the arm to a splint most skillfully. There were no more children in the camp — so we had the humiliation of returning to St. Patrick's without a single child. We received the promise, however, of some children and one had entered during our absence making the school enrollment in all 38. Now pray hard that one hundred Comanche, Wichita, and Apache children fill the school to overflowing. The school is admirably fitted for giving them just the education they need — Sisters to teach the boys and girls class work and housework and sewing to the girls, and a farmer to teach the boys the very trade they need, viz: farming. The 160 acres of farm land at St. Patrick's ... has been well worked. The barns overflowing with prairie hay, Kaffir corn, sorghum, wheat and corn and potatoes testify to the fertility of the soil and the industry of the farmer and boys...

St. Louis School at Pawhuska is a 15 mile drive from St. John's. It is a rough stony road and it was moonlight ere we drove before the entrance of this Girls' School for the Osage Nations. The building is of stone and a duplicate of St. John's. The Franciscan Sisters have every hope of obtaining the appropriation of $125 for each pupil as they did in former years. They are not yet sure of obtaining it, so pray still fervently. There are 72 girls — all full bloods — in the school. The Osages say they prefer the Sisters School to the National School which is a fine stone school 3/4 mile from St. Louis on the hill. The Agent threatens to send to St. Louis School for 20 girls who were in the National School last year. However, as the parents freely desired to send their girls to our school, if he dare to do this, the Catholic Bureau for Indians will surely force him to bring every child back. There is an elderly Sister — at St. Louis who was one of the Sisters sent to found the mission 14 years ago. She says she remarks the greatest improvement in the girls. She says she used to cry in bed the first years at the manners and unkindness of these little Indian Princesses. They are the children of wealthy Indians and very much spoilt by their parents who disdain all work. They rent out their farm to be worked by white men. I saw them in their blankets in Pawhuska, the Osage City. I shall not soon forget the regal repose of one chief, seated on a porch by the court house. The Sister tells me many of the first girls who attended the school are now married and they go to the Sacrament, and they visit the Sisters and they say, "Sister, I do not know how you stood us when we were young. We treated you so meanly." The girls all had a ball the evening we left and we had a reception of chiefs in the afternoon...

I am still dazed at the discovery made in our trip to the Indians wherein in their own land, their own specially reserved territory, so few comparatively Indians are to be seen. White people and white people, always and white Indians except in the unbeaten paths...[I] burn with a desire to bring the full bloods, what is left of them, somehow to the church, to educate them so that they may not be cheated out of their land by the teeming population of whites, so that they too may be fit to intermarry with good Catholic whites, and not the worst white element, and thus be saved unto generation and generation soul and body, mingled as Normans and Saxons were, so that future generations may not be able to discern difference of Nationality but that mingled into one Nation all may serve God on earth and praise Him eternally in heaven. If an awful effort be not made to save the full bloods, they must inevitably become paupers and die out...

Mother Katharine Drexel, S.B.S., to My very dear daughters in the B[lessed] S[acrament], 15 October 1902, Writings of Katharine Drexel, vol. 2, no. 144, Archives of the Sisters of the Blessed Sacrament, Bensalem, Pa. Printed by permission.

Great Basin Conflicts

35. A Spanish Priest Comments on Early Indian Catholicism, 1775

As seen in the diary of a Spanish priest, as the eastern part of the country entered the American Revolution, the western part already enjoyed a widespread Catholicism, a product of much earlier national contests played out in the Great Basin.

On this day the married Indian chanted the whole bendito (Benedictus) with little difference in intonation from that which it is chanted in the missions...I (asked) him eagerly who had taught it to him. He gave me to understand that the Yutas his neighbors knew it, for they had heard it many times among the Tiguas; whereupon he fell to chanting it twice over again.

> Francisco Garces, *On the Trail of a Spanish Pioneer, the Diary and Itinerary of Francisco Garces (Missionary Priest) in His Travels through Sonora, Arizona, and California, 1775–1776* (New York: Francis P. Harper, 1900), quoted in Bernice Mooney, *Salt of the Earth* (Salt Lake City: Litho Grafics, 1987), 16.

36. Protestant Clergy Remark on the Dangers of Catholicism in the West, ca. 1865

In part, Catholic identity was forged out of the forceful anti-Catholic sentiments articulated as intensely in the West as in the urban centers of the East. As seen in the remarks of two Colorado Protestant clergymen, deeply imbedded cultural practices often became the focus of the attacks.

[The Roman Catholics] are sure to take good care of the young of their own flock, while they exhibit a very tender solicitude for the lambs of other folds. In the larger towns before they have a church edifice they have a schoolhouse...They are not content with baptizing their children, and then leaving them to grow up in ignorance, or to be taught by irreligious instructors, or by those who do not hold to their own faith. They aim to have in the new settlements of a country better schools than any other religious body can have, and thus they contrive to compel Protestants to send their children to Romish schools. This is now done in Denver. Episcopalians are sending their daughters to the Convent because it is the best school in the Territory.

The people here are able and willing to pay liberal tuition. A school for girls in Denver, of a high order, with competent instructors, would be at once self-supporting...

Will you suffer me to go back again, singlehanded and alone, to stand there and see the immense tide of emigration pouring into this great State, as large in area as all New England and a part of New York; and behold infidelity sweeping through the land, and Romanism triumphant; and other zealous denominations spreading their systems with more or less of error; while I am powerless, because solitary, and solitary because the Church will "not come up to the help of the Lord against the mighty?" Is that to be the destiny of my Apostolic Mission? NO! NO! I don't believe it can be so. God forbid! There is too much godliness, too much of the mind of Christ in His people to allow it. God will surely crown our labors with a measure of success that will gladden every heart capable of rejoicing in the triumphs of Christ and His Church.

•

No wonder they ring so merry a peal for it tells also of a handsome fee for the well-fed priest, a fee too, not willingly given but extorted with utmost cruelty of oppression from the very poorest children [who] grow up unbaptized because of their parents being too poor to pay what is demanded and disowned by their mother when dead and secretly left in the Church at night that the priest may be compelled to bury them without a charge, which would deprive their parents of every worldly comfort!...

The ugly dolls, with tin crowns representing the Virgin and other Saints, the miserable daubs which picture our Blessed Lord, the Virgin, and the Holy Family, the tin candle sticks, the tin glitter everywhere, the box for the confessional, the super altar with its sacrarium — these are there and without doubt are valued by the people as aids in devotion not only, but as essential in public worship... The majority had learned no law save what the priests taught them, confession and mass, payment of a portion of all they had or could raise to the Church,... [offering them] nothing to elevate them to a higher state of civilization or make them men and women in our nation.

Bishop George Randall, *First Report*, and John Dyer, *Snow Shoe Itinerant*, quoted in Alice Cochran, *Miners, Merchants, and Missionaries: The Roles of Missionaries and Pioneer Churches in the Colorado Gold Rush and Its Aftermath, 1858–1870* (Metuchen, N.J.: Scarecrow Press and American Theological Library Association, 1980), 176–80.

37. Sister Frederica McGrath, D.C., Responds to Criticism in the Nevada Legislature, 1873

Sisters found occasions when controversy surrounded their work, as indicated in this letter. In it, Sister Frederica asked that a state allocation not be renewed for the Catholic orphanage at Virginia City, Nevada, because of criticism she felt had been directed at the sisters for their management of the facility.

The Sisters of Charity, grateful for past favors from the Legislature, conferred on themselves the Nevada Orphan Asylum and the Orphans render their thanks. They are also desirous of manifesting their gratitude for members of the present legislature who have shown a kindly feeling toward them and a due appreciation of their labors in their works of charity.

The Sisters established their asylum in 1867, when the State allowed but a heartless indifference for parentless children. What they have done since that time in their vocation is more public than private and is open for the public

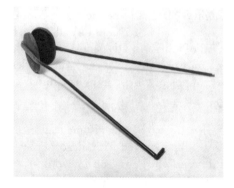

This nineteenth-century Communion wafer press used in Virginia City, Nevada, to produce the Host for Mass demonstrates that the preservation of well-known forms served to reinforce Catholic identity for religious and laity alike.

Credit: Scott W. Klette, photographer, Nevada State Historic Preservation Office, Carson City, Nev.

and private investigation. They have been duly acknowledged by previous legislatures and in some manner recompensed. Had they no other rewards, but that arising from their efforts in awaking a feeling of sympathy for poor parentless children from the people of Nevada, they consider themselves amply repaid. All know, though some reluctantly admit, they were the Pioneers in the state for the orphans. When they threw their doors open to the public, no questions were asked, there was no distinction of persons; no discrimination of creeds — distress and poverty directed their actions. The State, through her representatives, was aware of this, and not from charity, but a sense of justice, rewarded them.

But of late a hostile feeling has risen against them, still the hope to live notwithstanding this unfriendly opposition. They have been informed that members of the present Assembly were approached before election, and a qualification for election was an opposition to themselves and the orphans under their charge; such being the case, we most sincerely and respectfully request of your honorable bodies to withdraw the bill for the Nevada Orphan Asylum. If we are not entitled to the appropriation in justice, we do not look for it from the state in charity. Be pleased, therefore, not to say anything more about it in the present Legislature. Whatever has been said is sufficient and should anything more be said, it is entirely adverse to our feelings of propriety and rectitude.

The asylum has friends and these friends are good enough to see that neither ourselves or the orphans under our charge can want for food or clothing. We have no salary or wages; we have consecrated our life, our time, our attention, our care and all that this world could afford us, to help the distressed, the afflicted and especially the poor orphans, and we look for a recompense from a good Master who has promised a reward, even to the charity of a cup of cold water.

Very respectfully and humbly on the part of the Sisters of Charity.

Sister Superior Frederica McGrath, D.C., to the *Territorial Enterprise,* 19 February 1873.

38. The First Utah Priest Reports on the Catholic Presence among Mormons, 1876

As a pioneer priest living in the kingdom of the Mormons, Father Lawrence Scanlan (1843–1915) looked outside his Utah Territory for the funds he needed to construct a physical Catholic presence. He turned to Europe for mission funds, and his detailed reports brought him positive results.

As we are taught by our holy religion that the best and surest way to obtain new favors from Heaven is to render due thanks for those already received: so, I begin my report by sincerely thanking you for the very handsome appropriation of $1560 which you, in your boundless charity, have made us during the year. This, indeed seemed to have been sent us by Providence, as it came at a time when it was very much needed; and, I assure you that the good news caused many a fervent prayer to ascend to the Throne of Grace for you and every member of the Society.

With this short preface, I now proceed to give you an account of my stewardship, and lay before you how we have employed the talents you have entrusted to us, what we have been doing during the past year, and what we want to do with your cooperation and the Grace of God in the future, in this far off and all but pagan land.

Although a decade of years has scarcely elapsed since the small grain of "mustard seed" was first dropped into this large and then seemingly barren and unfruitful field of the great "vineyard of the Lord," yet, through your fostering care, our own feeble efforts and the life-giving sunlight of a benign Providence, it has already taken deep root, is extending its branches higher and wider every year and is still full of life, health, and vigor.

There are, at present, two churches in the Territory. The Church in Salt Lake City, which since its erection in 1871, lay under a heavy debt, is now free of all encombrances. Its congregation is steadily increasing, and many indifferent and lukewarm members are becoming less irregular in attending divine Services and in the performance of their religious duties. During the year, we had about 60 Baptisms, twenty of whom were adult converts; 12 marriages, chiefly "mixed" and at Easter, about 50 communicants.

I have just built a church in Ogden, the second city in the territory. It is a frame building 33 by 40 with a small tower in front and recess for Altar in rear. Its cost, when furnished with proper benches, will range from $1500.00 to $2000.00 with an indebtedness of about $500. It is sufficiently large to accommodate the Catholics of Ogden and the surrounding district for a long time to come.

In my last report, I had the honor of stating to you that we succeded in bringing to Salt Lake City and establishing therein a colony of faithful and devoted Sisters of the "Holy Cross." I hope the Catholics of this Territory shall never forget the generous support which you have rendered them in accomplishing this grand and glorious work. These good daughters of the "Cross," since their advent here, have been indefatigable workers, and have done more to remove prejudice and give tone and prominence to our Cause than we priests could have done in many years of hard work.

The Academy of St. Marys of Utah: This large and commodious brick structure, described in my last report, was opened for the reception of boarders and day pupils on the 6th of September 1875, from which time, it has been wonderfully successful — to the great credit of the good Sisters. The average attendance is about 100, and when we remember that the great majority of these are non-catholics [and] that there exists in the minds of non-catholics, generally, in this country a bitter prejudice against everything Catholic, this number must strike us as exceedingly large. But the Sisters, by their exemplary lives, their industry, their holy conversations, their solicitude and even love for the children and the good advices they give them, are silently — but surely, not only removing all prejudices from their minds, but even gaining their respect and admiration! Hence, during the past year many of the pupils expressed a desire to be baptized; I baptized about a dozen and refused to comply with the desires of many others, through motives of prudence and objections raised by their parents.

But, apart from the effect which the Sisters have upon non-catholic children, who can enumerate or comprehend the blessings which they have brought to our Catholic children? We priests have been laboring here for the last ten years, have held Catechism class once every week and have done all in our power to teach Catholic children the theory and practice of their religion: but, owing to the want of continual every day teaching, of a wholesome Catholic atmosphere, and, worse than all, the indifference, if not, scandalous lives of the parents, our efforts were all but fruitless! We never could collect more than two or three every year fit for first Communion! The Sisters are at work only a year, and note the contrast.

The Archbishop [Joseph Sadoc Alemany] paid us the honor of visiting us last July, when he had the pleasure of administering Confirmation, for the first time, in this land of Mormonism, to about 50 persons; and of witnessing the pleasing scene of about 40 children make their first Communion, all of whom have been gathered together, taught, and duly prepared for these Sacraments by the persevering efforts of the daughters of the "Holy Cross." Verily, the "Cross" is becoming a power in this benighted land, and the little "mustard seed" is already extending its branches and yielding abundant fruit!

St. Joseph's School for Small Boys: This is a neat little building, but sufficiently large, however, to accommodate, in a healthful and pleasant manner, from fifty to one hundred pupils. It is entirely separate from, but adjacent to the Academy. It is designed for the education of small boys of 12 years and under that age, and is also conducted by the Sisters. The average attendance is about forty, most of whom, also, are non-catholics. What I have stated respecting the girls school, apply with equal force and truth to this. The Sisters are giving the same good example, the same salutary instructions and training and educating the Catholic boys with the same fruitful and gratifying results!

Hospital of the Holy Cross: This is the crowning institution of our Church in this territory. Persons may, and do, hate the Catholic name, but, in spite of themselves respect and love its philanthropic spirit; its grand broad hearted charitable institutions. They may curse the priest, but must bless the devoted Sister of Charity — the angel in human form. They may and often do, close their ears and eyes to the teachings of the priest and spiritual directors, but they must open them wide to the inexorable logic of facts. They may listen for hours unmoved to the grand orator in the pulpit — wasting his eloquence in endeavoring to prove some grand dogma of the Church, or to portray the beauty or usefulness of some Christian virtue; and when he has finished, re-gard him as a hireling, a mere professional man, if not, a hypocrite: but, the poor emaciated Sister leaning over the bed of suffering, wiping away the sweat of death from the pale forehead of the dying man, soothing his declining mo-ments, softening his pillow, administering to his last needs, consoling him in his expiring agonies, standing by him as his friend, when perhaps his own desert him, encouraging him to enter with confidence on his long and mys-terious journey, alleviating his sufferings in life, and closing his eyes in the last long sleep of death — all these acts performed for no earthly reward, but through love of humanity, irrespective of creed, color, or country, and very often, to an enemy are sufficient proof, that even the most rigorous and seem-ingly repugnant maxims of the Gospel are, not only possible to be realized, but, are actually realized every day by hundreds and thousands of these de-voted creatures in the Catholic Church — All these, I repeat, speak indeed, true Christianity and with a logic and eloquence which the most bigoted and prejudiced cannot resist. And this is the logic and eloquence with which the Sisters in charge of the "Hospital of the Holy Cross" have loudly preached to the public, since its opening, and which has had already exerted a wonderful power in closing the mouths of many revilers of our Holy religion.

The hospital was opened on the 26th of October, 1875 in a handsome brick building which was then considered sufficiently large, but which is now too small to accommodate, in a proper manner, the increasing number of patients seeking admission. Being unable to purchase or build an hospital of our own, we had to leave the building for a few years, during which time Providence may supply us with the means to carry out His and our designs.

A hospital is an absolute necessity here, as there are a great many poor men of all creeds working in smelters and lead mines which are very unhealthy and cause a sickness known among miners as "leaded" or "lead disease" — the effect of inhaling arsenic and other poisonous matter through smoke, in working in smelters, and dust, in working in the mines. It is a very severe and painful sickness, and if neglected generally proves fatal. Over 500 patients have found

Here the Sisters of the Holy Cross, in a picture that might date to 1910, stand with their charges in the Kearns–St. Ann's Orphanage in Salt Lake City, the center of the Church of Jesus Christ of Latter-day Saints, which extended the sisters more goodwill than they had expected.

Credit: Archives of the Diocese of Salt Lake City. Reproduced by permission.

in this institution since its opening, a good home, kind treatment and nurses better than mothers — which is an abundant proof of its necessity. The average number in the hospital is about thirty.

So much for the past and present let us now turn our thoughts for a short time, to the future... The wants of this Territory seem to be multiplying every year. During last August, I visited the southern part of the Territory (about 200 miles from Salt Lake City) and received great encouragement from the few scattered Catholics and many non-Catholics there, to start a little mission with a church, schools, and hospital. I think a priest could do a great deal of good there, but, the distances between the places he would have to attend are so long and the travelling so expensive, that it would be very difficult for him, at present, to obtain a living. I merely refer to this portion of my mission as a growing place that will soon need our attention. Ogden, now having a church, ought henceforth be attended regularly every Sunday. But this cannot be done without another priest. We have, besides Salt Lake, which has service every Sunday, six other places to attend and to do justice to those places, there ought to be here, at least, 4 priests. Hence, one of our great needs, at present is more priests with some little provision made for their proper sustenance.

Again, a Catholic School is very much needed in Ogden, where, all the Catholic children are attending either Mormon or protestant schools. This should be attended to at an early date, otherwise, there is not only a danger, but a certainty, that many of our children there shall be perverted and forever lost to the church...

In conclusion, I again, in the name of the Archbishop, Sisters, Catholics and all interested in this mission, thank you most sincerely for your generosity and charity in the past, and in the name of the same parties express a hope that you will not abandon us in our struggles, but will stand by us to the end, and that we shall never prove ourselves unfaithful servants or unworthy of your kindness and generosity.

> Rev. Lawrence Scanlan to Archbishop Alemany for the Society for the Propaga-
> tion of the Faith, 12 October 1876, in Bernard McGloin, S.J., "Two Early Reports
> concerning Roman Catholicism in Utah, 1876–1881," *Utah Historical Quarterly*
> 29 (October 1961): 332–44.

39. A Report to Europeans about the Progress of Catholicism in Utah, 1882

Father Dennis Kiely's report to the French-based Society for the Propagation of the Faith demonstrates the complexity of trying to explain the environment faced by Utah Catholics to European benefactors.

As years pass by, it is a pleasure to be able to report more favorably, each succeeding year, the prosperity of the Church in this Territory. But a few years ago when making up our annual report for the "Society of the Propagation of the Faith," in a district embracing upwards of eighty thousand square miles, we could only report one Church in that wide-spread district. Those places, where a priest visited a few times each year, are today supplied with priests, who are aided in their missionary labors, by zealous, self sacrificing sisters, who have, in the missions thus far established, the pleasure of seeing their labors crowned with success.

Four years ago, the entire Territory of Utah formed one parish; today there are five parishes, all of which are under the immediate supervision of Very Rev. L[awrence] Scanlan. To keep pace with the rapid growth of churches, schools, and hospitals in the Territory, his Grace, Archbishop [Joseph Sadoc] Alemany saw fit, that the jurisdiction of its Pastor, who saw the Church cradled in its infancy, and who labored zealously to bring it, and its noble institutions prominently before its very enemies[,] should be extended, and in 1879, his Grace appointed Father Scanlan vicar-forane of the Territory of Utah.

In 1873, when Very Rev. Father Scanlan received his appointment as Pastor, the Church was in its infancy, and the great work accomplished by him in those years is marvelous.

In 1874 when I received my obedience to come to Utah to aid him in the mission, he was alone. With a few Catholics to aid him in discharging a heavy debt, which then encumbered the Church, the only one at the time in the Territory, the future prospect of the Church was anything but encouraging; but the good seed of the Divine Word planted by him in those years has multiplied manifold, and to your noble, and generous society is due the gratitude of every Catholic in Utah; for to your generous aid may be traced the foundation of the churches, schools, and hospitals, which today are to be found throughout the Territory.

In 1874 though numerically as strong, as any one Protestant sect, in point of prominence, we fell far behind the least among them; because we lacked the public institutions which they had, and gave them prominence among the Mormon people. To this point, my attention was soon directed, by Very Rev. Father Scanlan, after arriving here. "We alone," he remarked, "are without a school in Salt Lake, until this is done we will be in the background, the Church will not be fairly represented. 'There is a tide in the affairs of men which, when taken at the flood, leads to fortune.' This," he remarked, "applies to the Church here at present." This was the all absorbing thought of his mind, when I first came to Utah, and his first gleam of hope was realized when in 1875 he received his Archbishop's sanction to found a day and boarding school for young ladies, and more than realized were his most sanguine anticipations, when through your generous assistance, aided by the voluntary contributions of charitably disposed persons, he saw his first great work crowned with success in its noble undertaking. The Sisters of the Holy Cross opened school in a new three story brick building in Sep[tember] 1875. To the youth of Salt Lake the Sisters were at first an object of curiosity. More than once when passing along the streets, have I seen crowds of Mormon children following them; but their Christian example, aided by their effective work, soon dispelled the feelings entertained by them towards the Catholic Church, her institutions and noble band of workers.

The work begun by them in 1875 still continues to flourish, and with pleasure, do the few Catholics in Utah today look back, and contrast the Church of today, with that of eight years ago.

That prestige, which she has attained at present, and which gains for her the esteem, and admiration of all, is due principally to her schools and hospitals. Without these her light was hid under a bushel, through these like the early Church emerging from the catacombs, her beauty, and grandeur showed themselves in her great charity, and practical workings.

The very example, of a procession of Sisters, going to church, and wading through mud, or snow in the cold winter season, was not without its effect on the Mormon people, who, though wandering in the mazes of error, are religiously inclined, and are, and have been so attracted on Sundays, that they would come to services. Eight years ago six Mormons would not enter our little church in twelve months. Today many attend regularly on Sundays. The impression existing in their minds regarding the Church, her services, and ceremonies is fast disappearing, and they no longer see her [as] that terrible institution so much to be dreaded, as they were wont to regard her, nor are afraid to entrust their children to the charge of her schools. As a rule the Mormons are no more bigoted against the Catholic, than against the Protestant, whatever bigotry they do possess is inherited by them from Protestant ancestary [sic] rather than taught to them by the Mormon Church.

Here in Salt Lake, with less pecuniary aid, and less influence, than any Protestant church, when once established, the Catholic Church has shown more vitality, than all other churches combined. In 1874, the Protestant Episcopal Church (Church of England) had three schools, and one hospital with an annuity of over twenty thousand dollars a year for their support, and the influence of the richest of the non-Mormon residents of the place to back them up. The Methodist Episcopal society had the largest church, save the Mormon tabernacle, in Salt Lake, and a flourishing school with an annuity of over twelve thousand dollars a year for their support. The Presbyterians had their church and school with salaried elders, and teachers to carry on the mission. The Congregationalists enjoyed the same advantages. The Catholic Church alone was poor, depending on the voluntary contributions of a few poor Catholics, who were to be found traveling through the Territory or in the fastness of the mountains searching for their fortune.

To see the Church then as she really was, and contrast her with the Protestant, and let that contrast run along those years, that have marked the rise and growth of all non-Mormon churches, one can not fail to perceive in that contrast the vitality of the Catholic Church, in her vitality will be seen her strength, in her strength her truth. Her school, in Salt Lake today, is the finest and most flourishing in the city. Today she possesses the finest and grandest hospital, not in Utah, but within a radius of a thousand miles, and this hospital, it must be remembered, was founded at a time, when no apparent means of support were to be had. St. Mark's Hospital under the auspices of the Protestant Episcopal Church was founded three years previous. The support and influence of the non-Mormon population were on their side. They had possession of all that was worth possessing at the time, and the Sisters opening their hospital in 1875 had to depend solely on their own merits and ability to conduct an hospital. Once opened they had to engage in a fair contest, in an open field, with their more fortunate rivals, the Protestant Episcopalians. Public opinion, basing its judgment on the good accomplished by both institutions, was to decide which institution was superior. The work of the past seven years has decided the contest; for whilst the Protestant hospital has advanced but little, the Sisters' hospital has extended its salutary influence through Utah and the adjoining Territories. The former has nothing, save a small brick building, never intended for hospital use, to show the public as the result of its labor, and economy; the latter has succeeded in obtaining of a whole block of land (10 acres) in the healthiest part of the city, and within the past eighteen months, erected thereon the finest hospital, as already remarked, within a radius of a thousand miles. Protestants are wont to boast of their superiority over Catholics, but here in Salt Lake we apply the argument, from which there is no appeal, "contra factum non dater argumcutum."

In Salt Lake, the Sisters' school is the most flourishing and prosperous in the city. Not only is it self sustaining, but they have been able to save sufficient, to enable them to commence, next spring, an addition to their already large building, a work much needed for the accommodation of its many, and constantly increasing boarders, and day pupils. Of all the mission schools in Salt Lake, it alone is self sustaining, as it grows older, it grows more in favor with the public. Here again can be seen how a Catholic institution can gain the ascendancy over Protestant institutions, even though the latter possess more advantages, which they do possess in Salt Lake City, first in pecuniary matters, and secondly and principally in not having to fight that prejudice entertained by infidels against the Catholic Church. The works, and workings of the Catholic Church we present to all non-Catholics, and say to them, "if you believe not our church believe her works." This argument is not without its effect upon the thinking, and unprejudiced public, and more than once have men of reason and intelligence [remarked], "whatever truth, there is in religion, is to be found in the Catholic, and her institutions." I herewith send slips taken from papers published in this city, showing that greater praise is lavished on our schools by non-Catholics than I could bestow.

The prosperous condition of the Salt Lake mission applies equally to Ogden, the second prominent city in Utah. The school conducted by the Sisters is in a flourishing condition, and receives pupils from points 400 and 500 miles from Ogden. In 1875 a three story frame building 50 ft. x 50 ft. was erected there. Very Rev. Scanlan, at the time, but little expected, that so large a building would not be more than sufficient for many years to accommodate all who would apply there for instruction. During the present years, the numerous applicants as boarders was such, that the building was no longer sufficiently large, and a new two story building 50 ft. x 24 ft. was erected during the present year to make ample room for the accommodation of all applicants. As with Salt Lake, so also is it in Ogden. When contrasted with Protestant churches, her beauty, and grandeur, and superiority show themselves in her institutions. The last in the race, she is today the most prominent among the non-Mormon churches in Ogden.

In 1874, 75 and 76 when I visited Ogden monthly to say Mass, for a few poor Catholics, there was no church or school. Mass then was celebrated in a hall owned by the Spiritists. In this little hall Mass was celebrated for three years monthly, and during those years, often I did not have more than four persons in attendance, and the congregation never reached twenty persons. Catholics, long removed from Catholic influence were ashamed to identify themselves with the few Catholics then there, and not till the Church emerged from her nothingness, made her power and influence felt did they like the strayed sheep return to the flock, and today are good practical Catholics. The prominence, which the Church possesses today in Ogden, and the good, accomplished there during the past five years, are first traceable to your noble society, and to you gentlemen every Catholic in Ogden owes a debt of gratitude for first helping them to secure a lot and build a church, which they themselves, no matter how freely they gave could [not] accomplish...

375 miles south east of Salt Lake is a little mining camp called Silver Reef. In 1877, Very Rev. Father Scanlan first visited this place. Being the first priest, who visited there, he was received with open arms by the Catholics of the place. Having sojourned there for two weeks, he found the people well disposed, and willing to aid him in any work he would undertake for the Church. He determined, after returning to Salt Lake, and arranging other missionary work, which was progressing at the time, to go back to Silver Reef, and commence the erection of a church. This he did in the early part of 1878, and very soon his labors were crowned with success; for in three months he succeeded in building a church and hospital. Since 1878, a priest and four Sisters have been in charge of the mission. In connection with the hospital, the Sisters have a school, where the Catholic children of the district are being educated.

Traveling from Silver Reef to Salt Lake over bleak mountains, and barren rolling land is to be met another mining camp, whose inhabitants are largely composed of Catholics. It is called [Frisco]. In 1880, a little church was commenced and finished in this little town. Previous to its erection, the priest, who visited there occasionally, was subject to great inconveniences, trying to secure a suitable place to offer up the adorable sacrifice of the Mass [or] hear confessions. On one occasion, the writer, when about to celebrate Mass, had to hear the confession of a good Catholic in the open air, for want of a more suitable place, the hall in which I was about to celebrate Mass, being filled with people, many of whom were non-Catholics. This inconvenience, thanks to God, no longer exists, and we have today in Frisco a nice church.

During a visit there last May, a prominent resident of the place, and a school trustee, asked if the Catholics would accept the public school of the place, and send Sisters to take charge of same.

I mention this fact to show that the good work being done by the Sisters in Salt Lake, Ogden and Silver Reef, is appreciated far beyond the limits of these places, and to show also how their Christian example, and the moral and intellectual good accomplished by them in the past seven years are extending into the most remote and isolated parts of the Territory of Utah...

About 40 miles south east of Salt Lake at the foothills of the Wasatch Mountains is Park City with a population of 3000 inhabitants. Here within the past twelve months a new church with a parsonage has been erected. Last May Archbishop Alemany came from San Francisco, a distance of a thousand miles to dedicate the new church, and administer the sacrament of Confirmation. Notwithstanding the length of [the] journey and his fatigue, age and traveling, he felt that he was amply rewarded, and more than once expressed his surprise and agreeable disappointment to find in Utah, in the vastness of the mountains, so many Catholics. Hardy miners living in the mountains for years, and innured to hardship came to see the Archbishop. It was the first time in the history of the place, that a Catholic Bishop visited the place, and it was the first opportunity for years afforded many, to see a Bishop of the Catholic Church. Among the numbers, who were attracted to come to see his Grace, were many who approached the sacraments, and who would not otherwise do so. On Sunday he administered the Sacrament of Confirmation to over thirty persons, many of whom were adults. Being pleased with the Catholic spirit manifested by the people, and having heard the expressed wish of some among them, that a Catholic school should be there, to help them, to educate their children in the principles of the Catholic faith, his Grace promised that he would try, and get the Sisters to come, and take charge of a school. Faithful to his promise, he succeeded, and a school was opened there in the middle of September which is largely patronized by non-Catholic children since its opening.

This is a brief recapitulation of the history of the Catholic Church in Utah during the past eight years. It shows what has been done. Much has been done. The many churches, schools, and hospitals which dot the territory today are an exemplification of the parable of the mustard seed. Though much has been done in the past, much yet remains to be done, and whilst it is gratifying to be able to report the great progress of the Catholic Church in Utah, as shown in her churches, schools and hospitals, it is the earnest wish of every priest in the mission, to see established in those same missions much needed Catholic institutions.

In Salt Lake City is one of the finest and most promising openings for a "brothers day and boarding school," that could be wished for. This institution established, the Salt Lake mission would be well provided for, and the priests' earnest wish would be no dream of life but a glad reality. Ogden offers, if not better, at least a good inducement for a similar institution. Catholic parents wishing to send their boys to a Catholic boarding school, and young Catholic men who work during the summer and wish to attend school in the winter (of this latter class many are to be found in the mining camps) have no means of satisfying their wishes in Utah, nor nearer than San Francisco in the West, and Omaha in the East. The result thus far has been that many, who would gladly avail themselves of a Catholic school, go through necessity to the Protestant schools of this city. Protestants, realizing the great necessity of such schools, have made provisions for boarding as well as educating young men. We are last in the field, in this much needed institution, but we hope, D[eo] V[olente] with a little outside [assistance] to be able to report another flourishing institution for young men, and our Protestant competitors first in the race last at the goal. Notwithstanding the number of priests in the Territory, and the number of miles traveled annually by each one of them, there are yet in this Territory places so far removed from civilization that a priest has never visited them; and strange yet true in those remote places are to be found Catholics, with grown families, over whose heads the regenerating water of Baptism was never poured. Only last week an instance of this kind came under my notice, whilst traveling in a wild unsettled district. At a small station a young man stepped into the car, in which I was seated. He looked at me for some time, evidently wishing to speak, but apparently afraid to do so. I said to him, "Well my boy are you belonging to this place?" He answered, "No I belong to the coal mines way up in the mountains. Are you a Catholic priest?" he asked. When I answered "yes" with a tear in his eye he said to me, "Well priest I am a Catholic. My mother always tells me [to] say I am a Roman Catholic, and I do say it, when the Mormons ask me to what Church I belong." "Do you go to your duty?" I asked, and to my surprise the reply I got was: "What is that?" I next asked, "Do you go to the sacraments?" and here my surprise was still greater when he replied, "And what are these?" I said to him, "Why my boy did you not tell me you were a Catholic," and here he interrupted me saying, "Yes, yes, I am and my mother always tells me [to] say I am a Catholic." "And you do not know what the sacraments are[?]" He answered, "No."

"Baptism is a sacrament," I remarked, "you were baptized." He told me, "No." I asked his age. He said he was 17 years. His mother had always told him, when an opportunity offered he would be baptized, and as a proof that Catholic instinct was impressed on him, poor boy, before parting with me said, "If I go to you tonight will you baptize me?"

This is one of the many cases that comes to our notice occasionally. It will show the necessity of establishing other missions, to increase the facilities of reaching the most distant places. All the missions, thus far established, are doing a good work, and others, which will do as much, [can] be established, as soon as circumstances and the means entrusted to the Very Rev. Father Scanlan's charge will permit.

For what has been done thus far pray accept the thanks, and gratitude of every Catholic in Utah, and a share in the prayers of your unworthy but ever grateful child in Jesus Christ.

Father Dennis Kiely to the Society for the Propagation of the Faith, in Francis J. Weber, ed., "The Church in Utah, 1882: A Contemporary Account," *Records of the American Catholic Historical Society of Philadelphia* 81 (December 1970): 199–208.

40. Catholic Comment on Two Important Elements of Faith, 1917

When surrounded by a religion, Mormonism, that dominated all aspects of Utah frontier life, Catholics appeared to treasure the rituals of church tradition that gave witness to their faith. The two documents below indicate that Utah Catholics welcomed two common patterns of their faith — conversion and religious vocation — in the center of the Mormons.

Six converts to the Church were confirmed in the chapel of St. Mary's academy last Friday morning by the Rt. Rev. Joseph S. Glass, C.M.D.D. In the class also were two Catholics who had never received the sacrament and who were instructed with the converts in preparation for confirmation. All of the converts were recently baptized and received their first Holy Communion.

The converts confirmed last week were: Mrs. Olive Gaylord, Mrs. Clara Ryan, Mrs. Mary Agnes Sloan, Mrs. Henrietta Killeen, Mrs. Alice Bueter, and Miss Adelaide Sullivan. Mrs. Anna Ryan and John Ryan were also confirmed with the class.

Gaylord Bueter, son of Mrs. Alice Bueter, who was killed in an elevator accident at the Fifth East Hotel a short time ago, was to have been confirmed in the class with his mother. The boy was to have made his First Communion on the Sunday after the fatal accident occurred. He had been a faithful attendant at the class, and was much admired by all who knew him.

The conversions were fruits of the class of instruction started by the Very Rev. Frederick Maune, C.M. at the mission held in the cathedral last winter. The converts began attending this class, and later, when the missionaries departed, the Rev. Dr. S. Anzalone of the cathedral took up the instruction. Several others who were members of the mission class may yet become Catholics, according to Dr. Anzalone.

Another class of instruction for non-Catholics will be opened by Dr. Anzalone in the fall.

Intermountain Catholic, 24 November 1917, 19.

On one of the trains that left Salt Lake Tuesday was Marian Bruneau, one of the most popular and talented students ever graduated from St. Mary's academy. It bore her away from her relatives and friends, from the life she had known, to even greater friends and to a life she has chosen as the best. She has determined to spend her life in the service of her Master, and in a few days will enter the novitiate of the Sisters of the Holy Cross at the Mother House at Notre Dame, Ind.

When but a small girl, Miss Bruneau was brought from her home in Contact, Nev., by her parents and placed in St. Mary's academy, whence she graduated in 1915. Since that eventful day of June she has been taking a postgraduate course and teaching at the academy, thus preparing herself for the life of unselfish sacrifice she has chosen.

The audiences that have filled St. Mary's auditorium on numerous occasions have been thrilled by Miss Bruneau's voice in vocal and dramatic selections. She possesses a full, deep, and sympathetic voice that grips the heartstrings and holds them taut. Her dramatic interpretations have had the same effect. Little did the audience that greeted the Glee Club Monday evening at the entertainment realize that the sweet, strong voice which rose above all others was to be heard no more in bursts of song from St. Mary's stage.

Miss Bruneau is not the first of St. Mary's daughters to choose the "better part" and follow in the footsteps of her courageous teachers. Other names of fair students are enrolled under the banner of the Holy Cross, teaching in all parts of the country, doing good wherever they go, bringing to a religious order talents rare and helpful. Not the least among these Sisters will be Miss Bruneau, who enters the order equipped as only Holy Cross girls are in spiritual and mental advancement.

The prayers and best wishes follow Miss Bruneau that she may persevere, and it is hoped that some day she will be a member of the faculty of St. Mary's of the Wasatch, inculcating the precepts of religion and culture to the children of her classmates.

Intermountain Catholic, 24 November 1917, 19.

Catholic-to-Catholic Conflicts

41. Letter from a Missionary Leaving His Post, 1851

Letters often proved to be the only way for far-flung missionaries to convey their unhappiness to clerical superiors who lived hundreds of miles away. As shown in this letter from a priest who had worked in Iowa for nearly a decade, complaints were couched in the most gracious language.

I am sorry that I could not receive your blessing before I started for my long journey but I trust that you will not forget me in your prayers. I could not very well describe the feelings which agitate my soul on leaving a place where I have spent the nine best years of my life. The kindness of my good people literally brought tears to my eyes, but all is over at present. I am already over the worse part of my journey and happy to meet again an old friend, Mr. Godfert. Whosoever will take my place will find everything on a better footing than I found them myself nine years ago. I have left (in the parish register) some directions to enable him to get a support and to pay for the grave yard. As to spiritual matters, I have nothing to say except this: there are two ladies from Missouri who have married Americans by the name of Taylor. They live and own land 12 miles south west from the church of Saint Patrick. I have been informed by these two ladies that they have not been married by a priest, and of course, their husbands being not baptized, that their marriages are null. One of the husbands being in California and there being no witnesses at hand when I received information on that subject I could not straighten matters, but I have deemed it my duty to request you to have it done with all prudence and charity especially as the kind of confidence which the two M. M. Taylors have placed in me make it obligatory upon you and upon your assistants not to mention my name. Although absent from your diocese and from Garryowen I shall not cease to pray for the good people entrusted to your care. I am sorry that I have done so little to promote Christianity in your diocese; if I have not done as much as I intended in moments of zeal at least I depart with the hope of having done nothing to hurt the cause of religion in Iowa. With regard to my conduct towards you and of yours towards me, I will not deny that on perusing your former letters a few weeks before my departure I remembered many things which have caused me in different occasions a great deal of displeasure. There is no doubt that you have also your accounts against me; I will therefore ask forgiveness for all the trouble which I may have given you and return you thanks for the good will and kind care which you have so often manifested towards all your priests...I have burnt all the letters which I have hitherto retained and considering the difficulties which you had to encounter I am determined to erase from my memory all the past deeds and words which indeed have now and then cooled my affections for Dubuque. I sincerely wish you every kind of success and my prayers will always be that your good examples and missionary labors may continue to bring fruits of salvation in Iowa. When I say that I will pray for the welfare of your diocese I wilfully give you to understand that it is not my intention to resume again the active life of a missionary. I have of late seriously reflected on that subject and concluded to remain in France near some seaport where the English language is more necessary than in the interior of the country, and in case that I cannot find a place to please me I am determined to live in a warmer country than the extreme north of North America. I therefore humbly beg from you to send me my exeat pro quacumque diocesi ["let him leave for another diocese"] and promise you not to go anywhere. Notwithstanding the latitude of the word quacumque, without the consent of my good uncle, I presume that you will not rejoice at my request because I have not, I hope, notwithstanding all my failings, deserved to be expelled from your mission and I am well aware that it is always unpleasant for Bishops, especially in America, to train young clergymen for the ministry, and ever more so to replace a foreigner with another foreigner but I feel that I am not bound in conscience to undergo any more trouble to repay the expenses which you have incurred on my account. I have received from you about five hundred dollars for your congregations and I am willing to leave you all my improvements in Garryowen, to forgive the debt which the church of Cascade owes me and to leave to your missionaries the books and other objects which I have left in Dubuque if you comply with my request. Perhaps you will ask me what reasons induce me to take that step. I have already given one, namely that I hate the long dreary winters of Iowa. Another reason is that it does not agree with my health to ride on horseback and that it is impossible in Iowa to have other modes of conveyance from place to place. I found it also impossible even to get a canonical cook, but a far better reason which I can give you is the following. It is a step that I think necessary for my salvation. I have the right to save my own soul as much as the souls of others, and I find by experience that it is extremely difficult to be exact in the recitation of the office, to meditate, to study, to preserve the ecclesiastical spirit in a word to be a good priest in the missions of this country. You will undoubtedly answer that God did not require more than what is possible, that dispensations from the breviary have been granted etc., but all that does not satisfy my conscience. I am not at peace unless I have the certainty that I have done everything correctly and though I should find elsewhere the same occasions to prevaricate as in Iowa, I would still choose a place where at all events it is easier to rise after a fall and to be free from all doubts before we ascend the altar of God. You perceive that I am in earnest. I request and beg from you to pray for me that I may act for the best and to write to me at the Seminary of Brou-Bourg-en-Bresse (Ain, France).

> Rev. Jean C. Perrodin to Rt. Rev. Bishop Mathias Loras, 10 April 1851, in Rev. Jean Perrodin Papers, Archives of the Archdiocese of Dubuque, Iowa. Printed by permission.

42. Concerns about the Arrival of Nuns to the Minnesota Frontier, 1857

Father Demetrius di Marogna's letter to his abbot demonstrates the many ways lack of communication confused Catholic initiatives on the frontier. In this account, it appears several persons had reason to feel aggrieved by the conditions in Minnesota.

As P. Cornelius and I arrived at night, of the 28th, in St. Paul, whither we traveled to get the rights of citizenship for P. Cornelius, we were — not a little to our surprise — welcomed with the announcement: "The sisters came and are housed in the hospital." An hour later P. Benedict came in, who had paid us a visit in St. Cloud and St. Joseph. The less prepared I was for this hurried arrival of the Sisters, the more surprised and puzzled did I feel and I could hardly suppress to cry out "precipitate." Moreover, the whole affair is enveloped in an ominous cloud, so that I really don't know what to do with these poor girls. Neither from you nor from the superioress did I receive any advance notice. Neither from you nor from the superioress did they furnish anything in writing... I spoke with the administrator who was no less surprised than I and moreover also reluctant. [He said] I should take them along with me and take care of them. This I also did. In St. Cloud I had to rent a house, which was provided for me, together with a garden. The house has a ground floor of two rooms, besides a spacious refectory and kitchen; on the second floor is a large room, a smaller one, and a long one over the refectory where easily ten to twelve children's beds can be provided. A well, garden, and a cellar are also adjuncts. The rent is $250 per annum. I rented it for a year. I hope that the good Lord will pay the rent. There are four sisters and two candidates, besides Fini Leshall. Willibalda Scherbauer, Regoria Moser, Evangelista Kremeter, Gertrude Kapser, Marianna Welter, and Prisca Maier. A few days ago I finally received a notice from the superioress in Eire that Sister Willibalda was the leader of the first group. The last Friday's mail brought me also your valuable letter of the 28th of the foregoing month, which wants me to know what I hope to experience. You want a report as to how things are shaping themselves. I can only write to you how the things are standing now. As to future developments, nothing can be said at present, under existing circumstances. The matters stand thus: Six Sisters and Fini Leshall are here each provided with a trunk in which there are mostly books, as I understand. A house on main street, together with a garden is rented for $250, cheap for this place. The garden and yard is to be enclosed by a high, board wall, to form the enclosure. The Sisters desire to remain together, which is perfectly right. P. Cornelius is their weekly confessor. The direction of the Sisters I have taken over for the present, since we cannot leave them to shift for themselves. To whom should the poor children turn and be entrusted here, in this distant land and destitute of all their money? What I did up until now, I did because I considered it my Christian duty and because I thought it was wiser that an older priest should come in contact with Sisters who are also young yet, than our young Fathers whose heads are filled with commando [sic] words. As soon as you or the superioress will take over the worry of the Sisters from my hands, I will very gladly give it up. Yes, I have to beg you that something definitely be established because such a thing cannot be long drawn out. All of them look pale, emaciated, and ailing. The Sisters think that the superioress went to Germany. Should there be another group coming, we would have to put them to St. Joseph, where a house could be rented which we would have to improve at a cost of at least $300. The owner does not want this. In St. Joseph a parish house will be built which, when finished, the Sisters could occupy until they could build a little cloister for themselves...

All of us really don't know where we are at. Each one leads his own life, and acts independently; however, if anything is needed, we in St. Cloud have to be the goat. This is very detrimental in financial considerations... Wouldn't you be so kind, in case you write to Rome, as to include a request that we real soon would get a bishop for St. Paul. Under existing conditions, namely, the matter of church property, a bishop is indispensably necessary. Wherever I go, I am asked, "Isn't the bishop coming soon?"

> Father Demetrius di Marogna to Abbot Boniface Wimmer, 14 July 1857, photocopy of translation, Annals, Archives of the Abbey of St. John, Collegeville, Minn. Printed by permission.

43. The Hardships of Missionary Life, 1865

In the mid-1800s a variety of clashes taxed the strength of missionary priests. The conflicts and the stresses of missionary life rarely were expressed as directly as in the following letter from a Capuchin priest to his archbishop.

We must hold fast to what we have. This task is by no means as easy as is imagined in Europe. We are compelled to fight against many terrible enemies ... Even now the life of a missionary in the extensive Western States and Territories is hardly less strenuous. Not one of them can stay at the same place for any length of time ... One can imagine how tiresome and grinding such a life must be for an isolated priest. Not every bodily constitution is suited for the privation of such a missionary life. Even the best health is undermined in time by the apostolic efforts ... [C]ases of this kind, even if they are common in the West, seldom occur in the East where there are more missions ... The people of Europe have no real idea of the hundreds of demands made on the missionary. It is especially difficult to unite and keep together a parish consisting of Catholics of various nationalities, as the Irish, the Germans from the North and those from the South. It seems almost impossible to find men fitted with all the talents that are required for these varying circumstances ... What is feared most under such conditions by the single priest is the sense of isolation. He is human. His body demands decent care, his mind looks for relaxation, despondency may gnaw at this heart. At such times it will often be impossible to find a person from whom he can receive advice, consolation, and encouragement. Faults of temperament, hardly noticed at first remain hidden and unguarded and may slowly develop into abnormalities. At times avarice presses down even the best heart with the spirit of the times; at times, a quick quarrelsome temper repels and estranges the parishioners ... [T]hus, the end of a missionary who began with zeal, enthusiasm and pure love of God and neighbor may be really deplorable.

[There are] ... dangerous conditions ... [A]mong these I count ... the intermixture of nationalities, who are frequently antagonistic to one another in their religious and political views. More dangerous are the various sects who are united everywhere against the Catholic Church ... [T]he assistance of the state has been withdrawn from the Catholic Indian schools and our enemies are scheming with all their might to tax church property. All sects are tolerated; the Catholics alone are considered secret enemies of their country.

The most important ... and most difficult task of the Church at present is the maintenance of the parochial schools. There is hardly a German Catholic parish in the country without its own school. It was, and still is in part, different among the Irish, who send their children to the public schools without scruple and thereby make life much easier for themselves...[T]o obtain the sanction of the Holy See for this dangerous mode of education, they alleged that such a procedure would help to make the Americans better disposed towards the Catholic cause and that the union of the parochial and public schools would be the quickest road to conversion of this country. Older and newer experience...agree in telling us that good apples do not make rotten apples good, but that the rotten also infect the good.

What would the Catholic Church do in America without its parochial schools? Those Irish who thought that they could get along without them are even now experiencing the evil results. Their offspring, who have never learned to know and love the Church in her salutary institutions, are falling away by the hundreds, especially in the large cities, and are becoming a prey to the sects. The better German Catholics are fully convinced...that the Church can not be kept alive for any length of time without parochial schools.

Father Fidelis Steinauer to the Most Rev. Archbishop of Munich, 21 September 1865, in *Pioneer Capuchin Letters,* special issue of *Franciscan Studies* 16 (January 1936): 31, 43, 116–17.

44. An Account of a Group of Dissident Catholics on the Minnesota Frontier, 1871

In largely isolated western communities, far removed from church offices, the chance that a priest would falter in ecclesiastical obedience existed, a circumstance that could lead to conflict with the local bishop. As seen in this episode, Bishop Thomas Grace, O.P., dispatched F. X. Weninger, the noted Jesuit preacher of parish missions, to Rush Lake, Minnesota, to bring the errant back to the fold.

The train brought me very near the neighborhood of Rush Lake where I had to conduct a critical mission. It was concerned with nothing less than [the need] to bring back upon the right track a schismatic parish, fanatically inspired by the influence of an erring, old priest.

The matter appeared the more difficult because this man was sufficiently clever to surround himself with the appearance of holiness. It is this Joseph Albrecht whom the Archbishop of Cincinnati suspended on account of his extravagances, and who on his own responsibility dares to function as a pastor at this place in Minnesota. He came with a great number of people deluded by him in Ohio and maintains that the Pope had empowered him to exercise the care of souls through the jubilee (indulgence). In Baden Joseph Albrecht was formerly a kind of burgermeister in a village and unfortunately, without possessing any theological knowledge, was ordained a priest. Nevertheless, he has a good mouthpiece and knows how to deceive the common people.

I sought him out before I began the mission and discovered immediately that against his purblind obstinacy every kind of argument rebounded. Therewith I began the mission and where possible sought to clarify at least the people concerning the status of their affairs. The mission began during the week and with but fifteen families who had remained faithful to the Church and the Bishop and who observed the interdict hurled upon the church where Father Joseph functioned. They built for themselves a small temporary frame church, from where they met me in procession. What a small structure! Nevertheless, at the same time, what a miracle of grace! At the conclusion of the mission there remained only fifteen families on the schismatic side.

On the very first day of the mission, five of the most influential of the schismatic party announced themselves and wished to speak to me. These soon realized the sacrilege of the arrogant Father Joseph. Daily others followed them so that Father Joseph probably noticed that he would lose every hold (footing) if he would not go so far as to hear the confessions of his people — something he had not done up to now. He made every effort to spread the news that he would now also hear confessions, and indeed without episcopal permission. Thereupon I threatened him with excommunication which soon followed from the Bishop. Be it also known that Fr. Jos., in addition to appear affected by brain fever, continued on his way with a few zealots, the schism was, nevertheless, broken since nearly the entire congregation joined the little church where the priest appointed to Rush Lake conducted divine services. Here also in a short time, an imposing church will be erected since the members of the congregation who broke off (the schism) are prosperous. As the crowd of people followed the mission cross in procession at the close of the mission, it was a triumphal procession in comparison with the first at the beginning of the mission. This is the third schismatic parish which was directed back to the right path through the mission which I gave to them; namely, Buffalo, Trenton, and now Rush Lake. In all three the situation appeared very doubtful, nevertheless, grace emerged victorious.

A group accompanied me to the station of the Northern Pacific railroad, from where I left for St. Paul.

F. X. Weninger, *The Wanderer*, 6 January 1872, quoted in Wilfred P. Schoenberg, S.J., *These Valiant Women: History of the Sisters of St. Mary of Oregon, 1886–1986* (Portland: Western Lithograph, 1986), 72–73.

45. A Statement concerning National Clashes between Catholics, 1910

Immigrants of many nationalities brought a strong Catholicism to the farming regions of the American West. These groups often clashed, not over religious belief, but over language differences. As seen in the document below, teaching sisters, who had accepted a mission invitation in good faith, found themselves, through no fault of their own, suddenly in the middle of local language conflicts.

Dear Mother Provincial:

There has been a dark cloud over Heron Lake preventing me to express my feelings to you openly, but now, since the cloud burst, I will speak to you like an honest child.

You know not the sentiments of the Heron Lake Parish as well as I, therefore hear them.

I am German, English, French, etc. and never will make it a difference in treating sisters, be they Polish, Bohemian or Spanish, they all will and shall receive a "good treatment." Alas, I am not boss here. I am unsettled myself and read[y] for a jump, as soon as command will be given — this is what prominent men prophesy to me. Things have developed here according [to] the people['s] taste, and I am simply powerless. They are German, with a few exceptions, and want German sisters, or sisters who are "able in English and German." I am honest in stating, that the 55 children who attend school now, will partly go to the public school in fall if there is no change of Sisters. The solution is "no school." It is not my fault, I told Mother Agnes to notify the congregation here that you intend to quit teaching in Heron Lake, and spoke *not* for me, for, I have to jump "most probably" myself.

You certainly understand that a German parish and French Sisters, both for which it is difficult to converse together, cannot be in the intimate terms as they ought to. However, the German people also treat the sisters well, as far as I know.

Hoping you will understand the situation better now, and do what you deem best for you.

George Jeagen to Very Rev. Mother Hilarion, Provincial, 23 February 1910, St. Joseph School Records, Wild Rice, N.D., Provincial House, Sisters of Mary of the Presentation, Archives, Valley City, N.D. Printed by permission.

THROUGH A CATHOLIC LENS
A Photo Essay Depicting
Catholic Frontiers
Anne M. Butler

Images convey at least some of the ambiance of the American West. The photographs that follow capture elements in the Catholic component of the western experience. They show both lay and religious persons establishing and celebrating a Catholic presence across many western landscapes.

Early frontier churches, rudimentary though they were, served as the focal point for building the Catholic community of the West. With their simple crosses, the small chapels, such as this first Catholic church in Minnesota, gave a place for pastoral care and reminded Catholics that, even in the wilderness, the organized church reached out, creating eight dioceses in the West by 1840.

Credit: Francis. P. Clark Collection, Archives of Notre Dame University, Notre Dame, Ind. Reproduced by permission.

The frontier sketches of Nicholas Point, S.J., companion to Pierre-Jean De Smet, S.J., illuminated his letters from the mission field and captured many ways that missionaries and Native Americans mixed cultures and shared religions. This scene, recorded from Point's 1845-1847 stay among the natives of the Upper Northwest, shows Jesuits and an Indian family, blending funeral ritual, as they raise a cross over the grave of a Blackfoot chief.

Credit: De Smetiana Collection, Midwest Jesuit Archives, St. Louis. Reproduced by permission.

Relationships between missionaries and native people often spanned many decades and encompassed a variety of experiences, some connected to religious matters, but others to social and economic life. This photograph depicts the elderly Father Joseph Cataldo, S.J., seated with Indian men and women who seventy years earlier, in the 1850s, had worked together to build a Jesuit mission in Idaho.

Credit: Negative Number 816.04, Archives of the Jesuit Oregon Province, Gonzaga University, Spokane. Reproduced by permission.

Mother Philippine Duchesne, along with four other members of the Religious of the Sacred Heart, arrived in America in 1818, and twenty-two years later she began mission work among the Potawatomie Indians. Her experiences until her death in 1852 mirrored that of many frontier missionaries—she lived in extreme poverty, weakened by a meager diet, far removed from her superiors, hampered by her minimal knowledge of Indian language, but determined to win converts by her religious example.

Credit: Image of painting owned by the Convent of the Sacred Heart, Albany, New York, reproduced from a negative in the Archives of the Society of the Sacred Heart, St. Louis. Reproduced by permission.

Throughout Texas, Arizona, and New Mexico, Spanish-speaking Catholics found ways to preserve their Catholicism, even though they often had only irregular visits from traveling priests. The laity created devotional practices in the home, making religion a central component to daily life. In this 1876 photograph from New Mexico, a husband and wife stand by their home altar adorned with flowers and holy pictures.

Credit: SRC Misc. Collection, No. 24626, New Mexico State Records Center and Archives, Santa Fe, N.M. Reproduced by permission.

Church authorities overseeing the West worried that isolated clusters of immigrants would be lost to the faith or would convert to rival churches. Perhaps of least concern was the Catholicity among newly arrived Poles. They emigrated with a strong commitment to the church and although they engaged in some national quarrels, they celebrated their Catholicism and cherished custom, as seen in these early twentieth-century photographs of two Polish children, dressed for traditional children's roles, that of the altar boy and the first communicant.

Credit: The altar boy: No. 15955, Roman B. J. Kwasniewski Collection, from the Collections of the Dept. of Archives and Special Collections, Golda Meir Library, University of Wisconsin, Milwaukee. Reproduced by permission.

Credit: The communicant: No. 15521, Roman B.J. Kwasniewski Collection, from the Collections of the Dept. of Archives and Special Collections, Golda Meir Library, University of Wisconsin, Milwaukee. Reproduced by permission.

The African American congregation, the Oblate Sisters of Providence, founded in Baltimore in 1829, accepted a mission assignment to St. Louis, Missouri, to provide care to black westerners. There they established schools and an orphanage for black children, regardless of religious affiliation. Mother Mary Petra, O.S.P., managed the orphanage with skill, building its economic stability and good reputation by cultivating the support of influential and monied Catholics in St. Louis.

Credit: Archives of the Oblates of Providence, Baltimore. Reproduced by permission.

In the early twentieth century, the Catholic Church Extension Society outfitted and sent the St. Peter Chapel Car into the West to reach rural Catholics and to combat the anti-Catholic sentiment around them. Typically, the car stopped for a week in a small town, where services and lectures were well attended, as local residents of many persuasions crowded into the traveling churches and, happy for the spiritual diversion, greeted the migrant missionaries with warm hospitality. Here two priests stand behind a first communion class in Helper, Utah.

Credit: Archives of Loyola University of Chicago, Catholic Church Extension Society Photograph Collection. Reproduced by permission.

Perhaps one of the most widely recognized of women's religious congregations, the Daughters of Charity with their blue dresses and sweeping white cornets, arrived in San Francisco in 1855, after traveling from their mother house in Emmitsburg, Maryland, across the Isthmus of Panama to their new mission in the West. Within two years, they had, as this painting demonstrates, assumed a public place in Los Angeles and could hardly keep apace of the demand from Catholic families for their services, which included conducting schools, teaching catechism, and organizing their charges into such groups as the Children of Mary Sodality.

Credit: California Historical Society/Ticor Title Insurance, Los Angeles, Department of Special Collections, University of Southern California Library, Los Angeles. Reproduced by permission.

After pioneering into Montana in 1879, the Ursuline Sisters, under the leadership of Mother Mary Amadeus of the Heart of Jesus, opened missions among the natives of Alaska in 1905. Despite chronically poor health, Mother Amadeus traveled almost continuously to Rome, Seattle, and several Alaska locations before her death in 1917. Her vigorous commitment to publicizing the Alaska initiative encouraged the Ursuline missionaries, such as the one pictured here with native girls.

Credit: Bureau of Catholic Indian Mission Records, Archives of Marquette University, Milwaukee. Reproduced by permission.

Born in Belgium in 1840, Father Damien De Veuster, famed missionary to Molokai, helped to build community, bringing both spiritual and temporal order to the colony after his arrival in 1873. In this photograph, about 1880, nine years before his death from Hansen's disease, Damien is seen with the children's choir, formed of homeless youngsters, fellow sufferers, for whom the priest constructed dormitories close to his own quarters.

Credit: Hawaii State Archives, Honolulu. Reproduced by permission.

As the urban West spread, regions of Old World Catholicism felt the impact of modernization and the passing of the frontier. Here among the symbols of Spanish Catholicism, the guests at this 1890s wedding in the San Gabriel Mission of San Gabriel, California, enjoy the sophistication of a wedding so fashionable it could compete with any similar eastern event, while holding onto reminders of an earlier West.

Credit: California Historical Society/Ticor Title Insurance, Los Angeles, Department of Special Collections, University of Southern California Library, Los Angeles. Reproduced by permission.

The philanthropy of those who acquired wealth during the bonanza days of mining, stock herding, real estate speculation, and railroad building accounted for many of the Catholic institutions that dotted the West by the twentieth century. In 1907, the Catholic community of Omaha, Nebraska, watched as the coffin of John A. Creighton, benefactor of schools, hospitals, and convents, was carried from St. John's Collegiate Church and Chapel at Creighton University, constructed in large part with his money.

Credit: Archives, Creighton University, Omaha. Reproduced by permission.

Part 4

MIGRANT LIVES
TO SETTLEMENT

Introduction

Human mobility marked the growth of the West. Indigenous people, by choice and by force, moved through western terrains. Anglo Americans, African Americans, and European and Asian immigrants did likewise. People of many complexions and from many origins climbed the mountains, descended the valleys, and traversed the plains as they acquainted themselves with the nooks and crannies of the American West. The result produced, between 1840 and 1920, massive changes in the configurations of home and place, as well as the understanding of those terms, for evolving communities of westerners.[1]

The flocking of pioneers to the Overland Trail in the 1840s launched one era of this change. It was an odyssey that engulfed the country after the first thousand or so stepped out for the West in 1843. Yet, despite its unsettling characteristics, most travelers — native or newcomer — sought a destination, a hearth, a home for themselves and kin. In that home, far from cultural origins, each group hoped for its own familiar patterns to be reestablished. Families clung to traditions they had treasured for generations; they longed to send their children to schools with lessons and languages of the past; they thought to recite prayers in their own tongue and to sing the hymns of their ancestors in churches designed to replicate those they had left.

The expansion of the West represented more than fluidity and change for countless families. It also represented a passion for cultural preservation and the attachment to well-known traditions. These characteristics permeated the experience of the Catholic migrants, as fully as those of other pioneers and the indigenous faithful.

This era of frontier Catholicism, although part of the church's formal history, underscored the role of the Catholic laity in forging a western religious

---

1. For a thorough discussion of the complexity of western migration across time, see Richard White, *"It's Your Misfortune and None of My Own": A New History of the American West* (Norman: University of Oklahoma Press, 1991), 181–211.

identity. Great distances, small clusters of Catholics, and smaller numbers of priests, brothers, and sisters forced frontier residents to adopt an assertive role as guardians of their religion. Even as they flocked into America's eastern cities, inciting an intense concern from both the Vicar of Christ in Rome and militant Nativists in the United States, Catholic newcomers found an institutional church struggling for voice and place.[2] As a result, new circumstances and separation from the ancient centers of church power required flexible responses from Catholics as they settled into America's diverse regions.

For example, Catholics living in frontier regions developed new roles as religious activists on behalf of themselves, their families, and their communities. This lay initiative created a distinctly American and frontier aspect to Catholic identity.[3] It applied pressure to distant church administrators for an increase in regular access to the sacraments. It constructed the buildings that were tangible symbols of faith. It embraced local social needs across ethnic groups to connect the newcomer and the indigenous Catholic. It organized, sponsored, and assumed a public persona for Catholicism, changing the face of the church from a missionary agency in the West to a permanent social and spiritual force.

Some of the earliest records indicate that migrant Catholics wasted no time in voicing their spiritual needs in the West. Even as land-seekers filled the Pacific Northwest, early Catholic pioneers expressed their desire for a permanent religious corps in their communities. Such requests placed hard-pressed bishops in a difficult position. As Bishop J. N. Provencher indicated in 1835, missionaries simply were not available for many remote outposts. In addition, bishops confronted the dual challenge of staffing hamlets of European migrants while sending representatives to nearby Native American groups. Settlers' well-reasoned insistence, however, on the need for priests and sisters to come among them suggests that the 1838 letter of Bishop Joseph Signay, given below, was not entirely grounded in accuracy. If lay Catholics initiated the requests for spiritual care, it is possible that they did not live in the ignorance and depravity that far-distant, high-ranking clerics suspected. While pioneers in tiny villages may have been people of simple means and education, their commitment to religious education speaks to a sense of Catholicism undiluted by their frontier environment.

The experiences of Catholics as they navigated through this unfamiliar religious world were highly varied. Some migrants wearied midtrip and looked

---

2. Nathan O. Hatch, *The Democratization of American Christianity* (New Haven: Yale University Press, 1989), 4; Marvin R. O'Connell, *John Ireland and the American Catholic Church* (St. Paul: Minnesota Historical Society, 1988), 40–42; Thomas D. Coakley, D.D., "The Growth of the Church," in *Catholic Builders of the Nation: A Symposium on the Catholic Contribution to the Civilization of the United States* (Boston: Continental Press, 1923), 85–99.

3. For a discussion of this topic, see Thomas W. Spalding, "Frontier Catholicism," *Catholic Historical Review* 77 (July 1991): 470–84; and Timothy M. Matovina, "Lay Initiatives in Worship on the Texas *Frontera*, 1830–1860," *U.S. Catholic Historian* 12 (fall 1994): 107–20.

for places to settle along their route. Others saw opportunity as they traveled and decided to set their roots in these spots. Many hoped to find a niche in an area welcoming to Catholics, as seen in the 1840s memoir of Martin Murphy's son. Still others, especially those from Ireland, tired of the chilly welcome in eastern cities and sought out Irish colonies in the West, a forerunner of which was described by Father Samuel Charles Mazzuchelli, O.P., writing about Dubuque, Iowa. As a result, as migrants rode and walked across the trails to the West, some peppered the landscapes with new towns that counted Catholics among the first settlers.[4]

The impact on non-Catholics of these various Catholic experiences — the need for schools and churches, the desire for association with others of the faith, the activism borne of isolation — remains hard to measure. Nonetheless, the anti-Catholic American Protective Association rose in Clinton, Iowa, in 1887 and spread its unsavory message through western states. As with earlier negative feelings aimed at Catholics, anti-immigrant, antiforeign sentiments fueled this movement, as well as religious ones.[5]

Still, positive reactions toward a Catholic presence in the West were also evident. Small bands of traveling nuns, left stranded when no priest came forward to greet them or no promised convent materialized, expressed their lasting gratitude for the hospitality of welcoming Protestant families. Non-Catholics — whether influential businessmen or poor miners — happy for a hospital or orphanage supported Catholic institutions through regular donations to the local convent. Protestant women bonded with Catholic sisters, working on their behalf as volunteers and fund-raisers.[6]

Although conversion of Protestants to Catholicism did not occur with great frequency, some joined the church, as seen in the cases of Kit Carson and Peter Burnett, whose articulate memoir explained his actions.[7] At the same time, the rigors of maintaining a frontier faith took a toll, especially for the lone missionary who lacked the daily comfort and support found around a family table or in a large boarding house. That loneliness and separation from a religious network explain the discouraged account of Bishop Francis Norbert Blanchet, who traveled thousands of miles, often under the most extreme

---

4. For a thorough discussion of Irish colonization in the West, see John Lancaster Spalding, *The Religious Mission of the Irish People and Catholic Colonization*, 3d ed., Pamphlets in American History: Catholicism and Anti-Catholicism (New York: n.p., 1880), 116, 141–47, 160–74, 188–99 (microfiche copy), Theodore Hesburgh Library, Notre Dame University, South Bend, Ind.

5. Winthrop S. Hudson, *Religion in America* (New York: Charles Scribner's Sons, 1965), 240–47.

6. For a case study discussing this subject, see Anne M. Butler, "Mission in the Mountains: The Daughters of Charity in Virginia City," in *Comstock Women: The Making of a Mining Community*, ed. Ronald B. James and Elizabeth Raymond (Reno: University of Nevada Press, 1997), 142–64.

7. Kit Carson converted to the Catholic faith in Taos, New Mexico, in 1842. See Lynn Bridgers, *Death's Deceiver: The Life of Joseph P. Machebeuf* (Albuquerque: University of New Mexico Press, 1997), 132. Despite such a noted person's entry into the church, conversion rates remained slow through 1920, according to Thomas F. Coakley, "Growth of the Church," 99.

conditions, throughout the Pacific Northwest. His hardships in the region differed in time but not kind from those of other missionaries well into the twentieth century, as seen by the experiences of the Sisters of St. Francis of the Holy Family, who made their way to an Oregon frontier in 1919.

These various forces all contributed to the growth of settlement. As the nineteenth century marched forward and more areas took on the hues of permanence, the quest for stability did not seem to lessen for frontier Catholics. In the 1860s, Father Emmanuel Hartig, writing from Kansas, recorded how political turmoil touched the Catholic experience in that area. Fifty years later, Father Eli W. J. Lindesmith, an army chaplain in Montana, captured the economic forces destined to influence the Catholic life there. In all areas, Catholic sisters accepted requests for social service initiatives. Often they served as health-care providers, as seen in the early account of the Franciscan Sisters of Mary, immigrants who struggled to establish a community in nineteenth-century St. Louis. A great number took on frontier education, their legions only seldom receiving the acknowledgment found in the 1908 letter of John Rush to the Sisters of Mercy in Omaha, Nebraska. Each of these endeavors furthered community building as a Catholic experience.

These efforts of the Catholic Church to reach out through the West to its dispersed constituency continued well into the twentieth century. Although official proclamations and pronouncements that the frontier closed in 1890 can be found, the lives of western people suggested otherwise, as did the response of the institutional church. The demarcation between a frontier era and its conclusion proved as blurry in a religious context as in a secular one.

For example, the railroad era of the late nineteenth century spawned the use of "chapel cars," specially outfitted trains designed to carry spiritual services to remote areas. Until 1913, railroad companies granted free passage to the chapel cars, a financial saving that made it possible for economically strapped missionary agencies to maintain them. In an undertaking that captured the imagination of the nation, several denominations secured and reconditioned older trains into chapel cars, outfitted with a pulpit, a lectern, an organ, and stained-glass windows. By 1907, Catholics had joined the initiative and the *St. Anthony*, equipped with an altar, crucifix, candles, sacred oils, and vestments, rolled toward Kansas, South Dakota, Oregon, and Washington.[8] Catholics had bonded their original missionary spirit with the latest technology to counter religious isolation and to combat anti-Catholic sentiment in the deeply rural West; according to Father Alvah W. Doran, they did so with some success.

That desire to reach across space influenced other Catholic moves in the later frontier years. The networking of Catholics of various ethnic origins did

8. For a full treatment of the story of the thirteen American chapel cars, see Norman Taylor and Wilma Taylor, "America's Chapel Cars: Answer to the Golden Spike's Prayer," *Locomotive and Railway Preservation* 62 (November/December 1996): 36–45.

not confine itself to one or two western regions. As Catholics of various backgrounds traveled to work locations far from home, the church tried to provide a religious framework within the contours of the migrants' culture. Whether through the arrival of Spanish-speaking nuns to Arkansas or the arrangement for Spanish missions throughout Kansas, the ever-expanding intermingling of diverse Catholic cultures continued to be a western characteristic of Catholicism.

Across the decades of this frontier Catholicism, certain patterns repeated themselves in various locales. What began as a highly isolated and largely rural experience yielded to the emergence of camps and clusters that became the urban West. It was in these centers that Catholicism shed its most frontier-like aspects. Yet as that occurred, Catholicism acquired a presence and tone more reminiscent of its European and eastern origins. The primitive, early days of a Dubuque, Iowa, as described in 1837 by Bishop Mathias Loras, gave way to a stronger community spirit of Catholicism, as noted in the 1865 Christmas descriptions of Father Xavier Kuppens, S.J., from the Montana Territory and in the recollections of Father James Joseph Gibbons, an 1880s missionary to Silverton, Colorado. Also in the 1880s, Father Eli W. J. Lindesmith showed how the urban and rural worlds increasingly merged, as he answered the call of both. These writings indicated that not only was the West changing, but so was the participation of Catholics in urban growth. Catholics, as they had always done, took advantage of town building to strengthen their presence.

By 1914, Catholic stability allowed priorities to shift. Gone were references to the "primitive" and "depraved" among the Catholic population. Such terms had been replaced with language, as indicated in the regional newspaper the *Intermountain Catholic*, suggesting that Catholics should construct more solid religious networks through their marriages. Only a few years later, in 1920, the Denver Catholic schools made clear that its students should be among those setting the social standards for the community.

The West, however, continued to be a powerful force upon Catholicism and did not easily or unilaterally capitulate to modernization. Even as the church, especially in cities, returned to its more formal structures, it retained western themes. Perhaps most important among the western influences was a continuous overlapping of Catholic cultures that diluted the strongest efforts to maintain racial and ethnic separation.[9]

As migrants and settlers, Hispanics and Native Americans crossed western lands, and their experiences touched upon each other, whether they wanted such contact or not. While these associations inevitably brought conflict, they also brought exchange, adjustment, and accommodation. People came

---

9. A full discussion of this concept is found in Anne M. Butler, *Sowing the Seeds of Justice: Catholic Nuns, Race, and Texas,* Charles L. Wood Agricultural History Lecture Series, 97:3 (Lubbock: International Center for Arid and Semiarid Land Studies, Texas Tech University, 1997).

into contact with languages, customs, and values they had not known. Some they accepted; some they rejected. Either way, the process influenced religious practice as well as secular life. This brokering of cultures constituted a major element in Catholic communities in the West, and the result brought both difficulty and understanding to group relations. Within the brokering are contained some of the most painful accounts of religious interaction, but also some of the most inspiring. In them are indications that the West accepted a closer mixing of Catholic cultures in the nineteenth century than has been recognized in the twentieth century.

Although often depicted in negative terms — especially within the writing of the clergy — these lay Catholics appeared to be thoughtful and direct about their religious needs. When the established church could not support them on a regular basis, when priests and nuns came and left their small towns, Catholics assumed responsibility for their own religious practice. These experiences enhanced the organizational skills and ability of lay Catholics to negotiate their needs with the institutional church. The West, especially in urban centers, provided the laity with an opportunity to mark the parameters of Catholic life and to articulate the meaning of Catholicism for a community.[10] While early conflicts and turbulence may have once caused pastor and parishioner to feel uncomfortable in the West, ultimately these feelings lessened as Catholics crafted a religious identity that gave them a place within the American Catholic Church.

Out of the migration and settlement of the nineteenth century, Catholics honed their spiritual and intellectual definitions for the twentieth century. At the same time, western Catholics did not depart from church traditions in many areas. Frontier Catholicism — like frontier life generally — was fashioned out of an experience of physical hardship, but refined by the reassertion of traditional values. Frontier fluidity succumbed, as it always did, to mature community. As a result, Catholic identity in the West coalesced around a set of contradictions. On the one hand, western Catholics retained their attachment to the innovative life of the frontier era, adjusting to regional imperatives and cultural overlays. On the other, they mirrored the generally conservative social and political atmosphere of the modern West, supporting church directives on the role of the hierarchy, sexual matters, and constraints for women.[11]

Catholics' early western history rested on their ability to adjust their religious expectations and to adapt to new spiritual practices, within the demands

---

10. For a description of nineteenth-century Catholic immigration and settlement, especially concerning the Irish, see Charles R. Morris, *American Catholic: The Saints and Sinners Who Built America's Most Powerful Church* (New York: Random House, Vintage Books, 1997), 50–53, 80–85.

11. For a discussion of the political tenor of the modern West, see Clyde A. Milner II, "America Only More So," introduction to *The Oxford History of the American West*, ed. Clyde A. Milner II, Carol A. O'Connor, and Martha A. Sandweiss (New York: Oxford University Press, 1994), 1–7.

of a multicultural world. The West required this process of missionary priests, nuns, and brothers, as well as lay women and men — the native resident and the immigrant newcomer alike. Their accommodations to the spiritual textures of the West occurred over many decades, even as the church stabilized and Catholics generally renewed their commitment to traditional values and attitudes. The result has been a religious identity formed in frontier uncertainty and tempered by western conservatism. Out of nineteenth-century migration both religious and secular groups reorganized their understanding of power and the importance of personal agency; out of twentieth-century settlement they reaffirmed the ancient stability of the church. None of these notions can be eradicated from the context of western Catholicism. These divergent forces gave western Catholics of varying backgrounds a singular religious heritage with which to face tomorrow's West, one where issues of race, class, and gender will influence the spiritual configurations of the twenty-first century.

The Overland Trail

46. Instructions of Two Bishops to the Northwest Pioneers, 1830s

Across great distances and cultural differences, the Catholic clergy tried to organize governance for the faithful and conversion efforts for those outside the fold. These two letters demonstrate the difficulty of implementing such goals when those proclaiming them were far from the sites of implementation.

To All the Families Settled in the Wallamette Valley and Other Catholics beyond the Rocky Mountains, Greetings:

I have received, most beloved brethren, your two petitions, one dated 3d July 1834, and the other 23d February 1835. Both call for missionaries to instruct your children and yourselves. Such a request from persons deprived of all religious attendance, could not fail to touch my heart, and if it was in my power, I would send you some this very year. But I have no priests disposable at Red River. They must be obtained from Canada or elsewhere, which requires time. I will make it my business in a journey which I am going to make this year in Canada and in Europe. If I succeed in my efforts, I will soon send you some help.

My intention is not to procure the knowledge of God to you and your children only, but also to the numerous Indian tribes among which you live. I exhort you meanwhile to observe a good behaviour that God may bless my undertaking. Raise your children the best way you can. Teach them what you know of religion. But remember, my dear brethren, that the proper means of procuring to your children and wives some notion of God and the religion you profess, is to give them good example, by a life moderate and exempt from the great disorders which exist among the Christians beyond the mountains. What idea do you give of God, and of the religion you profess, to the Indians especially, who see in you, who are calling yourselves the servant of that great God, disorders which equal and perhaps surpass their own? You thereby prejudice them against a holy religion which you violate. When this same religion, which condemns all crime, shall be preached to them the Indians will object the wicked conduct of those who profess it as a protest not to embrace it. On receiving this letter which apprizes you that probably you will soon receive the priest whom you seem to pray for earnestly, renounce then at once sin; begin to lead a life more conformable to your belief, in order that, when the missionaries will arrive among you, they will find you disposed to avail yourselves of the instructions and other religious assistance which they shall bring you. I wish God may touch your hearts and change them. My greatest consolation would be to learn hereafter that as soon as this letter was read to you, you began to pay a little more attention to the great affair of your salvation.

Given at St. Boniface of Red River, on the 8th day of June 1835.

J. N. Provencher, Bishop of Juliopolis

•

My Rev. Fathers [Francis Norbert Blanchet and Modeste Demers]:

You must consider as the first object of your Mission to withdraw from barbarity and the disorders which it produces, the Indians scattered in that country.

Your second object is, to tender your services to the wicked Christians who have adopted there the vices of the Indians, live in licentiousness and the forgetfulness of their duties.

Persuaded that the preaching of the Gospel is the surest means of obtaining these happy results, you will lose no opportunity of inculcating its principles and maxims, either in your private conversations or public instructions.

In order to make yourselves sooner useful to the natives of the country where you are sent, you will apply yourselves, as soon as you arrive, to the study of the Indian languages and will endeavor to reduce them to regular principles, so as to be able to publish a grammar after some years of residence there.

You will prepare for baptism, with all possible expedition, the infidel women who live in concubinage with Christians, in order to substitute lawful marriages for these irregular unions.

You will take a particular care of the Christian education of children, establishing for that purpose, as much as your means will allow, schools and catechism classes in all the villages which you will have occasion to visit.

In all the places remarkable either for their position or the passage of the voyagers, or the gathering of Indians, you will plant more crosses, so as to take possession of those various places in the name of the Catholic religion.

Given at Quebec on the 17th day of April, 1838.

Joseph Signay, Bishop of Quebec

Francis Norbert Blanchet, *Historical Sketches of the Catholic Church in Oregon,* ed. Edward J. Kowrach (1878; reprint, Fairfield, Wash.: Galleon Press, 1983), 44, 46.

47. An Interrupted Migration by Irish Catholics, ca. 1840

Not all immigrants followed the Overland Trail to the Pacific Coast. In 1839 and 1840, Irish immigrants, mainly from Cork and Limerick, halted their travels and settled the area around Dubuque, Iowa. Father Samuel Charles Maz- zuchelli, O.P., spiritual mentor to the Sinsinawa Dominican Sisters, recounted the building of the first church in the area.

Among the most remarkable places whereon the tide of Catholic emigration had checked itself might be considered that section of country called Makok- iti, so called from the river that borders it. The place is situated about 20 miles from Dubuque. Many Irish families had settled there to gain with the sweat of their brow, that bread which was denied them in their own oppressed native land. Therefore, in the beginning of the year 1840, the missionary considered it his duty to go to this settlement, and to do his utmost towards the build- ing of a little church, and this, on account of the poverty of the people and the abundance of timber, could be built only of this material. He distributed among the 42 men of the settlement the labor of preparing a great number of beams, from 20 to 40 feet long; in the spring each of these men carried to the site of the church his own handiwork. As they were not in a position to contribute money, they gave their assistance many ways to lessen the ex- pense of building. Bishop Loras gave the sum of six hundred dollars out of the contribution from the Propaganda with which to procure some building ma- terials and pay the workmen employed by the missionary for the erection of the church, which was dedicated to Saint Patrick the Apostle of Ireland. The wonderful results of this feeble beginning were a sudden increase in the num- ber of settlers in the neighborhood of the church, so much so that the section whereon it stood was very soon occupied entirely by Catholics. When Divine Service was first held there in the summer of 1840, there were no more than 100 Catholics; three years later the parish of St. Patrick, where the zealous Reverend J. C. Perrodin regularly attended and officiated, counted 600 souls and possessed a school.

The Memoirs of Father Samuel Mazzuchelli, O.P., 254, quoted in M. M. Hoffman, comp. and ed., *Centennial History of the Archdiocese of Dubuque* (Dubuque, Iowa: Columbian College Press, 1938), 10.

48. The Conversion of a Well-Known Pioneer in the Northwest, 1844

In 1843, a large crowd gathered at Independence, Missouri, to begin the trek across the Overland Trail. The group selected Peter H. Burnett to lead the expedition, and his name became identified with the Anglo settlement of the Oregon Territory. In this document, Burnett explained what led him to convert to Catholicism, after his arrival in the Northwest.

In the fall of 1844 a Baptist preacher settled in my immediate neighborhood, who had the published debate between Campbell and Purcell; and, as the Catholic question was often mentioned, and as I knew so little about it, I borrowed and read the book. I had the utmost confidence in the capacity of Mr. Campbell as an able debater; but while the attentive reading of the debate did not convince me of the entire truth of the Catholic theory, I was greatly astonished to find that so much could be said in its support. On many points, and those of great importance, it was clear to my mind that Mr. Campbell had been overthrown. Still, there were many objections to the Catholic Church, either not noticed by the Bishop, or not satisfactorily answered; and I arose from the reading of that discussion still a Protestant.

But my thoughts continually recurred to the main positions and arguments on both sides, and, the more I reflected upon the fundamental positions of the Bishop, the more force and power I found them to possess. My own reflections often afforded me answers to difficulties that at first seemed insurmountable, until the question arose in my mind whether Mr. Campbell had done full justice to his side of the question. Many of his positions seemed so extreme and ill founded that I could not sanction them. All the prejudices I had, if any, were in his favor; but I knew that it was worse than idle to indulge prejudices when investigating any subject whatever. I was determined to be true to myself, and this could only be in finding the exact truth, and following it when known.

My mind was therefore left in a state of restless uncertainty; and I determined to examine the question between Catholics and Protestants thoroughly, so far as my limited opportunities and poor abilities would permit. In the prosecution of this design, I procured all the works on both sides within my reach, and examined them alternately side by side. This investigation occupied all my spare time for about eighteen months.

After an impartial and calm investigation, I became fully convinced of the truth of the Catholic theory, and went to Oregon City in June, 1846, to join the Old Church. There I found the heroic and saintly Father De Vos, who had spent one or more years among the Flathead Indians. He received me into the Church. The reasons for this change are substantially set forth in my work entitled, "The Path which led a Protestant Lawyer to the Catholic Church," from the preface to which the forgoing statement is taken.

I was the only Catholic among my various living relatives. None of my ancestors on either my paternal or maternal side had been Catholics, so far as I knew. All my personal friends were either Protestants or non-professors, except four: Dr. McLoughlin, Dr. Long, and Mr. Pomeroy of Oregon, and Graham L. Hughes of St. Louis. Nine tenths of the people of Oregon were at that time opposed to my religion. Nearly all the Catholics of Oregon were Canadian French, in very humble circumstances, many of them being hired menial servants of the Hudson's Bay Company. I had no reason for the change from a popular to an unpopular religion but the simple love of truth; and, as I have so long borne whatever of censure may have been heaped upon me in consequence of this change, I think I can afford to die in the Old Church.

Peter H. Burnett, *The Path Which Led a Protestant Lawyer to the Catholic Church* (New York: Appleton, 1860), 188–90.

49. A Catholic Family Seeks a Catholic Community, 1844

Catholics, like all other migrants on the Overland Trail, set forth with cultural baggage, hopes, and considerable rumor. This account from an early pioneer tells of his father, an Irish immigrant who, concerned about the religious education of his children, relocated to California because of its prevalent Catholicism.

The Murphy family runs away back, according to works on the subject, to the kings of Linster, though the family tree has not been made out to that extent. My father Martin Murphy was born in Wexford, Ireland. I don't remember the date of my grandfather's birth but the date will be on his headstone at Santa Clara. My grandfather was five feet ten inches high and weighed two hundred and ten pounds. He was an earnest Catholic and very strict in religious matters. In early times he used to ride from near Gilroy to San Jose in order to attend church every Sunday, a distance of twenty miles; he kept this up until within six years of his death. The Murphy family left Ireland because the western country afforded more and better opportunities for progress and development. The family left there sometime in 1833 and went direct to Quebec, Canada, where they engaged in farming; I was born there [March 1, 1841].

My uncles were all born there except Uncle Jimmy, and, my brothers were all born there except my younger brother James who was born here. My sisters were born here. The family left Canada for Missouri in 1841, for the same reasons that caused them to leave Ireland, with the additional cause that the country was cold and sterile and the occupation of farming was unprofitable. They went to Missouri about the time of the Platt purchase, having heard wonderful accounts of the fertility of the soil and the general outlook for that particular section. They resided in Missouri until 1844.

They were satisfied with the soil, but there were two drawbacks to protracted residence there. First, chills and fever and malaria, and second, the country was very sparsely settled, and the educational and religious advantages were very meager. We were located in the northwestern portion of Missouri, just above St. Joe.

They left Missouri for California in 1844. Among the party was Sullivan, now of San Francisco and a family named Townsend...A Catholic priest, Father Hookens [Hoecken], was with them some time on his trip through Missouri and told the family much of Californi[a,] saying that it was strictly a Catholic country, in addition to its many natural advantages and this it was that caused them to come here...We started with wagons and oxen, the younger men riding on horseback. It was a very co[u]rageous band. The crossing of the Red Sea was a mere circumstance compared to their journey.

They left in March, 1844 and arrived here in November...We travelled as far as Ft. Hall in company with another party whose names I have forgotten who left us there and went to Oregon. We met Indian tribes all the time but took them into camp and gave them lots of game and fresh meat and some-times we gave them a little bacon or an old blanket. Most of the party were pretty well fixed for that time, none of them being worth over two thousand dollars. Every night guards were put out and watch was kept until daylight. At one time a man named Shellenberger [*penciled out:* an Indian half breed], and a relation of Townsends, [*penciled out:* was filled with a desire to shoot an Indian]. One morning gathering up the outfit and packing the wagons a halter was missed and he accused a chief of the Winnemucka tribe of stealing it. Words followed and Shellenberger rushed to his wagon, seized his gun and was going to shoot when my father rushed in threw the gun up and took it away from him.

The Indians were given presents and pacified after this and things went on smoothly again. One of the party named Flambeauy was filled with the desire to shoot an Indian, he himself being half French and half Indian, and he had to be watched all the time to keep him from bringing trouble on the party, but nothing serious occurred. Grandfather was considered boss of the party and my father next as he was the oldest of four brothers...

The children of Martin Murphy Sr., were Martin Murphy, my father, James, John, Dan and Bernard, Margaret Mary, Ellen and Johanna. The chil-dren of Martin Murphy Sr., seemed to be men and women of strong common sense, and my opinion is that common sense is about as rare as genius. They seemed to be entirely devoid of peculiarities and took a practical reasonable view of everything. Martin Murphy Sr., was a devoted Catholic and my father followed in his footsteps in that direction. The family took an active part in all religious projects to build churches and schools or anything in that line both in Missouri and here...On coming here our first view was like that of our friend Moses in viewing the promised land. They could see the plains of Sacramento from the hills, and everything appeered fresh and green from the first rains (this was in November), and they thought they had found an

earthly Paradise at last. My father settled in the Sacramento Valley about eighteen miles this side of where the city now is, on the Mocosome River, now
called the Cosomnee [Cosumnes] River, on there until 1849...

Dictation by Bernard Daniel Murphy [1888], typescript in the Bancroft Library;
quoted in Charles Kelly and Dale L. Morgan, *Old Greenwood: The Story of Caleb
Greenwood: Trapper, Pathfinder, and Early Pioneer*, rev. ed. (Georgetown, Calif.:
Talisman Press, 1965), 340–43.

50. Church Conditions in the Pacific Northwest, ca. 1850

*Stereotypical perceptions of priests and nuns have served to obscure the per-
sonal and professional difficulties they encountered. While there were many
spiritual joys for missionaries on the frontier, there were also frustrations caused
by pioneer lifestyles and conflicting national loyalties, as demonstrated by
this account by Francis Norbert Blanchet, describing his mid-nineteenth-century
experiences in the Pacific Northwest.*

What constancy and strength of spirit missionaries must have when it comes to
the question of receiving affronts and opposition. This had happened in Oregon
when our Church was further aided by the arrival of the first missionaries...
This opposition became more furious as the faith continued to grow. Nothing
was too bad to say about the Church, the priests, and the Religious. In their
statements the Catholics were always represented as superstitious, drunkards,
ignoramuses and enemies of the republic. The Church was pictured as trying
to destroy the institutions of the country. And the people, ignorant of the
principles of our Mother Church, and being credulous, believed these rumors
going into transports of hate and rage. The children often acted on what they
heard from their elders and they would throw stones and mud at the crosses of
the church, call the missionaries insulting names and term the Catholic children
bastardy. Others, more daring, would knock on the doors of the convents,
run away and shoot guns at the windows. Some would tie ropes across the
sidewalks so that the Nuns and the Catholics would trip when they left the
churches after vespers. Prejudices were printed even in the newspapers of the
country. There the monstrosity of heresy manifested itself in all its deformity;
our sainted ceremonies were travestied, our pious habits ridiculed and even the
sacred vestments were dragged through the mire. Oh! But what patience was
needed in the midst of such vexations, insults, and outrages!

False rumors were leveled against the clergy and the Nuns and often believed for the while. Such accusations were difficult to quash at the time
and had to be suffered in silence and patience. It is difficult, if not almost
impossible to defend oneself against what was not true and did not take
place...

The second problem which troubles the heart of the missionary is to see
the widespread infidelities in married life. Pray heaven, that Catholics will
never be entangled in such criminal depravity! On the Pacific Coast there is a

divorce for every dozen or fifteen marriages. This will give some small idea of the public morality. Who could count the number of wives and husbands separated each year, thus scattering the children and depriving them of the means of existence? There have been cases in which husbands and wives, separated in the morning, were remarried that same evening...What will happen to a society built on such foundations? Will it not fall into ruins before long? This is not only the Catholic point of view, for it was shown by a recent Protestant paper of Illinois which wrote that it feared that the edifice of society will crumble and be destroyed.

Another source of affliction for the poor priest is seeing so many mixed marriages between Catholics and unbelievers. In certain quarters almost a third of the marriages are of this kind. Sometimes the marriage ceremony is performed by the missionary with trepidation, more often they are before a preacher or a civil officer...Also, one notices unhappily, that the Catholic in these mixed marriages, in many instances abandons his faith, turns his back on the Church and renounces the aid of his religion...

A fourth unhappiness which is not less poignant to the heart of the missionary is to see the religious education of the children neglected, not only by others but even by Catholic parents. There are those who are so little zealous in this regard, that the Nuns and the priests have had to teach the morning and evening prayers to children already eight, ten or eleven years old. It often happens that during the Sunday catechism, the children are playing at home, running in the streets, going for a walk, or going hunting...What happens? One meets older children incapable of making the Sign of the Cross, ignorant of the words of the catechism, and consequently incapable of being admitted to their first communion...What kind of Catholics will they make? They will be like their parents, lax and indifferent...I have promised myself never to advise Canadians to come here, or even to Oregon or California...

Drinking and gambling are large problems for the poor pastor. Although there are severe laws against gambling, there are many gambling games and the law is broken with impunity...In almost all the cities of Oregon and California there is a tavern for every hundred persons. There they go to spend their week's wages — even the Catholics — to the shame of all civil and Christian virtues.

Cursing and blasphemy are also unhappy crosses for the minister of God. It is a very common vice which is found in all classes of society and a vice which is corrected with difficulty.

The frequent violation of the Sabbath could perhaps be considered the seventh sword that cuts the heart of the missionary. Every summer there are many accidents on Sunday, as God looks unfavorably on the transgression of His holy day. Many go to spend the day in the country, perhaps to fish or to hunt. Often some Catholics would leave early during the Holy Mass...

Another desolation for a priest, charged with watching over souls, is the sinful negligence of a great number of former Catholics concerning their conversion. There are those who spend ten, twenty, and even thirty years without the advantage of confession. Sudden deaths, accidents of all kinds do not move them a bit. Some of them have the good fortune of having a priest to reconcile them with God before death, but how many pass to the Supreme Tribunal without preparation?

The ninth cross of a missionary, which is not the least, is the conduct of the Canadians on the Pacific Coast... Some are ashamed of being called Canadians and do not wish their origin known. They abandon the faith of their fathers. Others enter into secret societies to get in the good graces of the Americans to make advantageous marriages, or for pecuniary reasons... Of the ten or twelve thousand Canadians who are west of the Rocky Mountains from one to two thousand only receive the holy sacraments. The largest part never go to church, their children almost never go to catechism or to the Catholic schools. They almost never help build the churches or keep up the repairs. They do not deprive themselves of a glass of rum to sacrifice for the needs of their religion. Nevertheless, these are they who object the loudest against a collection for a school or church or to conduct a bazaar. These Canadians are careful to translate their names into English or to Americanize them, changing the pronunciation... Often their children talk their native language like a servant would but they speak English perfectly. One should be proud of the language of one's ancestors in which their pastors have taught them to love God and which they use when asking favors from the Eternal Father. Of course, there are many Canadians worthy of the name, who are good Catholics and who are not slackers when they are asked to help build churches, construct schools or support the church. I know many such in the south, the center and the north of Oregon, in the Territory of Washington, in California, and even in Idaho and Montana. Should a priest speak of a needed repair, they start fixing it enthusiastically. All prosper and one does not see them suffering when they make a few sacrifices. I say with pleasure that there are good Canadians who give honor to the country that gave them birth, and who attract the respect of all who know them. They live a life above reproach and occupy a distinguished place in society.

Francis Norbert Blanchet, *Ten Years on the Pacific Coast by Francis Norbert Blanchet,* ed. Edward J. Kowrach (Fairfield, Wash.: Ye Galleon Press, 1982), 32–36.

51. Sisters of St. Francis of the Holy Family Arrive in Oregon, 1919

The Sisters of St. Francis of the Holy Family from Iowa responded to the request of an Oregon priest, their former student, and opened schools in Shaw and Silverton. Their account demonstrated how a Catholic network helped to provide religious care to the West and inspire new vocations to the church.

Until 1919 the educational activities of our Sisters were confined to Iowa. In that year, however, came a call to the missionary spirit of our Sisters from across the Rockies. Father Francis Scherbring, pastor of Shaw, Oregon, a small parish of forty-five families, had applied in vain to a number of religious communities in the West for Sisters to teach the little ones of his flock. Nothing daunted by disappointment, he proceeded to build a school, trusting in Divine Providence to supply the teachers. Most Reverend Archbishop Christie humorously referred to the situation with the words, "He built the cage, and expects God to send the birds to occupy it." The event proved that the good priest's confidence had not been misplaced. Having spent his boyhood in Iowa, where he had attended a school taught by our Sisters, he at length appealed to Mother Coletta for help. Despite the fact that Father Scherbring had nothing to offer the Sisters but the assurance of a sublime opportunity for charity and the use of a two-story building designed to serve both as school and convent, and despite the further significant fact that a number of substantial Iowa parishes had applied repeatedly but in vain to Mother Coletta for teachers, four missionaries... were sent to Shaw in September 1919. And thus it came that the brown Franciscans, with something of that adventurous thirst for sacrifice characteristic of their Seraphic Father Francis, first turned their steps toward the land of the setting sun, where the harvest was white and the laborers deplorably few. God is constrained to bless unselfishness such as this. In the hearts of the people among whom the Sisters labor, the seeds of faith and virtue have visibly sprung up and flourished. Already, also, two pious young ladies of the parish have elected the "better part," and are now valued members of our congregation.

In 1921 Silverton, a mission whose plight was even more deserving of commiseration than that of Shaw, was taken by our Sisters. This town is of considerable size; but before 1920 the Catholic population was so small that priests from the neighboring parishes attended to the spiritual wants of the people. In that year, however, Father Joseph Scherbring, brother of the pastor at Shaw, was assigned to Silverton as its resident pastor. After a year of disheartening labor there, he recognized that the only solution of his difficulties lay in finding a more efficient way of winning the children. Encouraged by the generous manner in which our Sisters at Shaw had braved hardship, he applied to the mother house at Dubuque for Sisters; and to his great joy his request was granted. In the fall of 1921, Sister Mary Cortona Gloden, Sister Mary Edwina Goebel, Sister Mary Marita Wempe, and Sister Mary Doretta Diers set out for Silverton. The building in which they were to make their home was the old infidel university of Silverton, which was now to serve not only as convent, but as church and school as well. This building had stood unoccupied for twenty years thus, though presenting a stately exterior appearance, it was in a deplorable condition of interior decay. Nor had the depressing state of the parish treasury permitted much renovating to be done. The Sisters had much to suffer in this ramshackle home. The blasphemous obscenities scrawled on the walls by the infidel students who had once occupied the building emphasized the alien atmosphere of the place. Not until they had painfully removed these vile inscriptions could the Sisters think of feeling at home. The numberless privations, however, and the stony attitude of disapproval shown them only too plainly by many of the bigoted citizens of Silverton, could not make them falter. They faced the situation with serenity — even with gaiety. When school opened, sixty-five pupils presented themselves; and in a short time their number had so increased that Mother Dominica, on her first visit to the West in November, 1921, took with her Sister Mary Alfrieda Schwers as an additional teacher. What matter that, during the rainy season, the teachers and pupils were often obliged to shift their positions under the leaky roof to keep dry! The good work for God went on despite all this, and has borne splendid fruit in breaking down prejudice and in bringing back to the fold of Christ many who had strayed. Financial conditions have now considerably improved, so that the stern sacrifices of the first years of missionary labor there have been appreciably lessened.

Sister Mary Cortona Gloden, *The Sisters of Saint Francis of the Holy Family* (St. Louis: B. Herder Book, 1928), 171–74.

Migration to Settlement

52. An Invitation to Join the Catholic Settlements of Kansas, 1860

Political factionalism in the Kansas Territory prior to the Civil War was not the only concern of newcomers. In Catholic settlements, residents clamored for regular priestly services. In June 1860, Father Emmanuel Hartig, O.S.B., used a description of Kansas to entice a priest friend in Pennsylvania to come to the West.

Two weeks ago I spent about two weeks on a mission seventy-five miles from Atchison and found there large Catholic congregations, also a church and a nice new house for a priest. The people did not want to let me depart. I also found three other congregations who had already gathered materials for building churches, and they also wanted to detain me for a time to direct the building. I could not accede to their wishes but consoled them by telling them that I would use my influence to get them a priest as soon as possible. The good people were by no means satisfied with this, however, and they determined to send some men to Atchison without delay to ask Father Prior for a priest to take over the supervision of their building and to remain permanently with them. Accordingly, four men from the various congregations came with me to Atchison and were successful in obtaining a resident priest. I would have been happy to return with these good people, but the lot fell to

A mission call to the early frontier often evolved into permanent work, as affirmed by this 1910 photograph of students at the St. Louis School for the Deaf with Sister Borgia, whose Sisters of Saint Joseph traced their instruction of the hearing impaired to the 1830s.

Credit: Courtesy of Rose A. Flock. Reproduced by permission.

Father Severin [Rotter]. They will come to get him in a few days, and he now has a large field of action which extends over three counties and is more than a hundred miles in circumference. For the time being he has four congregations to attend. One, about sixty miles from Atchison, already has a church and a rectory. The other congregations intend to build churches within the year.

> Quoted in Peter Beckman, O.S.B., *Kansas Monks: A History of St. Benedict's Abbey* (Atchison, Kans.: Abbey Student Press, 1957), 119–20.

53. A New Congregation Established in St. Louis, 1872

The nineteenth century saw the formation of many new sisters' communities, most under conditions of excruciating poverty. As this 1870s account from the chronicles of the Franciscan Sisters of Mary in St. Louis, Missouri, shows, pioneer nuns, through remarkable dedication, paved the way for their congregations to grow into important service providers for Catholic families.

In the year of our Lord 1872, on the 16th of November, Reverend Mother Mary Odilia Berger, four Sisters and one candidate arrived in St. Louis from Germany ... Unable ..., on account of the already beginning "Kulturkampf" to remain longer in Germany, the five Sisters decided to immigrate to free America, and there continue their labors in the service of charity ... Thereupon, the five Sisters packed their scanty worldly goods, sailed from Hamburg on the 18th of October 1872, and after a stormy voyage finally arrived in St. Louis as above related ... The Ursuline Sisters very kindly offered the newcomers hospitality until they were able to procure a more permanent place of abode, which was about four weeks later. In the meantime, Reverend Mother Odilia went in search of some suitable house in the vicinity of St. Mary's Church, for she was desirous to establish the little convent in this parish. The Sisters had been in St. Louis about three weeks when Reverend Mother found a tenement house just opposite St. Mary's Church, the upper story of which was vacant. This she rented, and immediately set to work to furnish it.

Reverend Mother Odilia had but $5 in her pocketbook when she landed in St. Louis, but she put all her trust in Divine Providence, and succeeded admirably well in her undertaking. The Sisters' humble dwelling consisted of two rooms, a small summer kitchen and an attic. One room was used as a parlor and oratory at the same time. Reverend Mother Odilia possessed great ingenuity, and knew well how to improvise and economize; she made two altars out of the dry goods boxes which they brought with them from Germany, in which their clothes, bedding, etc. were packed. Upon one altar a statue of the Blessed Virgin was placed, and upon the other a statue of St. Joseph; both of these were brought from the dear old fatherland. The altar of the Blessed Virgin was placed in the parlor, and that of St. Joseph in the adjoining room, which served for a dining and sitting room. The furniture was in keeping with the surroundings. Reverend Father Faerber gave the Sisters a table and several chairs; the Ursuline Sisters donated a stove and six bedsteads. The rest of the simple household furnishings were given to the Sisters by several charitably inclined people.

The attic was used as a dormitory for the Sisters; it was unplastered and as the winter of 1872 was very severe, and no provision could be made for warming the apartment, the Sisters suffered a great deal from the cold. It was almost worse the following summer because they could not sleep on account of the stifling heat ...

The Sisters had not arrived one day too soon, to immediately begin active work. Small pox had just begun to rage with great violence. The Sisters, therefore, found plenty of work and immediately devoted themselves heart and soul, both day and night, to the nursing of the poor small pox patients. Reverend Mother and the Sisters and the candidate ... were frequently out at the same time, and they were obliged to lock up the house and leave the key at a neighbor's, so that when one of them returned she could obtain entrance.

They were often at one house for several weeks without being relieved. Sometimes it occurred that when a Sister came home, she found the house cold and the cupboard bare. This did not discourage them, for were they not laboring, like good Samaritans, nursing and caring for Christ's Poor? So great and constant was their devotion to this work, that it earned them, for a time, the appellation of "Small Pox Sisters"...

When in the following year, 1873, cholera became prevalent and in the fall of the same year small pox returned, the Sisters again were seen at the bedside of the afflicted. They feared no contagion, although frequently compelled to pass days and even weeks in the infected rooms of the poor. For it was preeminently to the *poor* that the Sisters offered their services with joyful predilection...

The Sisters were kept constantly occupied, and demands for nurses could not, by far, be satisfied. The cholera became prevalent in the summer of 1873, and it required the united forces of the Sisters to answer the numerous summons of charity. It was indeed a work of charity, since everybody else feared contagion, and many would have died for want of care and proper attention. The first to send for assistance was the milkman who had been bringing milk to the Sisters since their arrival in St. Louis, free of charge. The poor man took sick in the afternoon, and when he became aware that he had cholera, he immediately sent for a Sister. Reverend Mother Odilia responded to the call herself. She worked hard and exhausted every means in her power to save the patient, but the disease had taken so strong a hold of him that he died that night.

During the cholera epidemic of 1873, the Sisters nursed 78 patients. Many of this number died well prepared, among which were conversions worthy of mention.

It soon became evident that the Sisters must look about for a suitable home of their own; especially as several more young ladies, attracted by this quiet, happy and self-sacrificing mode of life, had applied for admission to the order. The ecclesiastical authorities here came to the assistance of the Sisters, by granting them permission to erect a large building on a vacant lot directly south of St. Mary's Church. This unexpected offer was gratefully accepted... This was the first Motherhouse of the Sisters of St. Mary, for by this name the Sisters were hence forth to be known.

Sisters of Saint Mary, Chronicles Book, no. 1, 1872–1916, pp. 1–4, Archives of the Franciscan Sisters of Mary, Motherhouse, St. Louis. Printed by permission.

54. A Chaplain Speaks for Building Catholic Institutions, 1883

A variety of businesses influenced western settlement. For example, railroad companies exerted control over the distribution of land and the shaping of communities, as demonstrated in this letter of Army Chaplain Eli W. J. Linde-smith, writing from Fort Keogh, Montana, to a railroad-town site agent in St. Paul, Minnesota.

I am sorry that at the time you came to Keogh, I was not at home. Colonel Price, told me that you desired me to write to you... During last spring and first part of the summer I went to Forsyth every other Sunday, and remained over several days. I came to the conclusion that a good congregation of Catholic people could be built up there in a few years, which at the same time would be an inducement to some of our Protestant friends to improve in building churches, schools, etc. The first thing is not a large fine church building and a big debt on it, not at all, that would be the way to prevent a settlement. But the absolute first thing nessary [*sic*] is a small church paid for. The second thing is, plenty of church room, a fine large place for future buildings, of church, school, parsonage, convents, colledges [*sic*], asylums, hospitals, and Catholic cemetery, etc. The more land the better, this is an inducement for such orders of the church, or such priests as have energy in them, and enterprise to desire to go to such a place to labor. My idea was, that the least the R.R. Co. would or could do, would be to give us at least a whole block; and that I would call, a small thing.

But one of your men wrote to me that the R.R. Co. would not do it; but would give us three lots, in the residence portion of the town, for five dollars. So then I selected three lots in Block Forty-nine (49), Numbers Seven (7), Eight (8), and Nine (9). If you will agree to make a warranted deed of them to John Bird Brondel; (who is Bishop of Montana) when the church is so far completed as to hold service in it, I will agree to finish it so far in two years or less; perhaps may be able to do it in a few months, the sooner the better for all parties concerned. The dimensions shall be at least forty (40) by eighteen (18) feet, and as much larger as the money will allow that can be raised. No debts to be made on the church. I will give all my services for nothing until the church is built and paid for. I want to put every dollar that can be collected right into the building. N.B. We can't get more from one other place. I would also most respectfully ask that the R.R. Co. give me a free pass only until the church is built and paid for, and then give me half fare. You will never get another Priest or Preacher that will do as much as I will and all that for the R.R. Co. and the people and nothing for myself but hard work.

E. W. Lindesmith to S. Taylor, 8 September 1883, no. 23, Diary and Accounts, E. W. Lindesmith Papers, Archives of the Catholic University of America, Washington, D.C. Printed by permission.

55. Expression of Gratitude to the Mercy Sisters for Their Service, 1908

The Catholic laity vigorously encouraged various religious orders to establish schools throughout the West. Over time, these schools and academies played a forceful role in stabilizing the Catholic presence, for which families expressed their gratitude, as seen in this letter from John Rush, father of thirteen, to the Sisters of Mercy in Omaha, Nebraska.

Thirty-two years have elapsed since my first child received her first lessons from you. From then until now there never has been an interval in which one or more of my family have not attended your excellent academy. Indeed so closely have the good Sisters of Mercy and my children been united that a separation at anytime would have appeared as regretful as it would be unnatural. Thirteen children of my household — ten girls and three boys — have drunk copiously at learning's fount, as it gurgles pure and fresh, and healthy, at the foot of Mt. St. Mary's.

And now my baby girl — Florence — will graduate in a few days while I shall be three hundred miles away. How I would like to be present! No event in the school history of Omaha gives me greater pleasure (and I have had some pleasant experiences), than the contemplated graduation of Florence Rush. Nothing but the imperative demands of duty, or sickness would cause my absence. Apart entirely from a father's natural pride and affection, there is another and perhaps as strong a motive; I wish to add my testimony to that of the many other parents, living and dead to the meritorious work of more than forty years, performed by your community of Sisters in the City of Omaha. For my own part, looking back retrospectively, I can say that God has blessed me with a splendid family, and He has provided for them a splendid school in which they have been properly trained for the battle of life, with all its toils and troubles. But more important still, they have lived in an atmosphere of religion and morals; they have been brought close to their Heavenly Father; they have been taught the rules of justice, temperance, honor, and truth. The ten commandments mean more to them than appears on the surface, and the performance of religious duties has to them, a higher significance than the mere performance of a perfunctory attendance at church. For this, their father thanks the Sisters of Mercy — those women who have devoted their lives, their talents, their energies to the service of God, and the betterment of His children.

John Rush to Rev'd Mother and Sisters of Mt. St. Mary's Academy, 7 June 1908, quoted in Kathleen O'Brien, R.S.M., *Journeys: A Pre-amalgamation History of the Sisters of Mercy, Omaha Province* (Omaha: Omaha Province, Sisters of Mary, 1987), 84–85.

56. Diary of a Priest on a Chapel Car, 1909

The vast distances and scattered population in the West allowed frontier conditions to linger into the twentieth century. Efforts by the Catholic Extension Society to contact church members using railroad cars converted to chapels had a major impact on Catholics and non-Catholics, as seen by the diary of Father Alvah W. Doran.

Oxford, Idaho, July 17, 1909

Being a convert, it seemed to me a strange coincidence that my initial missionary work on the St. Anthony Chapel Car should begin at Oxford. It can not be said, however, that Father Doyle and myself started much of an "Oxford movement." The town is nearly three miles from the railroad station. Fortunately, we arrived Saturday afternoon, and therefore could avail ourselves of the opportunity to ride over to the town in the rail-cart, and personally announce the service. The Mormon meeting-house was the only hall we could secure. There was not a Catholic in the place; all inhabitants are Mormons. After getting acquainted with every person in sight, we walked back to the car in the cool of the evening... Not until after the second Mass had been said on Sunday did the congregation appear in the person of Mr. Michael Casey, foreman of the section gang at Swan Lake...

The Mormons used their meeting-house in the morning and afternoon, but announced our evening lecture. We borrowed their choir and bible also. Both Father Doyle and myself delivered addresses on the position and claims of the Catholic Church, which were kindly received. Some time ago a Methodist minister, who attempted to preach here, was chased out of town. The Mormon bishop and ninety of his flock were present, counting the babes in arms, but not the dogs. We distributed a quantity of Catholic literature and discovered one young married woman, an "ought-to-be" Catholic. A number of Mormon young people visited the car. Three little Mormons became our very good friends, asking many amusing questions...

Downey, Idaho, July 19, 1909

Downey had been an entirely Mormon settlement, but with the irrigation canal surveyed and soon to be opened, land is being taken up. "Gentiles" are moving in, and as the usual consequence the town is booming. The car did its full work here, all services being held under its roof, with the assistance of an annex in the evening, a long telegraph pole lying beside the track. We remained three days, and the services were well attended, the audience including the Mormon bishop of this section. There is only one Catholic family there. A gentleman named Byrne claimed to be a Methodist, but we "smoked him out" as a "woodchuck" Catholic. Several persons, one an intelligent young man, an Episcopalian, acknowledged that we had started them thinking. While sitting out after the sermon and Benediction, one evening, enjoying the refreshing night air and a smoke, two young men of a squad stringing telephone wires through the town gave us a chance for missionary work; we found that they were both "ought-to-be's." Thereafter it became a saying with us that when we scratched anyone in this western country we usually found Catholic underneath. We drove eighteen miles one day and made two converts, ages six and three years. The father, a good Catholic, died a year ago, and the mother was willing to bring them up in his religion...

St. Anthony, Idaho, July 26, 1909

We could not omit this town, however much work our shortness of time compelled us to leave undone this trip in Idaho. The honor of the Chapel Car's

patron saint constrained us to preach his religion to a community as ignorant of it as they were of how their town received its good name. There are
a handful of the very best kind of Catholics here, and the foundations have
been dug for a church. We trust that our work will raise it above ground-level
soon. St. Anthony, pray for them! One family drove forty-eight miles each
day, living twelve miles from the town, and coming to both the Mass and the
evening services. At this place the opera-house had been lately burned but the
Mormons granted the use of their meeting-house. Thursday evening the Mormon choir had a rehearsal, and then remained to sing at our services. Average
evening attendance was one hundred...

American Falls, Idaho, August 15, 1909

I felt at home in this growing and thriving new community, for my only
brother, not yet a Catholic, lives here, and I had not seen him for four years.
The auditorium was placed at our disposal. Before we came Catholics had
heard Mass in the schoolhouse or in private houses, and were supposed to be
few in number. The car immediately gave them prestige and confidence. It
was undoubtedly disconcerting to the community for us to discover between
eighty and ninety Catholics in and around the town, making our membership list larger than that of all the sects. One thousand dollars was subscribed
for a church. Almost everyone in town attended one lecture, giving us a new
audience each evening except the last. Doctor Nee, dentist, a native of Boston
and graduate of Georgetown University, rendered invaluable services in getting
the people out and helping to organize matters. Father Van der Donckt, from
Pocatello, heard confessions in German. Thirty persons received the Sacraments, among them my dear father and mother, recent converts, who are
spending the summer with my brother.

"Mission Work on the Chapel Car," Extension: Magazine of American Catholic
Missions (November 1909): 13, 22.

57. Catholicism for Hispanics in the Twentieth-Century West, 1913 and 1914

*The frontier symbolized a place of opportunity for some, as well as a region of
racial diversity. These two twentieth-century newspaper accounts indicate that
the racial boundaries in the West may have bent as Catholics of differing cultures
moved about, in this case seeking opportunity in Kansas and Arkansas.*

The Mexican revolution has blown good to at least one person and that is
the Reverend P. Bandini, a priest laboring in the mission fields of Arkansas.
Father Bandini, recognizing that the great need of the Church is that the children be taken care of, has been planning a chain of parochial schools. He
has been thinking of this for a long while, and not only thinking of it, but

working for it. He traveled to the mother house of religious communities both in this country and in Europe, but evidently God's time had not arrived for he was not successful, as none could spare members at once. But Father Bandini did not give up. He wrote to the superior of the Sisters of the Incarnate Word in Mexico and requested that, in the event it became necessary for the Sisters to seek new fields of labor, some of them at least would come to Arkansas. That request although made over a year ago was not forgotten, and the very thing anticipated by the priest happened. The Sisters were driven out of Mexico and twenty-five of them were sent to Father Bandini for his missions.

The nuns were enthusiastically received by the townspeople, the proprietor of the hotel giving them a bountiful supper and the use of his rooms.

When September comes schools in three of Father Bandini's missions will be started.

At two missions he opened schools, but they will not be patronized until fall, when the scholastic year begins.

"I find it mighty hard, if not impossible to supply their needs until fall," said Father Bandini. "In September the worst will be over. I have no more money in the school fund, and I hate the thought of losing even one of these good teachers after my terrific struggle to get them."

Will you help Father Bandini in retaining them? If you will help him over this tight place, send your donation to the Catholic Church Extension Society, 1133 McCormick Building, Chicago and the Society will gladly forward it.

•

Rev. Rafael Serrano, C.M.F., of San Antonio, having returned from the missionary congress at Boston, Mass., has resumed the work he had undertaken upon the invitation of Rt. Rev. Bishop Hennessy of Wichita, Kansas, of giving missions to the Mexican people in that diocese. In speaking of his work there, the *Wichita Eagle* of Nov. 7 says: "In order to give the Mexican population opportunity to attend the church of their choice, Rt. Rev. John J. Hennessy, Bishop of the Wichita diocese, has secured the services of the Rev. Father Serrano, of San Antonio, who has spent most of his life among the Latin-American people and can hold services in the Mexican language. He will not only look after the Mexican Catholics of Wichita, but of all Mexican colonies in the diocese.

"Father Serrano has arrived in Wichita after devoting a week among the Spanish-speaking Catholics at Great Bend, Dodge City, Hutchinson, Newton, and Lyons. He has arranged for services in Spanish at the old Pro-Cathedral school. Next Sunday he will talk to the Mexicans of North Wichita at St. Patrick's Church.

"The new priest has been associated with the Cathedral of San Antonio for some time, being of an old Spanish order. He will go to Winfield, Wellington, and possibly Arkansas City next week."

"Nuns Driven from Mexico Welcomed in Arkansas," *Southern Messenger* 23, no. 8, 2 April 1914; and "Missions to Mexicans in Kansas," *Southern Messenger* 22, no. 41, 20 November 1913.

Bonanza Camps and Urban Centers

58. A Report from an American Bishop to His French Colleagues, 1842

An important fund-raising strategy of missionary bishops was to report on American frontier conditions to those who would never see the United States. In this letter, Mathias Loras, who came to Dubuque as the first bishop in 1837, described his western world to those who contributed mission revenues.

Thanks to the prayers of your associates, and to the zeal of my colleagues, the Church of Dubuque, which has been long sterile, promises, at length, a numerous posterity of children to the faith. If in all parts of the civilized provinces of the Union, the Catholics are rapidly raising new temples to Jesus Christ, the time seems also come when, in the north of my diocese, interesting Missions are about being opened for the savage tribes. You will allow me to relate some facts in support of these conjectures: whilst demonstrating the progress of religion on our continent, they will inform the readers of your Annals, if there be any among them who are ignorant of it, how the parishes are formed here, and how the new American cities rise up in the midst of the deserts.

At twenty-one miles to the north of my residence, there is a small establishment of eight or ten Irish families. But lately the country was only inhabited by the savages: at present it is no more than a solitude traversed by numerous flocks of deers and roebucks. In this place an old man was suffering from sickness, but too much exhausted to allow of his coming to Dubuque to seek the aid of my ministry, yet desiring with a holy impatience to receive the last sacraments before his end, which he believed to be approaching.

To call a Catholic Priest was for his children a sacred duty; they fulfilled it with zeal, and the next day I had passed the eight leagues that separated me from the poor dying man.

I shall not attempt to describe to you the joy of all the family; I was for each of its members — for the sick man in particular — the angel of hope and consolation. In spite of his weakness and acute pains, he wished to get up and kneel upon the bare ground of his cabin; I had to use all my authority to oblige him to consent to make his confession without leaving his bed. After this act of religion, he felt himself relieved; strength returned with peace of soul. "Father," said he to me, "like my ancestors in Ireland, I should be glad to repose in blessed ground, under the shade of the cross; the sanctified place would no longer be for me a strange land, and I should the less regret the tombs of my country." This wish was too Christian-like not to be granted. I promised him a speedy return, and in a short time after, I appeared again in the midst of this family, who were delighted to present to me the old man almost entirely restored.

This time my visit was marked by still more abundant consolation. A rustic altar had been erected in the enclosure of the farm; I celebrated at it the holy mysteries. Around this crib of Bethlehem I also found, in my worthy Irish, the adoring shepherds, and I had the happiness of giving communion to all who were of an age to receive it.

When the Mass was finished, I was shown, placed upon a sort of bearer, a cross of oak skillfully wrought, twelve feet long. As I could not, by any discourse, add to the emotions of those around, I confined myself to blessing this pious family, and the sign of religion they had presented to me.

This cross is now erected, in its majestic simplicity, at the crossing of the two principal ways of the desert, upon an eminence whence it may be descried at the distance of several leagues around; it appears to protect the land cultivated by our Christians, to stretch forth its arms to the savages, who inhabit the neighboring forests. Beneath it, according to the desire of those Irish, the old man and his children will be laid up in that sleep which will be broken only by the trumpet of the resurrection; there, will be assembled, as under a tutelary shelter, other Catholic families, cast by their adventurous character into those vast solitudes; the hostile tribes will, perhaps, one day lay down their ever-blood-stained weapons at the feet of the God of peace; and thus will, I hope, be formed a new parish, which heretics will not venture to visit, for they take flight at the sight of the cross.

It is not long since I took possession, in the name of the Catholic Church, of a city still in its infancy. When the former colonists wished to establish a town, often upon a usurped soil, they traced with the plough the trench that enclosed it, and then grouped their dwellings at hazard, without any other rule than the caprice or interest of the moment. We now proceed more methodically. The government purchases from the savages a considerable portion of land; commissioners are appointed to draw up a plan; they trace out, in the bosom of the forest, squares and streets in straight lines; some emigrants arrive at the place, and erect a few poor little houses; they are the first elements of a future town, which as yet exists only in the plan of the architect. When once the inhabitants have increased to a tolerable number, and that the opportunity seems favourable to realize some profit, the government thinks of selling the city of which it has marked out the foundations; a moderate fine is fixed on each lot of ground; it is moreover provided, that no person shall bid for the site already occupied by the first possessors; the other lots are disposed of

by auction, and the produce placed in the hands of the civil officers, who are
named to fill the duties of mayor and his assistant.

They were selling then the infant town of Belleview, situated on the Mississippi, at twenty-five miles above Dubuque, when I appeared among the
crowd of purchasers. The Protestants were numerous; nevertheless, the Catholic Bishop was received with marked favour. As it was easy to see that the
building of a church could not fail to attract new inhabitants to the rising
city, and give value to the neighboring ground, the commissioners offered
me immediately two spacious sites upon the quay, that runs along the river;
and I think that their generosity was very well-timed, for the sales have been
much more advantageous than they expected. I shall build there immediately a
temple to the Lord, if the society grant me the means; it will be an additional
monument to recall to my diocesans the benefits of your Association.

Dr. Loras, bishop of Dubuque, to the members of the Central Council of Lyons,
Annals of the Propagation of the Faith 5, no. 3 (London, 1842): 389–92.

59. Priestly Recollections of a Montana Christmas, 1865

*On the urban frontier, people found comfort in their familiar, long-cherished
institutions and cultural rituals. Perhaps nothing underscored this so much as the
desire to celebrate Christmas, as seen in this memoir of Father Xavier Kuppens,
S.J., as he recalled events in Helena, Montana Territory.*

Virginia City at that time was a very prosperous settlement, the centre of
various mining camps in the district. It was a wild place and could hardly
be called civilized. Communication with the States was very slow, most of
the goods were imported by ox train, from Ogden or Salt Lake. The stage
had only recently been established, but at prohibitive prices. There was as
yet no telegraph. The medium of commerce was gold-dust or nuggets, which
was weighed in small apothecary scales, or guessed at by a two-finger or a
three-finger pinch. Metal coin or paper currency were never seen. The population of the district was estimated to be about 10,000. There were hardly
any families in place; all were individual men of every nation, and tongue.
Some fifteen or twenty married couples was all that the place could boast of;
children were never seen. There were some refined persons, but they were
mixed and lost in the crowd. The refining influence of woman to leaven the
manners of the people was absent. The vigilance committee had been organized the year before, had in three weeks executed over twenty persons and
was now at the height of its power. They assumed to themselves the office,
not of protecting life or property, but of dealing out swift and summary punishment to any transgressor. The town had been elected the Capital of the
Territory, in place of Bannock, whose star had set when a few of its richest
claims were exhausted. General Thomas Francis Meagher had been appointed
Acting Governor, had arrived in the Territory during the preceding summer

and had taken up his residence in the Capital. The legislature was to meet in a couple of weeks for the first time in this new Capital, and many law-makers were already at the place before Christmas. Many miners were idle on account of the frost, and the approaching holiday season brought together an unprecedented numerous population. Every hotel, lodging house and cabin was crowded to its utmost capacity. The priest on his mission in those days, besides vestments, altarstone, and chapel, also carried some provisions and a couple of blankets; all his travels were on horseback, and few journeys were undertaken during which he was not obliged to camp out a few nights. When lodging was obtained it most generally was only a shelter under a stranger's roof, and a place to spread your blankets on the floor. There was no mail from the Indian Country where the priest lived and no notice could be sent of an intended visit.

In 1865 Father Giorda arrived in Virginia City a few days before Christmas and took up his lodging at the cabin of a good pious Catholic miner. He, in company of that worthy man spent all evening and all next day in trying to secure a place that might serve for a Chapel on that great Holy day. Any hall, dining room, large store, or large room would have been most gladly accepted, or rented at any price, for a place of worship on that day; but none could be secured, not even for a few hours of the early day before breakfast hour, no, not even a couple of hours in the forenoon during the quiet hours of business from nine to eleven o'clock could any room or hall be secured. Late that night exhausted, footsore and more heartsore after the fruitless search, the Father and his companion retired to rest hoping and praying for better success in the morning. What their prayers and reflections were on that night, considering the many points of similarity to a like occurrence in Judea, is a subject of reflection.

Late that evening in a place where the youth and the sporting fraternity of the town amused themselves by feats of dexterity and skill, or at cards and dice, some one mentioned that a Catholic priest was in town and had been trying all day to find a place for holding Catholic service on Christmas day and had not succeeded. This was too much for the hearers. The old faith, though it had lately shown few signs of life, now burst from the embers in a fair blaze. A firm resolve took possession of them all; a place must be found for the Christmas celebration; that was the verdict, and without definite plans they dispersed, determined to find ways and means in the morning.

The leader of the crowd, however, was not a man of procrastination prin-ciples. I forget his name and we will call him Mr. Hugh O'n. He wore the champion's belt, and had posted a standing challenge to any aspirant of hon-ors, and was ready to try issue in the ring according to the rules of the Marquis of Queensberry. Though late, Mr. Hugh O'n went to see General Meagher, the Governor, who was well known. Both were of one nation, country, both of one religion, and it did not take long to form a plan of action. It would be a shame, a burning and everlasting shame, if the Catholic religion could obtain no place of worship on Christmas day; and that in the Capital of Montana, and the Governor there. Both men were equally indignant. Shortly afterwards the proprietor of the theatre, the largest place in town, had his sleep interrupted and was compelled to listen to business propositions. A large amount of gold would be paid for the rent of the theatre for two weeks. This and other equally eloquent arguments brought consent and all dates and engagements were canceled. The actors were easily persuaded that a two weeks' rest during the Holiday season would give them a good rest — so necessary for their health.

In the morning a committee of two waits on Father Giorda, with a most pressing request that he come at once to the theatre and meet the Governor and Mr. Hugh O'n. The Father, overjoyed at all the news, did not know how to express his thanks in words, but we may be sure that the angels recorded his aspirations. Some few alterations in the arrangement of screens and seats were suggested, and then General Meagher by his supreme authority claimed Father Giorda as his guest, and all rights of individuals or promises of priest were declared void and null. Himself with two assistants would see to his comfort and entertainment. Mr. Hugh O'n took charge of the alterations of the theatre.

In a little while carpenters, decorators, helpers of every kind, friends of Mr. Hugh O'n, turned the theatre into a veritable bee hive. His quiet suggestions are looked upon as orders; loads of evergreens disappear in a few minutes and are seen in garlands, emblems or festoons. An immense cross is planted in front of the door to proclaim to the world the interior change. A large cross over the door and also one to surmount the roof proclaims that it is a place of Catholic worship. There is nothing subdued, or simple in manner in those decorations; they are bold, profuse, and aggressive. The interior decorations were equally profuse, all pictures or signs of a distracting nature are removed or covered under the evergreen wreaths and religious emblems of crosses, crowns, hearts, etc. An altar, communion railing, confessional, have been constructed, all decent and serviceable. And Mr. Hugh O'n directs and manages the whole transformation of the theatre into a Catholic church. And all day the news around town, and in the neighboring camps was very unusual and almost unprecedented. Numerous messengers on splendid mounts brought the glad tidings that the theatre had been rented, and that there would be Christmas service for the Catholics, that the priest was the guest of Governor Meagher. All items of interest, and the fruitless search for a hall, all were told hundreds of times, and every Catholic was most earnestly invited to be present. Messengers succeeded messengers; some sent directly by the Governor, some by Mr. Hugh O'n. Many volunteered and no Catholic was overlooked. From Summit and Central and Dobie town, and Nevada, the whole length of Alder Gulch and Stinking Water Creek. The commotion drew the attention of the whole population. There never had been such stir before; at the time of the discovery of gold at Last Chance Gulch, there had been a great stampede, but the preparations now appeared more stirring. But it was well known that there was friction between the Governor and the Vigilance Committee, no one knew to what extent, or when a storm would burst loose. At the time of the organization of the vigilance committee, and their first executions, there had also been seen an unusual number of persons bringing messages to their friend; but now there were joyful tidings, nothing secret or hidden. And the response to the repeated invitations, that had been lukewarm and faint-hearted from some in the morning, became warm, fervent and determined in the evening.

Towards the close of the day General Meagher came to see what progress had been made in the work at the theatre and congratulating Mr. Hugh O'n over his splendid work, was interrupted by the proprietor who had also come to see, and who expressed himself in no uncertain words that in his opinion his theatre had been utterly ruined for further business, by those exterior and interior emblems and decorations. The General and his lieutenant had never hesitated in any difficulty before, and now in answer to his complaint asked him to set his price on the building. It was accepted and the earnest money to make the bargain binding was paid on the spot. These men were not hampered by regulations of canon law, consultations, and delays in decisions of Bishops; they did not think it was necessary to speak to the priest about it. They knew their neighbors would all endorse the act, and that the angels would applaud.

The news that the theatre was bought for a Catholic church was the crowning event of that day, and was heralded everywhere; and then the further news that there was to be midnight Mass, and that a church choir was organized, and that it would be midnight high Mass, and that all were expected to help pay for the theatre was fresh news to be thoroughly circulated. On the morning of Christmas eve Mr. Hugh O'n was at his self-imposed task, the decorations needed a few finishing touches, the altar needed a little extra decorations, the candles were to be placed in proper and symmetrical form. The seats required a little more orderly arrangements. The holy water font at the door was not neglected, and visitors who came by the score out of curiosity, or from a motive to make sure that all reports were genuine, were all reminded by the sexton that no loud remarks or distracting behavior was tolerated. They were politely requested to kneel down and say some prayer, and stay a while to rest their souls. All day long a good number of persons were in the church, raising their hearts to heaven, not distracted by the stream of visitors that came and went away. All formed a firm resolution to be generous on Christmas day. The priest was free from the ordinary distracting cares of preparing all things for the altar and church. He could give his whole mind to his prayers and devotions, and spent all afternoon and night in the Confessional, till it was time for midnight Mass. Long before the appointed hour the church was crowded to its utmost capacity. Many unable to gain admittance resigned themselves to the inclemency of the weather, and knelt at the door, uniting their hearts to those who had come earlier.

As the hour approached the choir intoned the Adeste Fidelis. Mr Hugh O'n lit the candles and assisted the priest in vesting and by his devout reverential manner edified all. The clearness and correctness of his responses to the priest gave evidence of a careful, thorough Catholic education in his youth.

Father Giorda preached a most consoling sermon on the gospel of the occasion. After the gospel and sermon, General Meagher prepared to take up the collection among the congregation; and it has often been mentioned that he had a large white delft plate. This had been found among the latest invoice of goods in the territory. Up to that time a tin plate had been the orthodox receptacle for the offerings of the faithful. And on this delft plate were two spoons, a teaspoon and a tablespoon, with which members might [with] ease and despatch transfer the shining dust from their buckskin purse to the plate. There was no announcement whatever about the collection, the priest knew nothing about it. Every member of the congregation was thoroughly alive to the occasion. No member so devout that he failed to see the General or the plate.

The number and devotion of the worshipers, the earnestness in their prayers and all their actions, and especially the numbers of communions, attracted the attention of all. The whole atmosphere seemed to breathe a spirit of piety such as never had been experienced in Virginia City. On no previous occasion of a visit had Father Giorda or any other priest witnessed so consoling a sight. These men were oblivious to the world, past hardships and struggles were forgotten; the future did not trouble them, and for the present one and all were intent to join the Angels to give Glory to God in the highest. I doubt if the recording Angel could find anywhere on earth a more earnest congregation.

After Mass General Meagher requested all to remain in their seats a few moments and in words as only he could command presented the offering. In the name of the whole community, of every claim in this mountain district, in the name of every person present and in his own name, he presented this house to God, that his infant son might find a dwelling place amongst them and that his minister might take care of it. He offered to God and to religion the largest place and most suitable house in town. Would to God it were made of marble. This house henceforth is the House of God, a Catholic church, we give it and here is the price, in God's noblest metal, gold pure as it was washed from the earth yesterday; pure, it has not yet seen the smelting pot to receive its capacity of alloy; no Caesar or potentate has as yet set his image or superscription on it; it is virgin gold and has not been contaminated by any traffic or commerce; it never will be spent in a better cause; as God has given it in abundance without measure, so they return it to God, without weight, but plenty to secure the house, free without debt, as an abiding place to God forever. It would never be said of them that there was no place for

Christ... The priest tried to express his thanks, but was overcome to tears. Mr. Hugh O'n, his strong attendant, supported the frail form, and guiding his faltering steps, led him away.

> III Rocky Mount Mission Files, no. 17, Father Francis Xavier Kuppens's Account of Christmas Night in Virginia City, Montana, 1865, Midwest Jesuit Archives, St. Louis. Printed by permission.

60. Priestly Recollections of a Colorado Christmas, 1888

Burgeoning mining camps brought spectacular challenges to Catholics and their missionary priests. Church members preserved their faith in the absence of regular pastoral care, and when priests appeared, as seen in the memoir of a Colorado missionary, people of many religious convictions appreciated a religious celebration.

It had been snowing for three days before Christmas, and crossing the range was no holiday pastime; but as Silverton was in my jurisdiction, I resolved to brave the danger, say the midnight mass there on Christmas night, and on horseback return to Ouray, where I intended to say two masses on Christmas day, which happened that year to fall on Tuesday...

We arrived about one o'clock at Silverton... During the afternoon I called upon most of the families in town, and notified them that on Sunday we should have not only mass, but benediction of the Blessed Sacrament and a Christmas midnight mass. Mrs. Prosser had charge of the choir and was a musician of no mean degree. A convert, intelligent, pious and charitable, she was active in promoting Catholicity in that mining camp. The Silverton church workers were second to none in the state, and strange to say were nearly all women. Practical woman suffrage was in wholesome operation there long before it was embodied in the legislation of the state. The women attended not only the proper duties of the altar society, but in no small measure to the financial affairs of the church. Fairs and balls were organized and managed by them, the tickets were sold, collection made and the money put in the bank to the credit of the church. I am happy to know that their zeal has not abated, for word comes still that they are not wary of well doing.

I said that the church workers were, strange to say, nearly all women, for I do not forget that representative Catholic gentleman of Silverton, Barney O'Driscoll... Until his grandchildren grew to a sufficient size to wait on the altar, the colonel served mass every Sunday, and as long as he was around the camp the priest did not shovel snow from the church door or build a fire when the thermometer was twenty-five below zero... On this particular Sunday before Christmas the colonel waited, as was his wont, after mass to escort me to his log cabin which stood some distance from the church... A good dinner at his hospitable board caused me to forget the pangs of a long fast and the thought of impending dangers. At three o'clock on returning to the church we found it had narrowly escaped destruction in our absence. The candle which I had left burning before the Blessed Sacrament had emitted a spark which set the altar cloth on fire, and the fire went out just when the cloth was burned from the epistle side to the front of the tabernacle...The next day everyone helped to beautify the altar and the church. Boughs of green were conspicuous everywhere. With the paper roses that had been made by the ladies of the altar society we decked the pine — strange it was to see American beauties on pine trees, but the simple artists thought the effect was good and there were no others to be satisfied...

At twelve o'clock the church was filled to the doors with Protestants as well as Catholics. It is customary for the miner to come to town at least three times a year, at Christmas, Easter tide and on the Fourth of July, and if he is a practical Catholic, the church is one of the first places he visits...Most of the boys were in church that night, and there was a regular round of hand shaking and merry Christmas greetings before and after the services. A little after twelve the "Gloria in Excelsis" pealed through the little fane and was caught up by the choir until it rang out in sweet strains of music far up the streets of the town. I preached a short discourse on the Christmas holy day and the lessons that should be drawn from the event. I was unable to extend my remarks as I had to set out for Ouray immediately after the services. The services over, Fred soon had the two horses before the church door. We sprang into the saddle and many a God speed and merry Christmas followed us into the storm and wind.

> James Joseph Gibbons, *Notes of a Missionary Priest in the Rocky Mountains: Sketches* (New York: Christian Press Association [1898]), no. 2164, "Western Americana: 1550–1900: Frontier History of the Trans-Mississippi West," reel no. 212, 2163–70, filmed for the Beinecke Library of Yale University (New Haven: Research Publications, 1975).

61. A Priest's Montana Diary, 1880s

The experiences of Eli W. J. Lindesmith as an army chaplain in Montana under-scored that the urban and rural frontiers overlapped. The demands made on a priest were varied, but what Catholics sought, often under irregular circum-stances, were the sacraments and rituals of their faith, as seen in these excerpts from Lindesmith's diary, with its many Latin abbreviations.

Marriages

June 1, 1882, At the house of James Gloster, on the north of the Yellow-stone River, five miles from Glendive, I married John J. O'Brien (a drayman and native of Mass. was a soldier, 60, E, 11th In. One year in the Territory) and Addie Butler (native of Minn., one year in the Territory) In presence of James and Margaret Gloster.

June 1, 1882 (at the house of James Gloster, on the north side of the Yellow-

The environment of the West complemented the beauty of the traditional ceremonies of Catholicism, as seen in this turn-of-the-century outdoor Mass offered by Anselm Weber, O.F.M., in New Mexico.

Credit: Archives of the Franciscan Friars, Province of Our Lady of Guadalupe, N.M. Reproduced by permission.

stone River, five miles from Glendive) I married James Taylor (native of Mass., saloon keeper in Glendive, twenty-two months in Montana) and Elizabeth Gloster (native of Toronto, Canada, seven months in Montana) In presence of John and Ann Lee. (On Deer Creek, one mile from the Yellowstone River and one miles [*sic*] from Gloster's Butte, the highest peak in the neighborhood, Davison Co., Montana). The marriage took place at three (3) A.M. then Mass, and sermon on "Marriage." Next very good music and a dance and a few Irish gigs on the green in front of the house, followed by breakfast, and the guests returned home; in number 19 and two babies. The reason the marriage at this early hour was, the train I went on was seven hours behind time, and my returning train was due at 7:00 A.M.

July 5, 1882 (At the house of Mrs. Mary Johnson, in Miles City) I married Mr. James Stanley (whom I baptized at the same time) and Miss Ellen Madden, in the presence of George H. and Ellen Catharine Johnson.

November 30, 1882 At my private quarters and chapel, I married Michael C. O'Brien and Miss Bridget Hertz. In presence of M. C. Haleran and Delia Haleran. The married parties are natives of Ireland. He is a R.R. man. She is not long from the old country.

Baptisms

October 3, 1880 (at public school house) Baptized Margaret, Natum July 9, Ex John Carter, uxor Mary Custella.

May 12, 1881 (in a little log hut near the printing office on Main Street) Baptized Francis James, Natum about February, ex William Nichols, et uxor. Sponsors, babies [*sic*] sister and a strange man. They all left the next day, no one knows where.

June 26, 1881 (at parents' ranch, two and a half miles [2 1/2] south of Miles City, on the east bank of Tongue River) Baptized John Kenedy, Natum Sept. 14, 1879, ex Michael Hurley, et uxor Ellen Kenedy. Sponsors, Charles Arthur, Com. 1st Serg., 5th Infantry, et Mary Barteman. (Those present were 15 children, 13 adults, 3 soldiers, Quartermaster Sergeant, and Commissary Sergeant. According to Indian custom, we had dinner first, then the Baptism).

July 31, 1881 (at public school house) Baptized Robert Cobb, natum April 28, ex Robert Matthews (a non-Catholic), et uxor Mary Jane McCanna. Sponsors Edward Flinn et Bridget Johnson (Residence at Matthews Ranch, 20 miles below Fort Buford in Dakota Territory on the Missouri River. A three week trip for this Baptism).

March 12, 1882, Jane. Born November 28, 1881. Baptized March 12, 1882. Child of Daniel O. Connell and wife Mary Butler. Sponsors Charles and Ann Payette. (This was the first child baptized in the new church).

March 24, 1882, Sarah Caroline. Born November 20, 1881. Baptized (at Glendive) March 24, 1882. Parents, Henry Devoe and wife Margaret Lenihem. Sponsors, Michael and Ann Slakhery. (The baptism was performed in the dining room of the R.R. hotel.)

Sick Calls

November 17, 1880, A Stranger in jail with delirium tremens.

November 29, 1880, Bridget McCanna, widowed mother of Michael McCanna.

January 3, 1881, A Fancy Woman.

May 1, 1881, Solomon Wills, pork packer.

May 5, 1881, Solomon Wills, pork packer.

May 9, 1881, Solomon Wills, pork packer.

May 26, 1881, Solomon Wills, pork packer.

Burials

September 14, 1881, buried Jeremiah Cox, age about fifty years, died on the 13th, fell dead in the yard, was buried by the county, he was a shoemaker and citizen, but had been a soldier in the regular army, 5 infantry, U.S.A.

October 11, 1881, buried in Miles, a R.R. man, who came to the hospital at the Post on the 8th and died on the night of the 9th; he was found dead in bed on the morning of the 10th. He was supposed to be a Catholic because he had Catholic books.

February 14, 1882, James Johnson, age 42, native of Ireland, County Mead. Died on the 13th February, buried on 14 Feb, He was the first corpse taken to the new church. He died of pneumonia; was buried with the honors of war . . .

February 28, 1882, Jane Roche, wife of D. S. Foner, age 30 years, 9 months and 15 days. Died Feb. 25, buried Feb. 28. Native of Minnesota, came here Sept. 22, 1881 from Waterville.

March 19, 1882, Catherine Elinor, child of D. S. Foner and wife Jane Roche. Age one month and two days. Died March 18. Buried March 19.

> E. W. S. Lindesmith Diary, first book, Miles City, Mont., 1880–83, file folder 21, E. W. S. Lindesmith Papers, Archives of the Catholic University of America, Washington, D.C. Printed by permission.

62. A Marriage Appeal to the Catholic Youth of the West, 1914

As the West urbanized, the concerns of Catholics shifted from primitive missionary conditions to cultural and religious preservation. This article from the Intermountain Catholic *newspaper captured the recognition that increased populations, less isolation, and better communications suggested new priorities for western Catholicism emerging from its frontier era.*

Why do many Catholic girls marry non-Catholics? Because first they keep company with them and thus have their affection entangled before they are aware of it; second, they are misled by material advantages, such as better homes, more comforts, less work, more pleasures, costlier dresses, attractive manners. But that is not all: they do not think or reflect that marriage is not necessary, but salvation is . . .

They do not know what they are facing: disappointment, torture of soul, often a life of sin, the practice of race suicide, and other practices against duty and conscience. They lack the proper ideal of marriage and motherhood, the right idea of their obligations and responsibilities. They try to escape advice that is unpalatable; they will learn by no experience but their own; they never speak to their suitors about religion.

Why do these Catholic girls not marry Catholics? Because Catholic young men are often unable to offer the requisite inducements of sobriety, industry, responsibility, and ability to support a wife. Frequently, they do not keep pace with the girls in culture and aspirations; they do not develop intellectually. Ask Catholic girls why they do not marry Catholics and they will inquire: "Where are the desirable young men?" The answer is that they avoid marriage because they are not leading chaste lives. The social evil makes sin too easy and should be stamped out, not regarded as a necessary evil. Marriage would be more common if the social evil were not so prevalent.

Why do Catholic young men avoid marriage? Many, no doubt, have good reasons to decline marriage, but many avoid it because they are selfish, cowardly. They say they cannot afford to marry. If their parents had reasoned as they do, the young men would not have been born. Let them live frugally, cut out drink and gambling, lead clean lives. Let them save with a view of marriage. They claim that girls are too extravagant and expect too much. Apparently non-Catholics who marry them do not think so. Usually the girls are more economical, reasonable, and self-sacrificing than the men.

The men do not keep company with the right kind of girls who know how to make themselves respected. Parents are too indulgent and do not inculcate responsibility by obliging their sons to support the family. The sons soon consider their means too little for pleasure. An epitaph for such a young man would be: "He led a selfish and sinful life; was useless to parents, family and himself, his country, his Church, his God; shed no tears, for he shirked the duties of a man and a Christian."

It is natural for young men and women to marry. If a large number fail to do so, something is wrong. Catholic young men must be blind to let others carry off the rich prizes of refined, educated, high-minded, virtuous, talented, good looking, healthy girls, fit helpmates for any man.

> M. P. Dowling, S.J., "Why Do Catholic Girls Marry Protestants?" *Intermountain Catholic,* 5 September 1914, 2.

63. The Urbanization of Western Catholic Education, 1920

As the frontier faded, Catholic institutions in the West took on the tone of well-established agencies. Gone were the extremes of the pioneer days, replaced by schools and churches that enjoyed large congregations and solid financial support. The transformation this caused can be seen in the student policy of the Denver Catholic schools articulated by Hugh L. McMenamin, rector of the Cathedral of the Immaculate Conception.

It is our privilege to have a child of yours in the Cathedral High School, and whilst we appreciate the privilege, we feel the grave responsibility.

Through many years we have maintained a standard of deportment and morality in our school of which we are very proud. The lamentable reports that come to us from other schools, make us feel well repaid for our own care and vigilance.

We recognize the fact, however, that we are helpless without the co-operation of the parents, and that we may have your co-operation is the purpose of this letter, a copy of which is being sent to all the parents.

Unlike most schools, we take cognizance of the conduct of our pupils even after school hours and even though their conduct be perfect in school, we must refuse to retain them in our school, if they conduct themselves in any way unbecoming even whilst away from the school.

We have, therefore, formulated the following rules and regulations, and respectfully ask you to help us in their enforcement.

1. Repeated instances of absence from school, or tardiness in arriving, except for grave causes, will not be tolerated.

2. Pupils of the Cathedral High School may not attend dances or parties of any kind without permission of the school authorities.

3. Should they desire to have a party, even in their own homes, they will obtain our permission and submit to us the names of their guests.

4. The girl pupils may not under any circumstances leave their homes alone with one escort, not a member of her own family. This applies to auto-rides, going to theatres, etc.

5. Any boldness or extreme fashions in dress, or "dolling up" either in or out of school, will not be tolerated.

6. The use of tobacco in any form by the boys is absolutely forbidden.

7. The first offense of profane or indecent language by any pupil will be followed by dismissal.

In justification of the above seemingly stringent rules let us say that high school pupils are still children and we insist upon treating them as such.

If in your opinion our rules are too severe, or if you do not feel inclined to co-operate with us in enforcing them, we beg of you have your child attend some other school. As for us, we must refuse to accept the responsibility of training the child along any other lines.

> Hugh L. McMenamin, Rector, Cathedral of the Immaculate Conception, September 4, 1920, "Records of the Cathedral School," Office of the Cathedral School, Denver, reprinted in William H. Jones, "The History of Catholic Education in the State of Colorado" (Ph.D. dissertation, Catholic University of America, 1955), 242–43.

Part 5

THE PACIFIC SLOPE —
"WHEN OTHERS RUSHED IN"

Introduction

Though all three states entered the United States as foreign territories, California, Hawai'i, and Alaska have distinct religious histories involving the settlement of Catholics and the development of the institutional church. The documents in part 5 reveal the diverse ethnic origins of each region's evangelization, as well as the roles played by clergy and hierarchy, women religious, and laity of differing nationalities. Cultural pluralism characterized the church in these regions from their earliest days. Further, each territory struggled to obtain personnel and finances from Europe and later from the United States to establish parishes, schools, hospitals, and other charitable and educational operations. Alaskan Catholics labored against greater odds to staff their remote and sparsely settled territory and confronted frontier conditions longer than almost anywhere else in the United States.

From the time of Spanish colonization of California in 1769 until conquest by the United States in 1846, Catholicism in the area possessed a distinctive Hispanic character. Spanish and later Mexican Franciscan priests were the sole clergy in the territory until expelled members of the French Congregation of the Sacred Hearts arrived in 1831 from the kingdom of Hawai'i. The twenty-one missions begun by Blessed Junípero Serra, O.F.M., formed the foundations of the church, along with chapels at four Spanish forts and parish churches at San Jose and Los Angeles. The Holy See erected the Diocese of Both Californias in 1840, with Francisco García Diego y Moreno, O.F.M., as bishop. He resided at Santa Barbara until his death in 1846. Though he founded the first seminary in the state, a chronic lack of funds and an aging clergy hampered García Diego. Similar circumstances initially stymied the next bishop, Joseph Sadoc Alemany, O.P., named bishop for the entire state in 1850 and first archbishop of San Francisco in 1853.

The onslaught of population during the Gold Rush initially overwhelmed Alemany's available personnel, but the determined Spanish-born prelate steadily recruited priests and religious to serve his vast diocese. The foundation of the sees of Monterey–Los Angeles in 1853 and Marysville in 1860 (transferred to Grass Valley in 1868, and to Sacramento in 1886) extended the hierarchy. Alemany and his brother bishops welcomed diocesan clergy from Ireland and Dominicans, Jesuits, Vincentians, and Christian Brothers to staff parishes, missions, and schools. Women religious who volunteered for service in California between 1851 and 1854 included the Dominican Sisters of San Rafael, Sisters of Notre Dame de Namur, the Daughters of Charity, the Sisters of Mercy, and the Presentation Sisters. In 1871, Thaddeus Amat, bishop of Monterey–Los Angeles, recruited the Sisters of the Immaculate Heart of Mary from Spain, while in the following year Alemany approved the establishment in San Francisco of a new order, the Sisters of the Holy Family.

While Hispanic Catholics predominated in the southern portion of the state until the 1880s, Irish, Germans, Italians, and persons of other nationalities constituted the laity in the San Francisco Bay area and in the interior valleys from the time of the Gold Rush onward. California Catholics encountered less prejudice than elsewhere in the nation, though the Daughters of Charity recorded their difficulties in San Francisco. The hierarchy regularized the worship, devotional practices, and lifestyles of these throngs of Catholics, though church institutions also adapted to the needs and desires of the laity. By the end of the nineteenth century, the church in California was well established, particularly in the northern portion of the state and in the cities.

In Hawai'i, the French members of the Congregation of the Sacred Hearts arrived in the island kingdom in 1827 and received a hostile reception from well-established American Congregationalist missionaries. Expelled twice, the priests and brothers returned to stay with the aid of a French frigate of war in 1839. Early evangelization inspired the lay "apostle of Maui," Helio Koaeloa, who converted and trained highly successful native catechists, including his brother, Petero Mahoe, as well as Cecelia Kanakaole and Helio Kaiwiloa. For their faith, early Hawaiian Catholics suffered persecution, such as the *pakaula* (the tying with ropes) on Maui in the 1840s. Catholicism nonetheless spread to all the islands, and the second vicar apostolic, Louis Maigret, SS.CC. (1847–82), recruited the Sisters of the Sacred Hearts in 1859, ordained Blessed Damien De Veuster, SS.CC., and later assigned him to Moloka'i to minister to the victims of Hansen's disease.

Amid the dramatic changes which beset Hawai'i in the later half of the nineteenth century, King David Kalakaua invited the German-American Sisters of St. Francis of Syracuse, New York, to work with those suffering with Hansen's disease. Mother Marianne Kopp, O.S.F., and companions arrived in 1883 to minister in Honolulu, and in 1888, she and two sisters began work at Kaluapapa, Moloka'i. With Hawai'i's annexation by the United States in 1898, five years after the fall of the monarchy, the vicariate eventually became a suffragan see of the Archdiocese of San Francisco. Portuguese and later Filipino plantation laborers swelled the numbers of island Catholics. By

1909, there was emerging evidence of an American identity for the Catholicism which French missionaries had founded and which native catechists and French, Belgian, and German-American religious had propagated.

While still a Russian territory, Alaska had first been included in the jurisdiction of a Roman Catholic bishop when the See of Vancouver Island was established in 1847. Beginning in 1873, Bishop Charles S. Seghers of that diocese visited five times, until he was murdered in 1886, along the Yukon River. Paschal Tosi and Aloysius Robaut, two Jesuit priests Seghers had invited to visit in 1886, received permission to remain in Alaska from the superior of the Jesuit Rocky Mountain Mission, Joseph M. Cataldo. The Jesuits founded several missions, beginning at Nulato in 1887. Five years later, Pope Leo XIII named Tosi to head the newly created vicariate apostolic which encompassed the entire territory of Alaska.

The same year that Tosi and Robaut arrived, so did the French-Canadian Sisters of St. Anne, who commenced a hospital and school in Juneau and then a school at Holy Cross mission in the north. The Sisters of Providence opened a school in Nome in 1902, and the Ursulines from Montana staffed St. Mary's mission at Akulurak in 1905. A limited Catholic population scattered over vast distances long characterized the church in Alaska. The great expense of maintaining missions and schools in remote areas prompted repeated appeals for aid by religious leaders such as Mother Amadeus Dunne of the Ursulines.

The Jesuits remained the principal source of clergy for the church, and relatively few native vocations to the priesthood arose. In the late 1960s, Bishops Francis D. Gleeson, S.J., and Robert L. Whelan, S.J., began a permanent deacon training program among the Central Yup'ik Innuits. To date, over forty men have been ordained in the Diocese of Fairbanks for the church in Alaska. Two letters from one deacon candidate, Michael Nayagak, express important characteristics of the identity of the Catholic Church in the state that prides itself as the nation's "last frontier."

California: Reestablishment and Growth

64. José De la Guerra Describes the State of the Church in California, 1849

After the war with Mexico, Bishop John Hughes of New York City sought information on the church in California. Hughes wrote to José De la Guerra y Noriega (1779–1858), a prominent layman, retired commander of the Spanish fort in Santa Barbara, and close friend of the Franciscan friars of the missions. De la Guerra described both the history and present challenge facing the church with the onset of the Gold Rush.

Great is the satisfaction I have felt upon receiving the letter which Your Illustrious Lordship deigned to address to me under the date of December 12, both because of the honor you have condescended to bestow upon me, and the pleasing information of your acquaintance with my daughter and son-in-law, as well as that by it I have proof of the great interest which Your Illustrious Lordship and the other bishops of the United States take for the spread of our Holy Faith and for the comfort of us who profess it in this remote region of California. Wherefore, I hasten to answer it, expressing, however, the regret that my answer will not reach you by the month of May, because it took four months for your letter to reach me; nevertheless, no matter at what time my letter will arrive there, I feel that the information which you solicited will be of some use. Wherefore, I give it according to my knowledge of the points contained in your questionary.

1. Bishop of California

In the year of 1836 a bishopric was established in the department of both Californias and His Holiness appointed as the first Bishop of this new diocese the illustrious Señor D. Francisco García Diego, who ruled it until his death, which occurred on May 1, 1846; after which the miter was transferred to a Franciscan at the request of the deceased, so that at the present time there is no bishop in this vast diocese. And for this reason I am greatly pleased that Your Illustrious Lordship is desirous of soliciting the Holy Father to appoint a successor to this See, which has been vacant now for over two years.

As to what you add, that it ought to be occupied by a Spanish priest, I judge that to be fitting, because the Catholics of this country are almost all Spanish-American, with whom the Spaniards are in sympathy; however, if this might not be accomplished, I think at least that as an indispensable requisite the bishop or bishops who are appointed should be proficient in Spanish.

2. Episcopal See

In this diocese there is no one place that can correctly speaking be called the episcopal see. I understand that when His Holiness was pleased to appoint the aforesaid bishop, he recommended San Diego as his see, or the adjacent mission to the north, San Luis Rey. But His Lordship decided otherwise, for lack of resources and for other reasons which he doubtless made known to the Holy Father upon informing him of his determination; wherefore, from the very outset he established himself at Santa Barbara and took up his residence in the adjoining mission bearing the same name, calling it his *hospicio*. There he resided until his death, and it has always remained the abode of the governor of this miter.

3. Number of Catholics

Regarding the number of Catholics living in this province, I shall only say that before the discovery of gold, they could be calculated at about twenty-five or thirty thousand, but since then the influx of people from the Spanish-Americas, and such as are expected from every part of the continent, Oceania, Asia, etc..., has made it impossible to form a judicious estimate of how many will be in this country within the next six years.

4. Number of Indians

In order to give you a clear idea respecting the number of Indians, I divide them into two classes: Christian and Gentile. The first comprise about ten to fifteen thousand, but of the second, their number cannot be calculated because there are many tribes occupying regions little known and who, because they are accustomed, like the Bedouins of Africa, to have no fixed residence and like these they may be classified as errant; for which reason it is difficult to have any satisfactory information about them.

5. Clergy

The whole clergy that at present exists in this Alta California consists of four secular priests, four outside priests, one Dominican religious, and seven Franciscans. Of these latter, one is the governor of the miter as already stated; another is the Commissary Prefect here of the College of San Fernando, who is about to depart for that capital (Mexico City) at the request of the Guardian of that College, and of the remaining five, only two are capable of giving their all to their ministry, the others being too old and too infirm. The Dominican belongs to the Missions of Baja California, which province he left, so I am informed, because of some revolts there, for which reason I presume his stay here will be of short duration. Of the four alien priests, two were sent here at the request of the Rev. P. Gobernador of this Miter by the Illustrious Lord Bishop of the Sandwich Islands; another was sent by the Illustrious Lord Archbishop of Oregon, also at the insistence of the aforesaid Gobernador; while the other came here on his own account, and who, because he acknowledges no prelate, will, it is feared, become discontented for any reason whatever and leave the country. Of the four secular priests, the one is always so sick that he is often unable to celebrate Mass, but the other three fulfill their ministry.

This then, Most Illustrious Lord Bishop, is the number and circumstances of the priests, both religious and secular, living in this extensive land, from which it can easily be understood how great is our need for an increase in the number of priests to administer to us.

As conclusion to this paragraph it remains for me to make known to you, with due respect to the Mexican priests, that the information which has been given to Your Illustrious Lordship regarding their conduct during these latter times does not correspond with the facts, because no one has left the country since 1844, and if then and afterwards one did leave, it was because he had served his time limit and returned to his college, and even then only those left whose health suffered from these climates.

6. Actual Conditions of the Missions

The actual condition of the missions is little less than nil, because some are entirely abandoned and their buildings in a very ruinous state; others are in the hands of private individuals, while the remainder (those less destroyed) have been rented out, and their rentals (except this Mission of Santa Barbara which is half for religious service and church administration, the other half for the Indians) are divided in three equal shares, one for divine cult and church administration, another for the Indians, and the third for the establishment of a charitable program in the favor of the Indians, which latter, however, has never been realized.

This then Your Illustrious Lordship, in summary, is the state in which the missions exist at the present time, which not so long ago were rich; but since day by day they are gradually being demolished and are consequently heading for total ruin, it is to be presumed that even this very scanty aid which they now yield towards divine service and for the support of their ministers will soon cease.

7. Property of the Churches

This consists of the church buildings, furniture, lots, jewels, etc., used for divine service, all of which still exists, although some of the churches, for lack of ministers, are closed and are in consequence continuously deteriorating; however, their belongings have been transferred to the churches still in use.

Ecclesiastical Property. Strictly speaking, there is no ecclesiastical property in California, because what came uder [sic] that term is in Mexico City or in some other states of the republic, which consists of various estates, urban and rural, called "Pious Fund of California," by whose revenues, at one time abundant, the religious missionaries of both Californias were able to sustain themselves; and now that the aforesaid revenues have greatly decreased, they could nevertheless be of invaluable service if their rents could be acquired. But unfortunately I look upon their acquisition as very difficult now that the political state of California with Mexico has changed radically from peace.

These funds were placed at the disposal of His Lordship, the bishop of the diocese, and his successors by the law of February 19, 1836. Afterwards, however, the government took them over again, and at present they are in its hands.

Since to give Your Illustrious Lordship a complete idea of these funds would take up many pages, for the sake of a better understanding of the subject I am sending Your Illustrious Lordship a *cuaderno* published by our deputy to the

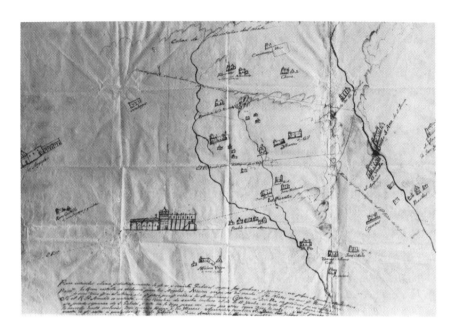

Map showing the divisions of territory served by the parish priests of Los Angeles, San Gabriel, and San Juan Capistrano. Traveling much like Methodist circuit riders, clergy-men rode on horseback to bring the sacraments to their far-flung congregations. The map locates the prominent "Californio" and Anglo-American *rancheros*. The notations referring to "Padre Amable" [Petithomme, SS.CC.] and "Padre Pedro" [Bagaria] of San Juan Capistrano suggest that this map dates from 1854.

Credit: California Historical Society/Ticor Title Insurance, Los Angeles, Department of Special Collections, University of Southern California Library, Los Angeles. Repro-duced by permission.

General Congress which, especially in the article entitled "fondo piadoso," as also in the discourse given by the aforementioned Señor Diputado on May 30, 1844, can give you an idea . . . of the nature of these funds, their sacred purpose, and their state during that period.

Furthermore, there is a small hacienda consisting of about twelve leagues, northeast of this town, established by the deceased illustrious bishop, which consists mainly of cattle numbering about two thousand head, together with a piece of land four or five leagues square, whose establishment, both on the part of the government granting it and of the Lord Bishop in soliciting and promoting it, was for the purpose of founding and supporting schools and colleges. Wherefore, it cannot be called ecclesiastical property, though that land is administered by the Church under the direction and supervision of this sacred miter.

The foregoing, Illustrious Lord, is all that I can say relative to the information which you ask of me in your welcome letter which I have the honor to answer.

With that I feel I have complied to the best of my ability with the wishes of Your Illustrious Lordship, and which I hope our Lord and Savior will bring to a realization. Meanwhile, with a prayer for the conservation of Your Illustrious Lordship's health, I kiss your sacred ring.

José De la Guerra to John Hughes, 18 August 1849, Santa Barbara, quoted in *El Gran Capitan: José De la Guerra*, ed. Fr. Joseph A. Thompson, O.F.M. (Los Angeles: privately printed, 1961), 221–25. Printed by permission.

65. The Daughters of Charity Arrive in San Francisco and Face Opposition, 1852

In 1852, five Daughters of Charity of St. Vincent de Paul traveled from Maryland to San Francisco in response to the urgent pleas of Bishop Joseph Sadoc Alemany, O.P., for sisters to care for orphan girls in his see. This memoir combined both a daily journal and later recollections in a document that describes the primitive conditions and opposition the first sisters encountered in the early days of the Gold Rush.

Wednesday

Our last, long and dreary night is over. — At two o'clock in the morning we were aroused by cries of "San Francisco in sight." It would be hard to describe our joy at the hearing of such welcome news, and our anxiety to set foot on the sandy shore of the far famed "Golden Region." It was four o'clock P.M. when we left the steamer. Mr. Eugene Kelly, coming on board, was soon recognized by Sister Francis [McEnnis], as an old and true friend, whom she had known for many years in St. Louis. He was delighted to see her, and immediately offered his assistance to take us on shore, and attend to our baggage; but as Mother Eteinne [Hall] had given us orders not to leave the vessel until some of the Rev. Gentlemen would come for us, so we watched and waited in vain, but not one seemed to think of us, or expect us; and fearing night would overtake us in the ship, Sister Francis availed herself of Mr. Eugene Kelly's kind offer, — shortly after we were let down in small boats, and rowed to shore, where we were the gaze and laughing stock of a crowd of men, who had never seen a cornette, and not even a female for many a long day — we were obliged to endure this humiliation till Mr. Kelly succeeded in procuring carriages to take us to our future home. But Oh! what a home for the poor, sick and tired Pioneers. After much riding up and down, and round sand hills that seemed interminable, the driver halted before a destitute looking shanty, and Mr. Kelly said, "Sister Francis, I think this is the place." In a moment the door was thrown open, and an elderly gentleman, in a torn and worn cassock, stepped out, surrounded by a crowd of dirty, ragged children who ran to look at us, and then went back. The Sisters were alighting even without an invitation, but Sister Francis was as if paralysed [*sic*], and remained seated. Father Maginnis (for so it proved to be) came up to the carriage and said: "Are you the Boss?" This was almost too much, however, we bore it, and be assured, that the soil on which we were to labor, was well watered with our tears. We hastened to get into the house, and there the picture of desolation was completed — not a chair was to be seen, wooden stools, the work of Father Maginnis, supplied their place. A large barrel of wine stood in the middle of the floor, and a few cans of preserved fruit were scattered here and there. Up stairs, there were seven cots, with thin straw mattresses, and little pillows of goats' hair, without sheets or blankets, or any to be had. Although sick and tired, we had first to arrange our little furniture to the best advantage. Father Maginnis' kind and fatherly care can not be forgotten by the first Sisters. He took the blanket from his own bed and gave it to us, and the meal which had been prepared for himself, sent it to us, as we had no convenience to prepare victuals for ourselves that day.

About five o'clock P.M. the Vicar General paid us a visit, and in a few moments, Sister Francis recognized in him, an old friend, Rev. Father Liberea, who immediately took her aside, and begged of her not to tell who he was: for once he had been a member of the Congregation of the Mission, but had severed the ties that bound him to it. He cordially welcomed us to the strange land, and hoped that soon our prospects would be brighter...

October 1852. We opened School about the first Monday in October, six weeks after our coming. Fifty girls, or thereabouts, presented themselves, but the number augmented each day. The five Sisters assembled in the principal room — Sister Francis came forward, and named each one, as Sister Fidelis, Sister M. Sebastian, Sister Corsina, Sister Bernice, and I am Sister Francis. The class rooms served as dormitories during the night — every morning the beds were taken away, and as duly rearranged at evening twilight...

Owing to the influence of the Catholic Community, in 1850 & 1851, and the difficulty of obtaining, or procuring competent teachers, the denominational system was introduced by the civil Authorities, and retained for some time, with most important advantages to our holy religion. On the 25th of September, 1851, an act was passed by the State Legislature, empowering the City Authorities to establish a number of gratuitous, educational establishments, known as the Common Schools, to be maintained by the taxation of the people. They were divided under the headings of the "City and Ward Schools" both of which received their pro rata of the State educational fund. The better which were exclusively for the benefit of the Catholic Community, were so called from the Wards into which the city was divided, where the Schools were established. The Annual amount received by the Catholics for their respective departments, amounted to close on forty thousand dollars. In 1853, our School was admitted as the School of the Seventh Ward. Four of us being employed as teachers, three were allowed each one hundred and twenty five dollars per month, and Sister Francis an additional twenty five dollars each month, as she did the principal share of the writing, and superintended the general conduct of the School.

According to the customs of public Seminaries, at stated periods, the gentlemen, Board of Education, came to inspect the School, and examine the teachers. In our regard they made the trial consist of a few simple questions, always manifesting the greatest respect for the Sisters. During one of these visits, the President, Mr. H _____ addressing Sister Corsina, said: "Madam, how would you govern children?["] Sister replied: "Sir, I would teach them to govern themselves." This elicited his approval in somewhat of a speech. On another occasion, Mr. S _____ inquired of each Sister how long she had been teaching, and receiving for an answer, Twenty, twenty-five, thirty years, etc. — the gentlemen took up their hats, saying; "that persons engaged in the business for such a length of time, were surely equal to the task." We were afterwards obliged to associate with us several, Catholic young ladies, as our pupils increased so rapidly, and while waiting for more Sisters from St. Joseph's. These Assistants, were recognized by the Board of Examiners, and we paid them a regular Salary.

"California: Roman Catholic Orphan Asylum (San Francisco, 1852 to 1910)," 19–20, 22, 25–26, in Daughters of Charity of St. Vincent de Paul, Western Province, Archives of the Seton Provincialate, Los Altos Hills, Calif. Printed by permission.

66. Last Will and Testament of Rosa Ruiz De Ávila of Los Angeles, 1854

Like many other members of Los Angeles's ranchero families, Rosa Ruiz (1789–1866) endeavored to maintain her Spanish Catholic heritage on the southwestern frontier. However, as Ruiz illustrates in her will, oftentimes the religiosity these Latino(a) Catholics practiced reflected the region's popular devotional beliefs rather than hierarchical church teachings.

In the name of God Almighty. Amen. Let it be well-known that I, Rosa Ruiz of fifty-nine years of age, native of this State of California, legitimate daughter of Efigenio Ruiz and of Rosa Lopez Monrial; finding myself by the mercy of God, in my entire consent and complete memory, believing and confessing in the mysteries of the Holy Apostolic Roman Catholic Religion that I profess, and fearful of death which is so natural in every human creature, so that when God Our Lord calls me to judgment I will be prepared with a testamentary arrangement, and so that I will not have in that anxious hour temporal possessions, I grant[,] do and order this my testament in the following form.

Firstly, I commend my soul to God who created it from nothing, and I send my body to the earth from which it was formed, it being made a cadaver I wish that it be shrouded in the habit of St. Francis and that it is buried in the Pantheon of the Catholics.

I order that the day of my burial in the hour [of my funeral] or, if not, in some immediate time[,] that mass be said for my soul with my body present.

I order that fifty masses be said for the good of my soul.

I order that another fifty masses be said for the souls of my Parents and benefactors, and for the blessed souls of purgatory.

1st I declare that I am married to Don Antonio Ygnacio Ávila,[1] in whose matrimony we have for our legitimate children Francisca, Acencion [*sic*], Juan, José, Rafaela, Concepción [*sic*], Pedro, Pedro Antonio, Marta y Pilar, of whom Acencion, José, Pilar and Rafaela have died.

2nd I declare, that when I married I did not contribute to the matrimony any quantity [of property] in any respect, but after I was married I inherited part of a farm that is adjoined today with that of Don Antonio María Lugo, that of the heirs of Don Miguel Prior and that of the widow of Vicente Sanches [*sic*].

3rd I declare that in the good times of my age, my husband and I have acquired through our work, care and economy the interests that we today possess, and my husband well-founded in this association of our goods, he has ordered in his testament that they adjudicate to me half of them, leaving me in the happiness of my_____.

> Rosa Ruiz, last will and testament, 13 February 1854, in Del Valle Collection, Seaver Center for Western History Research, Los Angeles County Museum of Natural History, Los Angeles. Translated from the Spanish. Printed by permission.

67. The Daughters of Charity Arrive in Los Angeles, 1856

Arriving in 1856, the Daughters of Charity of St. Vincent de Paul were the first women religious in Los Angeles after the Spanish colonial period. They established institutions to care for orphans, to educate young women, to nurse the sick, and to feed the poor. The author of this memoir, Sister Angelita Mumbrado (1833–1923), left her native Barcelona as one of Bishop Thaddeus Amat's early recruits for the newly erected see of Monterey–Los Angeles, where she served for over forty years.

The priest who instructed me was a zealous religious and relative of ours. One day he told me that Bishop [Thaddeus] Amat had arrived from Rome and was in the city looking for students to take with him to California...As soon as the Bishop saw me he asked if I would like to go to California with him. Without thinking I said, "Yes"...At last I took courage and asked, "Papa will you permit me to go with Bishop Amat to California?" He said "No"...I pleaded that I was very anxious and that I felt a hand pushing me as if our

---

1. Antonio Ygnacio Ávila (1760–1858) married Rosa Ruiz at the Mission Santa Barbara on 6 February 1803. Ávila was born in Villa del Fuerte, Mexico, and his family was one of the first to migrate to California. Not only did Ávila accumulate great wealth during his lifetime, but he also served as the *regidor* of the *pueblo* of Los Angeles. He was buried at the Los Angeles Plaza Church on 26 September 1858.

Lord wanted to me to go...My father called me and said, "My child I cannot give you my consent, neither can I prevent you from going..."

I felt very brave. It was the Hand of God that supported me...We left the city of Barcelona on the twenty-third of April, in the year eighteen fifty-five...[W]e had hardly entered the vessel when I began to be seasick...The bishop soon perceived that I was sick and asked me if I wanted to go back. I told him my sacrifice was made already and I was going to continue on the journey.

On the sixteenth day of May we started for the United States...On the fifth of June we entered the Seminary...During my Seminary I was often sick due to the change of climate, but I was never discouraged. I felt happy to be in the community...I am the only one of the three who persevered ...We received the Holy Habit on October thirteenth [1855]...

We started early on the morning of the eighteenth of October. There were five of us — three Spanish sisters and two of the three American sisters whom the Superiors had generously given for the California Mission...We had to go to New York in order to take the Steamer for California...We encountered a very bad storm at sea. The steamer was packed and all of the people were sea sick, even the sailors...On the Pacific we had a dreadful time. They put us on deck with a crowd of people. It was so hot we could scarcely breathe...

We arrived in San Francisco at five o'clock in the morning on November fifteenth...You can imagine what a sight we were after being one month at sea without changing our clothes...The Bishop left us in San Francisco and went through the Diocese to find the best location for us. He saw Monterey was not much of a place so he went to Los Angeles and decided that was the place for us and for him.

We were so anxious to begin our work that we left San Francisco without waiting to be told. The steamer brought us to San Pedro but as there were no public conveyance of any kind at that time, we did not know how we were going to get to Los Angeles. Fortunately a lady who had traveled with us was met by a man with a wagon. She offered to take us with her...The ride was splendid but as we neared the Los Angeles River the wagon stuck in the mud...We were there a long time, when some travelers came to our aid and we at last arrived in Los Angeles on the fifth of January, 1856...[T]here was nobody to meet us...There were no streets, no people were around and only a few houses could be seen here and there...

The house was quite small...[W]e had no beds...[T]here was nothing [to do] but to go out to the carpenters and fill some sacks with shavings...Later a good lady gave us some wool to make mattresses...The carpenter made six beds and then we were grand...The room where the children slept was used as oratory, classroom, sewing room and parlor. Only God knows what we went through but nevertheless we were happy.

In all kinds of weather we had to cross the zanja in a small boat to go to

Mass... The first Mass we heard... was chanted by the Indian boys, who were taught by a Brother of the Sacred Heart.

One day Father [Blas Raho] came to the house and said he had a very sick man for us to take care of... We [had] hardly room for ourselves. He said we must find a corner as the man had to be cared for or he would die... Father brought the man and he got well. That was the beginning of the hospital in Los Angeles...

Oh, those happy days in California. The long walks on dusty roads that charity and duty required us to make were a great pleasure to me. I remember the first act of charity that we performed in Los Angeles. A poor Indian boy who had worked for our neighbor... died. The coffin was put on a wagon and we four Sisters walked behind it. It was a very long walk over a dusty road but that was the only way to bury the dead in those days.

> Sister Angelita Mumbrado, D.C., "Remembrance of My Youth" (typescript,
> [1917]), 3, 4, 5, 6, 7, 8, 10, Daughters of Charity of St. Vincent de Paul, Western
> Province, Archives of the Seton Provincialate, Los Altos Hills, Calif. Printed by
> permission.

68. Letter of a French Missionary in Southern California, 1856

The diverse peoples on the California frontier received the ministrations of religious from many nations. The French missionary priest Father Edmund Venisse of the Congregation of the Sacred Hearts describes the first years after his ordination when he served in Southern California. He later worked in Hawai'i and in Chile.

Writing from Chile on the 20th of June, 1856.

I was ordained priest at San Francisco by Mgr. Joseph Alemany. I soon after set out for Pueblo de Los Angelos [*sic*], where I spent two years as a schoolmaster, teaching a little of everything to a few poor children... After having spent a few days at Sainte Inez, I returned to Los Angeles to revisit the good cure, Father Anaclet [Lestrade, SS.CC.]. I assisted him to the best of my ability, not, in this instance, in the capacity of schoolmaster, but as Missioner. Our church, some time ago too spacious, was now too small; the labor was immense, and would have fully occupied two additional priests. Always on the move, sometimes on foot, sometimes on horseback, day and night, I often went a distance of seventy miles, in the exercise of my apostolic ministry. San Fernando, another Mission intrusted to Father Anicille, was the one I most frequently visited. These good people, composed almost exclusively of Indians, have been without priests for eight or ten years. On each occasion that I visited them, I offered up the Holy Sacrifice, taught the catechism, heard confessions, baptized the children, and attended the sick. Poor California Indians, how they are deserted, and how deplorable is their condition! The contact of civilization is daily decreasing their numbers, through the destructive agency of brandy. Some of the white population even kill them merely for the sake of trying their pistols. Our little town alone is almost the weekly scene of eight or ten murders; but it is especially on Saturday night that these atrocious crimes are committed. How often I have already had to hear the confessions of these victims mortally wounded! One day, I arrived just in time to attend an unfortunate being, who was rolling in the street in a pool of blood; for several days, the doctors declared that there was no hope of his recovery. I continued, however, to attend him, and in less than a month his wound was healed.

I have been much surprised to find that savages die without agony. Their reason is but feebly developed, but the little they possess remains to the last breath; with only a few minutes to exist, they speak as if they were but slightly indisposed. Those who live among the white population die prematurely; those who dwell in the desert often live over a hundred years ...

However, during the few hours of leisure that the active life of a Missioner allotted me, I was able to teach music to some children, who manifested considerable talent, and we were thus enabled to have a Mass sung every Sunday. On great solemnities, we had also the assistance of an Indian band, the remnant of more prosperous days, when the Franciscan Fathers taught the arts with success. It would be difficult to conceive the effects of these Masses, simple in character, religious, sustained by an accompaniment in which even mingled, with any discordant notes, and yet with delightful contrasts, the joyous violin, the melancholy flute, the silvery triangle, the gay tambourine, and even at intervals the big drum. For my part, I was always deeply moved; I was in reality at Los Angelos — *with the Angels.* Sometimes, also, we had the services of a Mexican troop, who asked for admission to the choir. We had then a splendid Hispano-Californian Mass in two parts. The interludes were filled up by select pieces of pleasing harmony, well chosen, executed upon two flutes and two guitars. The preparation and direction of the choir was a very laborious undertaking for me, but I did not feel it; I was happy, I was contributing to render our festivals more solemn, and my exertions as a Christian Orpheus had the effect of attracting numbers of the faithful to our church.

On the feast of the Holy Sacrament [Corpus Christi], we erected with branches of green oak and palm leaves several *reposoirs,* which are still decorated with birds' nests, with garland of pure white, formed by the most splendid flowers of the country. Our processions were very simple, but in no way deficient either in the number of attendants nor in the piety of the faithful. We could not, it is true, even have any pretensions to equal that which I witnessed at Rio Janeiro [sic], in 1849 ...

Immediately after my return to Pueblo de Los Angelos, Mgr. [Thaddeus] Amat, Bishop of Monterey, anxiously expected for upwards of a year, also arrived. He was received with emotion and enthusiasm. The bells were rung, and the Indians, dressed in their finest costumes, joined by numbers of the *roncheros* [sic] (farmers) who had come from a distance, formed a joyful but respectful procession in the streets; at the pontiff's approach, they all knelt down to receive his blessing, and were much edified by his simplicity and extreme kindness. His immense diocese promises great success. Seven Seminarists are already forming a nucleus, which must soon be further developed, and, united with the zeal and efforts of six Sisters of Charity recently arrived, will, with the aid of God, no doubt revive that Christian faith in ancient times propagated here by the generous disciples of St. Francis, and which was never extinguished in California...

"Extract from a Letter of M. Venisse, Missioner-Apostolic of the Congregation of Picpus," *Annals of the Propagation of the Faith* (London) 19 (1858): 39–46.

69. Constitution of a Purgatorial Society in Los Angeles, ca. 1860

Confronted with the clashing of devotional and institutional beliefs, Father Blas Raho, C.M. (1806–62), pastor of the Church of Our Lady of Angels in Los Angeles from 1856 to 1862, established a purgatorial society, the Piadosa Asociación para las Animas del Purgatorio. A new devotion for his Mexican congregation, the purgatorial society represented the convergence of differing Catholic identities on the California frontier.

1. The souls that are suffering in Purgatory ask for the assistance of our prayers and sacrifices with these words of holy Job: "Take pity on me, take pity on me, at least my friends, because the hand of God has struck me." The charity and the duty are our helping obligation. — Coming to Heaven, do not forget your benefactors. We will have many intercessions in heaven with souls we have freed in Purgatory.

2. In order to help the blessed souls of Purgatory, this pious association is established in the Church of Our Lady of the Angels. All the faithful will be able to participate in the same.

3. On Monday of every week, the holy Sacrifice of the Mass will be offered and applied for the safety of the souls of Purgatory, a response at mass will be sung. On the first Monday of each month, the Mass will be sung.

4. In order to participate in the benefits of this association, each one should contribute alms of one peso a month, or twelve pesos annually.

5. At the time of the death of one of the members, who for a year has paid the contribution each month, three masses will be celebrated for the repose of his soul.

6. The money that is received will be used to pay the expenses of the Church of Our Lady of Angels and the debts of the repairs of the same.

7. The Pastor will name the collectors that collect the contributions from the faithful and all those will be collected in a separate book.

"Piadosa Asociación para las Animas del Purgatorio," Coronel Collection, Seaver Center for Western History Research, Los Angeles County Museum of Natural History, Los Angeles. Translated from the Spanish.

70. Synod Legislation Changing Hispanic Religious Customs in the Diocese of Monterey–Los Angeles, 1862, 1876

The decrees of Bishop Thaddeus Amat's diocesan synods in 1862 and 1876 sought to bring frontier ritual practice in Southern California into close conformity to the practices of the institutional church. These statutes specifically prohibited certain Hispanic folk religion customs and reflect Amat's seminary experience in St. Louis and Philadelphia prior to his epispocacy in Monterey–Los Angeles (1856 to 1878).

30. Pastors should be especially alert that other abuses, once common among us but now, due to the zeal of priests, quite infrequent, not be brought back anew, but rather totally eliminated; and we strictly forbid them to permit the faithful to put in the Church, which is a house of prayer, any scenes, such as "The Shepherds" [*Los Pastores*] on Christmas day, and "The Jews" at Passiontide and Holy Week, or the like; rather they should see to it that this is not done even outside the Church, for the sake of avoiding the scandals that often result from them. It is our wish that processions, if any should take place and local circumstances permit it, be restricted to those approved by the Church; and pastors should permit nothing in them contrary to the Roman Ceremonial of Processional, and whatever is prescribed should, as far as possible, be exactly observed, so that, in accordance with the intention of the Church, they may be helpful in cherishing and enkindling the true devotion of the faithful. Priests should also know that they may not use Blessings other than those noted in the Roman Ritual without special faculties.

31. In carrying out the bodies of the dead from home to church and from church to cemetery, the parish priests should permit nothing alien to the Roman Ritual, nor should they do honor with their presence, and so they should warn their parishioners that they should abstain from the use of [fire]arms unless perhaps the dead were military people and it happened that they were buried in their military garb or their military apparatus, nor should they permit them (bodies) to come into the church nor to be taken out of it whether they are of little people or adults except on a bier, well closed, in the exception of the case of poverty or if they happen to be Indians and no other way could be provided. Moreover, the parish priest should take care that the parishioners abstain themselves from the use of fires commonly on the occasion of the funeral procession *"cohetes"* [fireworks] and altogether they should refrain from the abuse of these people who gather in the home of the dead person until the body is carried out [who] indulge in dancing and drinking, which in truth we disapprove as bringing them down as from gentility.

Constitutiones: In Synodo Diocesana Montereyensi et Angelorum Prima Latae Et Promulgatae (San Francisco: Vicente Torras, 1862), decrees 30 and 31. Translated from Latin.

•

X. [On Baptism]

We wish that, in accordance with the prescription of the Roman ritual, a name be given them of the Saints reigning with Christ, and we disapprove the practice of giving them the venerable Name of Jesus, the Divine Persons or mysteries. They should urge the faithful to have the baptism in their own church, and guard against sponsors being presented who are unworthy or were rejected by other priests...

> *Constitutiones: In Synodo Diocesana Montereyensi et Angelorum Tertia Latae et Promulgatae* (San Francisco: P. J. Thomas, 1876), decree 10. Translated from Latin.

71. Archbishop Alemany's Dispute with the Jesuits over Parochial Property, 1862

The Spanish-born bishops of nineteenth-century California engaged in ongoing conflicts with several religious orders over the ownership of real estate. Archbishop Joseph S. Alemany of San Francisco, for example, sought title to the property from the Jesuits at St. Ignatius parish. The following two documents are drawn from the voluminous correspondence in which Alemany eventually removed the parochial status from the Jesuit church, while the Jesuits retained title to the property.

San Francisco, Sept. 10, 1862

Very Rev. Dear Sir,

I think it is time that I should comply with the wishes of the Church, which directs the Bishops in the United States to have parroquial or proparroquial [*sic*] churches in their name. This I should doubtlessly have done long before; but desiring always to avoid anything which might have the appearance of unfriendly feeling, I have put that off. Not to fail, however, any longer in this duty, I feel obliged to state to you, that I believe the Deed of your church in this city should be in my name, and that unless it be conveyed to me within twelve months, I will consider you not much interested in keeping the parish in the same church and myself bound to let said parish cease in said church.

Of course, this is not intended to give trouble to anybody: had we marked out more clearly the boundaries of the respective rights of regulars and seculars, perhaps we might have avoided the little trouble which now seems unavoidable. I think, therefore, that the defining now of those boundaries in a way clear to both parties is the only means of dissipating such troubles now and hereafter.

> Archbishop Joseph S. Alemany to Burchard Villiger, S.J., San Francisco, 10 September 1862, as quoted in John B. McGloin, S.J., *California's First Archbishop* (New York: Herder and Herder, 1966), 198.

•

This is therefore my statement: Our Father General not allowing us to invest your Grace with the title of our Church, has made use of the common right which is granted by the Holy See to all religious orders, which can possess property of their own. As our Churches are an essential part of our Colleges which we are authorized by the Holy See to possess as our own, Father General, I believe, wisely, thought that the Holy See would contradict itself if allowing us on the one hand to possess Colleges, she should on the other oblige us to dispossess ourselves of the same by vesting the Bishops with the title of our own property. He concluded, therefore, it not to be according to the will of the Holy See that the title which your Grace required from us should be given. And that Rev. Father General has been true in thinking so, it seems evidently proved also by this, that the Holy See allows those religious Orders who, according [to] their institutes, are enable[d] to have Parishes, to possess those Churches as their own; and therefore though the Ordinary has the right to visit them, his visit however is limited by ecclesiastical laws only to what concerns the Sacraments and parochial duties, but he cannot interfere with what concerns the property. And this is the reason, I think, by which the Holy See approving of the Decrees of the Council of Baltimore, with regard to the 5th Decree, made the observation:

In order that it may appear that, by this decree, the Bishops do not wish to injure in any way the Regular Orders, it might be added: "Preserving intact the privileges of the Regular Orders, according to whatsoever has been decreed in Canon Law and the Constitutions of the Roman Pontiffs." And, in accordance with such observation, the words — "The privileges of the Regulars," etc. have been added to the 5th Decree...

Our Father General therefore having considered all these things and regarding the 5th Decree of the Council of Baltimore as not affecting us, has deemed not only to be his right, but also to do according to the mind of the Holy See, not allowing us to invest your Grace with the title of the Church. And although on these principles he could perhaps have insisted upon your Grace not to withdraw from us the Parish, in view especially that the Holy See has temporarily enabled us to have Parishes — what we could not, according to our Institute — to supply the want of due foundation for the support of ours, he nevertheless would not. He has preferred that we should submit ourselves to the care of Divine Providence for our support rather than make any opposition to your Grace, to whom our Society is so much indebted for the true liberality with which your Grace has endowed Sta. Clara College.

I beg humbly of your Grace to accept these few words, as I have written them, in a friendly spirit, not to condemn in any way what your Grace has thought in his wisdom to be his duty to do, but only to show the truth of things, as it is in itself on our side.

Felix Sopranis, S.J., to Joseph Alemany, San Francisco, 2 October 1863, as quoted in John B. McGloin, S.J., *California's First Archbishop* (New York: Herder and Herder, 1966), 210–11.

72. Christian Brothers Adapt Their Course of Studies for American Students, 1868

The traditional courses of studies offered in European schools and colleges required adaptation to meet the more pragmatic educational desires of American Catholics. The following account testifies to the successful efforts of the Brothers of the Christian Schools as they commenced teaching in California.

The Pacific mail steamer Montana has brought this week an important and long desired accession to the cause of Catholic education in California. Among her passengers was a community of Christian Brothers, who have come from the East at the invitation of the Most Rev. Archbishop to take charge of St. Mary's College and establish there the system of education which has already borne such excellent fruits in both Europe and America. As the community is sufficiently numerous to form a teaching staff adequate to all the wants of the College, and everything has been prepared for their reception they purpose entering on their educational labors next week...Their success in instructing the mind and disciplining the hearts of their pupils is too well known to need any panegyric from our pens, and the rapid growth of the order in the United States shows more clearly than words can tell, how admirably it is adapted to meet the wants of the American Catholic population...Indeed, the original object of the venerable founder of the Brotherhood of the Christian Schools was to provide for the primary education of the poor in human knowledge and religion, and to this end, the efforts of his followers are still mainly directed. The wants of American society, however, needing such a modification of the rule, in this country, as would permit of the education, the Brothers have established colleges throughout the country, in which the full course of humanities is taught.

[San Francisco] *Monitor*, 15 August 1868.

Hawai'i and Alaska

73. Hawaiian Catholics of Moloka'i Request Priests for Their Island, 1857

Written in Hawaiian and first published in French, this letter expressed the desire of Hawaiian Catholics on the island of Moloka'i for the ministry of a priest. They wrote to the superior general of the Congregation of the Sacred Hearts whose members had worked in the island kingdom as the sole Catholic missionary group since 1831.

Molokai, 27 May 1857
To the Very Reverend Euthyme [Rouchouze], Head of the Priests of the Sandwich [Islands],

Receive our greeting.

We, your brothers in the Lord, want to communicate to you our thoughts. Sixteen years have passed since we embraced Roman Catholicism, nevertheless, no priest has yet to come to live permanently among us. This is why we appeal to your heart.

Fr. Aubert [Bouillon, SS.CC.], or one of his companions, comes to see us once a year, the rest of the time we are without mass, confession, communion. There is no one who can administer the sacraments of Penance or Extreme Unction, no one who can teach our children.

We are more or less two hundred Christians in Molokai and there is a big gulf which separates us from our priests. We are hungry and there is no one who can feed our souls; we are thirsty and there is no one to refresh our hearts. There is no one to wash the blots of our consciences, no one to encourage us towards the good, no one to open the eyes of heretics and pagans, no one to defend our religion from the outrages made against it. This is why our compatriots persevere in their errors and that they say: When your priests establish themselves here to stay, we will convert. Thus, reverend Father, give us good and wise missionaries so that they may oppose the Calvinists and Mormons, strong missionaries so that they may climb the high mountains of our island.

Please receive, very respectable sir, our greeting and felicitations.

[Signed]

Annales de l'Association de la Propagation de la Foi (Lyon) (1857): 470–71.
Translated from the French version of the Hawaiian original.

74. Catholics on Maui Build a Church, 1865

Catholic-Protestant rivalry in Hawaii includes its humorous moments, as this excerpt from a letter reveals. Leonor Fouesnel, SS.CC. (d. 1902), was a Belgian priest serving on the island of Maui when the Catholics of Keanae sought to build a chapel for their village in the mid-1860s. This chapel still stands.

When there was question of building a new chapel at Wailua-Nui (Keanae), our Protestant neighbors had been working for two years on the erection of a new temple. They had a hard time getting the necessary material. There is no beach in this region and consequently no sand. Rocks abound, but the lime-boiled coral — as well as the sand — has to come from the sea. One has to dive for it as deep as six to ten feet.

So we gather our neophytes and tell them to get the necessary materials, sand and coral, so as not to delay the work of the two Brothers who would soon arrive to build their church. A day was chosen and set for all to go down together and begin the diving and hauling. But on the appointed day a fierce storm was raging and it was only four days later that the ocean calmed. All of our people went down armed with iron bars to loosen the coral. What a surprise greeted them when, coming to the assigned place, they found the shore heaped with coral.

Of course, they went to work with a will, and soon gathered coral enough to take care of the whole building. The Protestants looked on spellbound, but did not dare take the coral that seemed to belong to the Catholics. However, the next day they hurried down to gather what we had left behind. But (and I was the eye-witness to this) when they arrived at the shore, all at once the sea took to a sudden swelling and washed away the last vestiges of coral.

In the meantime our people had worked hard, and when all the coral was at last hauled to the place of construction we had a sufficient quantity to put up the walls. However, we were in need of some more coral in order to plaster the walls. So it was decided to go down again and this time to dive for the small amount we still needed. On the very day appointed and for the length of time necessary, the wonderful event related above repeated itself.

Again the Protestants hurried down to the shore early on the following morning, but once more huge waves rose and took back the remainder of the coral, leaving behind this time a huge quantity of white sand, unknown to that locality, for a distance of ten miles.

An old influential Hawaiian then warned his Protestant fellowmen: "Hands off! God has sent it not for us, but for the Catholics." And so, after the coral, we have been hauling sand a whole day.

This wonderful event had never taken place before and never happened afterwards. Of course, I do not want to see in it anything of a miracle, but I simply want to relate the bare facts I myself saw.

The Hawaiians of this district were simply wonderful in this enterprise. They not only gathered coral and sand with their bare hands, but as if in procession, the priest leading, the men with their wives and children went up into the mountains to saw and carry piece by piece the necessary wood for the construction of their church.

When Brothers Arsene and Charles arrived, it took only a short time to build the church, a memorial to which one and all had so generously contributed. For the entire enterprise was the work of human hands, save for two oxen and an old cart used to fetch rock and tree stumps. Finally the new chapel was ready and was blessed by Rev. Father Modest Favens, SS.CC., Provincial-Superior of the Sacred Hearts Fathers in Hawaii.

A couple of days later the good Brothers left and also the kind oxen. And, such wonderful service had these animals given, it was hard to part with them. Not a few women began to weep, while the willingness and strength of the good animals were extolled in the most tender Hawaiian eloquence, and the drivers of the oxen were told to be kind to the poor animals and by no means ever to whip them.

Letter of Father Leonor Fouesnel, SS.CC., 31 July 1865, in *Lettres Lithographiées* (1870), 255–61. Translated from the French.

75. Father Damien Describes the Life of a Missionary in Hawai'i, 1869

Famed for his later work on Moloka'i for those suffering with Hansen's disease, Blessed Damien De Veuster (1840–89) first arrived in Hawai'i in 1864 and labored as a missionary for thirty-five years. He describes for the superior general of his order, the Congregation of the Sacred Hearts, the weekly routine, the personal attitudes, and the challenge he faced in ministering to the native people who embraced Roman Catholicism.

From the depth of the solitude whither I have withdrawn for some days, in order to restore my physical and moral strength, I will try to execute my annual duty, rendering you an account of the mission which the Lord has entrusted to me.

In my previous letter, I gave you the details of our arrival to these beloved islands, of our ordination, likewise my installation on the great island of Hawaii. I was at first placed in a district near the great volcano, which I often had the chance to see. I myself witnessed certain sacrifices which a poor Kanac made to this ancient divinity, a day when I found myself with him on the edge of the crater; I took the opportunity to give him a little sermon about hell. In the month of January 1869, it was necessary to part company with my first neophytes, and this separation seemed to me more painful and sorrowful than leaving my own parents, because of the heartfelt affection which I felt for these dear Kanacs. Rev. Fr. Clément [Evrard], weak in temperament, could not accustom himself to the climate and to the great hardships of the district which had at first fallen to his lot. With the consent of His Grace, Msgr. [Louis] Maigret, we made an exchange. Fr. Clément took my post and I took his. It was the feastday of St. Joseph when I left for my new destination. We were now 32 miles from each other. On my first round, I was convinced that in order to serve all the different Christian communities of this huge district well, hardships will be very necessary; it took me six weeks to visit all of them. From the time of Rev. Fr. Joachim Maréchal, there have been 15 chapels built there with leaves of pala. Unfortunately, they all fell in decay; so that prayer gatherings nearly everywhere take place in Kanac huts. It is there, too, where the missionary must preach, receive confession, baptize, and sometimes say the Holy Mass, especially during Easter time.

Because this region has been without a priest since the death of Rev. Fr. Eustache [Maheu], *the brambles and thorns there cut off the head well above the good grain,* which our first missionaries had sown and cultivated there carefully. Heresy and idolatry have played havoc there. Nevertheless, next to these two great evils, I have the comfort of finding some good souls in all quarters of this district which is 24 miles in length. At the place whence I write you these lines, I have a church in a forest, built by our brethren, from the time of Fr. Eustache. It is beautiful inside: it has a vault supported by pillars, three altars, three chandeliers adorned with flowers made by the hands of the good Fr. Eustache himself; its modest steeple includes a bell. My little presbytery, although of leaves of pala on the outside, is rather suitable for the floor plan within; a study for work, a bedroom for me and my schoolmaster who lives with me, a little dining room as well as another little room for welcoming everyone, it is hardly exuberant. There is a small Christian community here which is progressing rather well. In the morning and evening, my Christians from the surrounding area regularly come to prayer. Those for whom the dwelling is more distant, *pray at home,* as they say, on rising and retiring, and do not come to church except on Sunday. On the great feasts like Easter and Christmas, if the weather is good, one comes from very far: on those days the church is too small. On the last feast of Easter, I had 30 adults to renew in the waters of holy baptism, and several apostates to reconcile. *It is good enough to encourage the poor missionary, and to make him long for his destiny like our dear brother students of Picpus.*

Next Sunday, I am going to a Christian community 1.5 miles from here. There are almost 100 Christians, with a Catholic school; the schoolmaster is paid 2 F[rancs] 50 C[entimes] a day by the government. Where shall I say Mass for these poor people? In the schoolhouse. And what is this schoolhouse? A little hut of straw, of which the entrance door is nothing but 4 feet in height; the roof is perhaps 10. The wind comes in from every side; it is at the point when sometimes, during the Holy Mass, the candles are suddenly extinguished. 40 pegs are set up simply, on which some planks are placed which I cover with a sheet, and that is it! From early in the morning, some Christians come to confess. Having neither chair nor confessional, I set myself up as I am able, to continue thus until 9 o'clock. Then, at the sound of a trumpet, which is nothing more than a big shell found on the shore, everyone comes in and the divine office begins. Nearly everyone has learned the prayers of Mass by heart; led by their prayer leader, they begin to recite them together aloud. At Mass, I usually preach on the gospel of the day, and at rosary, I explain the catechism. It is in these little chapels, my Very Reverend Father, that the most good is done. I have another Christian community of pretty near the same kind, where there is also a catholic school. But the difficulty is in reaching that post. There is no way to get there by land, and the sea is usually bad. I have been told that Rev. Fr. Eustache went there only twice a year. Because I love the Christians of that place very much, I wanted to go there to spend the first Sunday of last October. On Sunday, the sea was rather calm. Early in the morning, I went down to the sea to catch a small Kanac boat; it is simply a tree hollowed out inside. I took care to make an act of contrition before getting on. Leaving the sort of little harbor one finds there, we set out for the said community. Suddenly, the man who was steering cries out and tells me in Kanac: we are doomed. In fact, our canoe, at most half a meter wide, turns upside down, and there we had to swim. Fortunately, in my childhood I practiced a little. Because my two boatmen knew no more than I how to make the canoe right itself and emerge from the water, we had to return to port swimming with one hand, and pushing our boat full of water with the other. Long after some fears and difficulties, we reached the place whence we left. My things having been fastened in the boat at departure, I lost nothing. Only my beautiful little breviary which I loved so much, because it was complete and at the same time very light, was completely soaked with sea water, and now it is out of condition to be of use to me on the trip. That was enough for that day; and so I waited until the following week to set out for the mountain. On the fourth day of the trip, sometimes by horse, sometimes on foot, even after having swum across a small branch of the sea, I finally reached the goal so longed for. God gave me much comfort among the Christians who live there as if in a cloister, apart from the rest of humanity. All are baptized, with the exception of two or three. I arrived just in time to give holy baptism to an infant which was just born, and which departed immediately for heaven.

Permit me now, my Very Reverend Father, to lead you on to another point in my district; it is 15.6 miles from here. There has never been a chapel in that place. On my first visit, a good number of catechumens there received holy baptism. All I asked of them in recognition of the pardon which the good Lord granted them that day was that they build a little chapel. They promised, and they have kept their word. Since some of those among them are woodcutters, they went to the mountain and cut very beautiful trees for building, not some kind of hut, as all our Kanac chapels are, but a chapel entirely of wood cut by their own hands. Everything is ready; but who can erect the chapel with these materials in a suitable manner? A foreign carpenter costs too much here. Having chosen the best possible of my plans, I myself began the work with two Kanacs. When these poor people are directed, they do not lack in skill. Until now we have not been too unsuccessful, and last Tuesday we raised the frame. On the facade there is a cross two meters high. When I return from here, I hope to adorn the exterior with beautiful planks which our Kanacs have cut and carved themselves, and to finish the whole interior. A certain American, I hope, will be willing to buy me the windows; and we will have there a beautiful little chapel in the middle of a little Christian community no less beautiful. I thank the good Lord for this with all my heart.

Because my district is too large for only one priest, my intention is to prepare a residence in the part opposite that in which I usually reside. Of the kind which later, when new assistance comes for us, Monseigneur can give me a colleague and return me there less solitary. Awaiting him, my Very Reverend Father, I will go in turn to see Rev. Fr. Charles [Pouzot] at Hilo and Rev. Fr. Régis [Moncany] at Kaua. Pray, my Very Reverend Father, and *say prayers* on my behalf, poor missionary of 29 years, that God keep me safe amidst all these dangers to which I am exposed, and that I continue, to my final breath, to defend the cause of Our Divine Savior and of his spouse the Holy Roman Church.

I have the honor of being, etc.

F. Damien, priest, miss. of the Sandwich Islands

Damien De Veuster, SS.CC., 23 October 1869, in *Lettres Lithographiées* (1870), 274–80. Translated from the French.

76. Robert Louis Stevenson Defends the Reputation of Father Damien, 1900

After the death of Blessed Damien De Veuster, SS.CC., in 1889, Reverend Charles M. Hyde of Honolulu questioned the virtue of the "Leper Priest" of Moloka'i. Robert Louis Stevenson had visited the island and, upon reading Hyde's attack, penned this defense of the deceased priest. Stevenson's Open Letter *reveals the keen — and at times bitter — competition among Christian missionaries in the Hawaiian Islands in the nineteenth century. This same Hyde is portrayed in Stevenson's famous* Dr. Jekyl and Mr. Hyde.

I know that others of your colleagues look back on the inertia of your church, and the intrusive and decisive heroism of Damien, with something almost to be called remorse. I am sure it is so with yourself; I am persuaded your letter was inspired by a certain envy, not essentially ignoble, and the one human trait to be espied in that performance...

Your Church and Damien's were in Hawaii upon a rivalry to do well: to help, to edify, to set divine examples. You having (in one huge instance) failed, and Damien succeeded, I marvel it should not have occurred to you that you were doomed to silence; that when you had been outstripped in that high rivalry, and sat inglorious in the midst of your well-being, in your pleasant room — and Damien, crowned with glories and horrors, toiled and rooted in that pigstye of his under the cliffs of Kalawao — you, the elect, who would not, were the last man on earth to collect and propagate gossip on the volunteer who would and did.

I think I see you — for I try to see you in the flesh as I write these sentences — I think I see you leap at the word pigstye, a hyperbolical expression at the best. "He had no hand in the reforms," he was "a coarse, dirty man"; these were your own words; and you may think it possible that I am come to support you with fresh evidence. In a sense, it is even so. Damien has been too much depicted with a conventional halo and conventional features; so drawn by men who perhaps had not the eye to remark or the pen to express the individual; or who perhaps were only blinded and silenced by generous admiration, such as I partly envy for myself — such as you, if your soul were enlightened, would envy on your bended knees. It is the least defect of such a method of portraiture that it makes the path easy for the devil's advocate, and leaves for the misuse of the slander a considerable field of truth. For truth that is suppressed by friends is the readiest weapon of the enemy. The world, in your despite, may perhaps owe you something, if your letter be the means of substituting once for all a credible likeness for a wax abstraction. For, if that world at all remember you, on the day when Damien of Molokai shall be named Saint, it will be in virtue of one work: your letter to the Reverend H. B. Gage.

You may ask on what authority I speak. It was my inclement destiny to become acquainted, not with Damien, but with Dr. Hyde. When I visited the lazaretto, Damien was already in his resting grave. But such information as I have, I gathered on the spot in conversation with those who knew him well and long: some indeed who revered his memory; but others who had sparred and wrangled with him, who beheld him with no halo, who perhaps regarded him with small respect, and through whose unprepared and scarcely partial communications the plain, human features of the man shone on me convincingly.

> Robert Louis Stevenson, *Father Damien: An Open Letter to the Reverend Dr. Hyde of Honolulu* (Boston: Alfred Bartlett, 1900), 10, 11–13.

77. Dedication Speech for the School of the Sacred Hearts Sisters, 1909

Subsequent to the annexation of Hawai'i to the United States in 1898, differing national attitudes emerged among Catholics there, as expressed in these remarks of John A. Hughes (1860–1952), Irish-born member of the territorial legislature. Hughes delivered the dedicatory address at the opening of the convent school of the French-based Sisters of the Sacred Hearts at Kaimuku on 5 September 1909.

The inauguration of Catholicism in these islands was an event of great importance to Catholics, it was one of the most important in their history. Since then our church has made many notable movements, each of them standing out like milestones to mark our progress. There was the coming of the Brothers [of Mary, i.e., the Marianists] of St. Louis College and openings of their school, the arrival of the Sisters of St. Francis to devote their lives to the afflicted ones at Molokai and their children; the building of schools, churches and orphanage, all meeting the demands of the time and bearing willing testimony to what our church can accomplish in a land where men are free and despotism is unknown. And yet giving due credit for all the good that has been done, and to those that have done it I submit that the opening of this school, whilst not the most important, is the most progressive step Catholicism has yet taken in this Territory — pregressive [sic] because schools are primarily the hope of our country's life, the beacon light of a nation's progress. The opening of this school marks a new era along lines of noblest endeavor, for here, irrespective of creed, is imparted to all who desire, an education embracing the highest ideals, an education that not only fits our children for the duties and responsibilities of this life but also for that greater life that lies beyond the tomb...

On coming into this school you will note that the only banner that flies to the breeze is our country's flag, the Stars and Stripes, and it is right that it should be so, for in all earthly affairs there is no dual allegiance here. This is an American school, whose watchwords will be Faith and Fatherland — a faith whose fundamentals teach us to love our neighbor and our God, a patriotism that teaches us to love our country, to preserve its institutions, to keep our leaders honest, virtuous and true.

Hawaiian Star (Honolulu), 6 September 1909, 1, 3.

78. Father Joseph Cataldo, S.J., Reviews the History of the Church in Alaska, 1903

Veteran missionary Joseph M. Cataldo, S.J. (1839–1928), left his native Sicily to enter the Society of Jesus in 1852 and spent a lifetime among the native peoples of the United States. An impressive administrator, recruiter, and fund-raiser, Cataldo was also an accomplished linguist who mastered numerous native tongues. His attitudes toward non-Catholics reflect the highly competitive nature of missionary activity in that era.

It gives me pleasure to comply with your request to send you an account of our Alaska Mission, where I have been the last two years and where I spent fourteen months in 1896 and '97. I must premise that I have little free time for writing and that I am not skilled in writing English. However, your readers are welcome to the little I am able to do for you. Let me begin with a fact which will explain much of our work in this Mission.

Archbishop Seghers, you will recollect, first visited Alaska and then returned to get missionaries for the great field he saw before him and which had been entrusted to him by the Holy See. Could he have got the missionaries he asked for, the Church to-day would have splendid missions all over Alaska. Unfortunately the several Religious Orders he asked, including the Society, all answered, "Hominem non habeo" [I have no man], so the sects took possession of the most important places. They have at present forty or more missions as they are called, or government non-sectarian schools as they call them in public. In fact these are all bigoted establishments with boarding schools supported for the most part by government money. Our Society has eight missions in Upper Alaska, — Eagle, Nulato, Koserefsky, Kuskakwim, Akulurak, St. Michael's, Nome and Council. Eagle, Nome, and Council are mostly for whites; St. Michael's for both Eskimos and whites. I will give you an account of each mission...

II. Nulato, the highest place in the Yukon I ever reached — about 680 miles east of St. Michael's — is a very important mission, being the centre of many Ten'h Indian villages (Tihne), and is the door to the great Koyoukuk mines. Besides, it is the nearest place to the mouth of the Tanana River, on the shores of which several gold and copper mines have been discovered. On account of these mines there was last year a great influx of miners, and a railroad is about to be constructed to it from Cook's inlet. The village has a U.S. Post Office; one of our Fathers being postmaster. The Nulato Indians at St. Peter Claver's Mission, for this mission is under the protection of the Apostle of the negroes, number about 1500 and are all Catholics, or well disposed towards the Church, with the exception of a few Russian schismatics and Protestants. At Nulato itself there are about 150 Indians and thirty or forty whites, who unfortunately do not give edification to the Indians. However, even among these whites, there are conversions. The year before last we baptized six of them and they continue the practice of their religion, even there are those who are faithful to the Communion of Reparation on the First Friday of the month. Whilst I was among them some died a holy death. We have at Nulato two Fathers, two Brothers, and three Sisters of St. Anne, who teach a day school for the boys and girls of the village. One of the many difficulties here is the Ten'h language, the most difficult of all the twelve languages we have been obliged to study in the Rocky Mountains and Alaska.

III. Koserefsky on the Yukon, 245 miles below Nulato, is a little village containing about two hundred Ten'h Indians, and some few Eskimos, this being the dividing line between Ten'h and Eskimos. Here we have a mission called "The Holy Cross Mission." It has a boarding day-school, the boarders coming from different villages below (Eskimos), and from above (Ten'h). There are about one hundred pupils, some thirty-five being day-scholars. Of the boarders, the boys live in our house, the girls in the Sisters' house. These Sisters belong to the congregation of St. Anne and are seven in number. The boarders, both boys and girls, compare well with our Indian boys in the boarding schools of the Rocky Mountains, in learning and piety. The teachers, the Brothers as well as the Sisters, praise highly their pupils and some are enthusiastic about them. These pupils they claim are "the best in the world" and this not only in school, but also as workers in the house, on the little farm, in the saw mill, in building log-houses, in taking care of cattle, horses, etc. They become good singers in school and in the church and some of the girls learn to play the organ very well. This Mission has wonderfully improved spiritually and materially since I was there six years ago on a visitation. Besides the flower garden and the vegetable garden, which have attracted the admiration of a number of visitors going up and down the river in the steamboats, they now raise oats and barley, and hay enough to support a dozen head of cattle and some horses. This mission takes care of 1200 Indians and Eskimos and employs three Fathers and five Brothers. As at Nulato there is a Post Office[,] one of Ours being the Postmaster. If we could get twelve strong Brothers who understand farming, the great problem of supporting the children, who number from one to two hundred, would be solved in less than three years. The same is true for the Mission of St. Peter Claver at Nulato, its climate and soil is as good for farming as those of Koserefsky...

VII. Nome, about fifteen miles north of Cape Nome, is a little town of whites, made up of frame buildings in this respect like many of our Eastern towns. Its population is about three thousand in winter and six or seven thousand in the summer. It was begun in 1899 when gold was found on the sea coast, and the next year nearly all the tents were replaced by frame buildings. As among these miners there were many Catholics from Montana, Idaho, and Washington, they asked for a Father several times and with insistence. For some reason or other no resident priest could be obtained till the summer of 1901, when a Father of the Society [of Jesus] from California arrived and at once began to build a church and residence. Another Father was sent in September, and before Christmas they had finished the church and residence. The church has a seating capacity of 350, has a high spire with a large cross, which has attached to it nine electric lights. It is visible in the darkest nights twenty miles away and has been the means of saving many a miner's life during our long winter nights. It is called by the Eskimos the "White-man-star, that saves the lives of lost people." During the winter of 1902 the Fathers organized the choir, the Ladies' Altar Society, and the Devotions for the First Fridays and the Communion of Reparation. At Easter they had one hundred communions. In July 1902 four Sisters of Providence and Charity came from Montreal and began taking care of the sick, till they had in August their own Hospital. Here they have been doing good work for the souls as well as the bodies of the poor miners, many of whom meet with accidents in the mines. In July of that year Father Devine of the Canadian Mission, who had come as a missionary to Alaska, was appointed to take care of the people in the little towns about Nome, as Teller, Goldrun, Candle, Solomon, Council, etc. In the beginning of November the last steamer left Nome for Seattle, and the people settled down into winter quarters. We then re-organized the choir, the Altar Society, and also established a young men's club, composed of good Catholics and called the Nome Young Men's Institute. We also began a course of lectures on Sunday evening which were concluded by Benediction of the Blessed Sacrament. God blessed our work and we reaped much fruit. At Christmas the midnight Mass was so well attended that the church was packed and many could not get in at all. Some forty received Communion at this Mass and all remained for the second Mass of thanksgiving. During Lent several marriages were made valid *coram Ecclesia,* and at Easter we had more than a hundred and fifty Communions. We heard many confessions, fifty of them being those who had not approached the Sacraments for from five to forty-five years. One of them went about praising and thanking God for the happiness he felt in being reconciled to God, and induced his friends to follow his example, promising them the same peace he had experienced. Besides, some of the miners, who had not been Catholics, were converted, baptized and received their first Communion, two of whom were children of Protestant preachers. The following fact will show how firm was their conviction and how sincere their conversion. A person of some standing in society having heard of the conversion of these children of the Protestant minister, sought one of them out, and said that bad news was being circulated in town about him, that it must be slander and that he had come to him to learn the truth. The convert replied,

"I know what you mean. They say that I have been converted to the Catholic Church; well, there is no slander, it is the truth and I am proud of it and I will tell you more. Yesterday I received my First Communion and I feel such peace and happiness as I never felt before and could never have imagined possible."

"Such being the case," replied the gentleman, "we sever all relations and I shall have nothing more to do with you." And so it really happened...

In instructing these sick patients we took occasion to instruct their relatives and friends who visited them, and thus we had a little school of twenty Eskimos. One difficulty we had was the language. Of course very little could be done in English and they did not understand my Eskimo Language, which I had learned five years before and had almost forgotten. They could not even understand what I read from my old books, because this Nome dialect — though the same language — is as different from the Akulurak dialect, the one which I had learned, as French from Latin. Hence I had to learn with the help of an interpreter the Nome dialect and to translate the prayers and the catechism. In this way we were able after some weeks to have a regular school in both English and Eskimo, having the first reader, the prayers and the catechism in both languages. We were going on pretty well, new pupils came to school and a good many came to the church on Sundays, when the preachers grew alarmed. They started meetings, called in white preachers from their so-called missions — Eskimo preachers and squaw-men preachers — held camp meetings, etc. and forbade the Eskimos to enter our church or come to our school. Those who knew us remained firm in their belief and asked to be baptized; but we could get no more of these poor Eskimos to come as they were afraid of the preachers. Before I left I had the consolation of giving first Holy Communion to three Eskimo adults, the first Eskimos to receive Holy

Communion in Nome. They received our Lord with great devotion. I gave my little knowledge of their language to Father [Bellarmine] Lafortune, who was to remain in Alaska, and who is very zealous. He continues the school, and we hope little by little, our Lord will open the way for us to establish an Eskimo Mission somewhere near Nome...

Letter, Joseph Cataldo, S.J., 17 November 1903, published in "Alaska," *Woodstock Letters* 33 (1904): 28–35.

79. Memoirs of a Missionary about Students at Holy Cross Mission, Alaska, 1907

The ordinary joys and challenges of missionary life in Alaska in the late nineteenth century emerge in these reminiscences of Jesuit priest Aloysius Parodi (1835–1928). The Alaska mission of the Jesuits grew out of the missionary work of their Turin Province in the Northwest and in California. Parodi served eight years in Alaska, and this section of his memoirs describes the talents of a native convert at Holy Cross Mission, located on the Yukon River.

There was also a young indian at the school of Holy Cross who was really a genius, his name was John. One day he saw a violing [*sic*] printed in a catalogue. He told F. [Paschal] Tosi that he thought he could play that instrument. F. Tosi knew the boy and sent to San Francisco for a violin. The violin came and in a few days John was playing the violin like a professor. Then John saw a picture of a modern harp. He told F. Tosi, and F. Tosi sent for the harp, and John could play the harp like a neapolitan [*sic*]. F. [William] Judge had brought a grinding organ along...John's greatest affliction was the pagan condition of his father. F. [Aloysius] Robaut was going after him, and John was praying and receiving often Holy Communion for his father's conversion, but it was of no use. After John's death, F. Robaut was not in need of going after his father, but he came after F. Robaut, and in a short time he was made Catholic. It is not the first time that children have been the salvation of their parents. John had a great influence in the conversion of his sister Tatiana...John's death has been a great loss for Holy Cross Mission. He had been the right arm of F. [Rafael] Crimont, helping him in the house, in the Church, in the garden, in the next village called Koziorefski, and every where and in every thing. John was acolite [*sic*] in the Church, serving every morning at F. Crimont's mass wearing the cassok [*sic*] and surplice, and with the cassok [*sic*] on he was buried by F. Crimont. Painting, carving, fixing cloks [*sic*], transcribing by lithography hundreds and hundreds [of] copies of F. Robaut Prayers and songs in the eskimo language, were John's delight. He was the only helper of F. Crimont in preparing the magic lantern apparatus. John's glory was shining at exhibitions and entertainments. Strangers were moved to tears hearing little children talking and singing in english, and the delightful sweet strains of

John's violing [*sic*], playing like a disciple of Paganini, whilst Tatiana, a school girl, was playing the organ.

"Reminiscences and Reflections of Rev. Al. Parodi, S.J.," 3 October 1907, 41–42; Jesuit Oregon Province Archives, Gonzaga University, Spokane. Printed by permission.

80. Mother Amadeus Dunne, O.S.U., Raises Funds for the Ursuline Sisters in Alaska, ca. 1912

This excerpt from a begging letter depicts the hardships the Ursuline Sisters faced in Alaska early in the twentieth century. Mother Amadeus of the Heart of Jesus Dunne (1846–1919) wrote to supporters in 1912 to appeal for funds to continue Ursuline efforts. Beginning in the 1880s in Montana, Dunne ad-ministered far-flung missionary efforts to provide native peoples with schools adjacent to Jesuit church stations.

As far back as 1905, I had sent three of my nuns from Montana into the in-terior of Alaska, and there had they been laboring unknown to all but God, where a tiny stream, meandering away from the known world, bends for the 48th time in its sluggish course from the old Yukon to the Kwemeluk. Ab-solutely unknown they were, for St. Mary's Mission becomes conscious of the outer world only when the "St. Joseph," a tiny boat, built and manned by the Rev. Jesuit Fathers, drops down upon it in July or August bringing the year's supply of provisions. The coming of the boat is the epoch making event and here where they cannot be reached by telegraph or telephone, and where mail comes only when some friendly indian brings it, do the Rev. Jesuit Fathers and the Ursulines weave out the mysterious design of Mission life — the pattern whose beauty no man shall see till the Master hand shall stop the loom and reverse the web. Eight months of the year does the river be frozen, and the snow heap up, while the children lead their busy school life, and the parents trap the Walaerine and fox and descend beneath the snow into their subterranean dwellings.

The Innuits have well defined customs from which they may not depart, and one of these, which makes education difficult is this: the parent may not correct or punish the child. Hence our little ones come to the convent with a great idea of their importance, and with their native stubbornness weighted with years of inherited formalism and it requires wisdom and patience, and all the power of convent discipline to train these little wild ones of the snow. But when the work is done, and it is done, day by day, thank God! and we see the little ones joyously studying and plying the useful arts of housewifery, and sitting down with us every morning to the Holy table, and stealing into the chapel for silent talks with our sacramental Lord, then does the cold seem less cold, the solitude, the privations less deep, less heavy . . .

You know then dear friend, how as Provincial of our order in the North of the United States, I had in 1905 sent three sisters to St. Mary's Mission, and how in 1908 I had opened a house with three more at St. Michael's — Then how in 1910 I was sent as her Delegate by our Mother General in Rome to Alaska "The great country" there to live and there to die, and how, after a most cold and stormy winter at St. Michael's, your dear charity nailed the wind rocked cabin "St. Ursula's by the Sea" and made it habitable and beautiful in the radiance of brother love — and ah! how the little home now hangs thoughts of you! But, pursuant of my duty I longed to see our nuns down the Akularak. Yes, I had long desired to visit the blessed spot amid the igloos. At last the opportunity came with the "St. Joseph" and I read the angel written history of my first missionaries, confirming them in their blissful, salient purpose, "He who tholes [*sic*] overcomes" — whilst I myself tasted the sweetness of the deep solitude, the utter unworldiness. I had not done so long, when a dispatch from our Prefect Apostolic called me away to open a school at Valdez. It was harder to leave St. Mary's than it had been to reach it. A little three horse power gasoline launch carried us up the winding Akularak, to what our Indians call the "Quislok" or old river — probably the original channel of the mighty stream. But when we reached this point of the Yukon delta the waves were so high and the sudden storm was travelling so fast that our tiny boat could not venture across so we faced about and returned to the Mission making it vocal with joy of nuns and children to see us so soon again. And there we were compelled to await five days the abating of the storm. But this time we crossed the "Quislok" and sped down the "Apenkar" to the "Quispak" or Yukon. The trip had been a long one, and as we glided up the giant stream, the sun just dipped below the horizon to arise ere we had missed it in crimson splendor. Look upon the scene with me, dear friend! The great and glowing silent night with the almost midnight sun trailing its glory along the waters edge; the stalking curlew, the leaping porpoise, the splendor of the Arctic light, and a little boat, the "St. Mary" is speeding along bearing two Jesuits and two Ursulines, and as we cross, a weird voice calls out from across the broad world of water: "Kalekat! Kalekat!["] (Some writing! Some writing!) It was one of our school boys who was speeding down the river to the Mission, as we sped up away from it. He was in his fishing smack and by his voice and his gestures we discovered that he had some Mail! Some Mail! Some Mail! . . .

Letter, Sr. Mary Amadeus of the Heart of Jesus, Superior of the Ursulines of Alaska, St. Michael, Alaska, 1912; Ursuline Archives, Ursuline Centre, Great Falls, Mont. Printed by permission.

81. A Native Alaskan Writes His Bishop about the Eskimo Deacon Program, 1970

Conditions long associated with frontier circumstances — vast distances and scarcity of clergy — have persisted in Alaska. To cope with these challenges,

Bishops Francis D. Gleeson, S.J., and Robert Whelan, S.J., instituted the Eskimo Deacon Program, which they adapted to the circumstances in their Alaskan dioceses. One candidate, Michael Nayagak (1900–1975), expresses his perception of the training and its goals.

Oct. 31, 1970

Robert L. Whalen [*sic*], S.J.
Bishop of Fairbanks

Dear Robert L. Whalen, S.J.

I was so grateful in receiving your letter. Since you've been handling this letter, I'll always keep it all the time.

Ever since I got back from Bethel, I've been looking forward to seeing you all again in Dec[ember].

"When I think of all the things we have to learn it seems real hard for me, but if God helps me I'll probably understand most of it."

I can't seem to find a rightful way to lead people. But be assured that I'll be of help to you.

Since I started [to] get this kind of schooling, I seem to be a guy that has his eyes closed. But I will always follow you until our meeting last [*sic*].

"Ever since I started working in the Church, even though I have never seen our Popes, I try my best to help them all I can. It seems that I had known all along that I'd be working to be a deacon."

Later on, we'll probably find a better leading of the people. And some day, a guy who has mind will find it and never forget it [*sic*].

You'll probably won't understand it, but I'm saying these the best I can.

When you say Mass, please include us in your prayers that we may help God in the right way.

Sincerely Yours in Christ
Michael Nayagak

•

December 18, 1970

Dear Reverent Whelen [*sic*],

I was most happy to have received a very nice and thoughtful Christmas card which you sent.

It makes us happy that you remember us in your daily prayers. That brings good and happy thoughts to us.

I am working very fine as a deacon here, and I will continue to put my heart into the work, that is joyous to me. With a thought of helping our church, I have been giving holy communion to the people, and also along with our parish priest, Father Jacobson.

I hope to see you in the up coming meeting, at Bethel.

To me, since I've been, or started giving the holy communion, the people have been behaving much better. And it seems there is a calm change in them.

I know that with your help, there will be more people won over to, or come closer to God, and I know this will be, if we keep up work. And I hope the other fellow deacons will put their whole heart into their work, and I want them to.

On behalf of the Chevak people, I would like to say, that we will all try to make Christmas a real joyous and peaceful time.

I will remember you in my prayers and I am sure that is a well brought up Christmas gift.

May God bless you dearly,
Michael Nayagak

Michael Nayagak to Robert L. Whelan, S.J., 31 October 1970 and 18 December 1970, Chevak, Alaska; Archives of the Diocese of Fairbanks, Alaska. Printed by permission.

Part 6

THE SOUTHWEST

Introduction

Spanish colonial expansion in the seventeenth century introduced the first permanent Catholic institutions in Texas, New Mexico, and Arizona. Missions to native peoples and settlements of Spanish-speaking Catholics extended Spain's empire north from Mexico and west from the Mississippi Valley. By 1789, when George Washington assumed the presidency of the United States, Catholics had lived a century and a half in the southwestern corner of the continent. Franciscans and Jesuits had established missions with varying degrees of success in southern Arizona; along the Rio Grande from Isleta and El Paso up to Santa Fe; in eastern Texas, inland from Matagorda Bay; and around San Antonio. Settlers had founded communities in these same regions, defended by a series of *presidios* (forts) against attacks from indigenous peoples such as Apaches and Comanches.

With the secularization of the missions between 1794 and the early 1830s and with Mexico's independence in 1821, few clergy were available to replace the withdrawing Spanish Franciscans, particularly in the more heavily settled region of New Mexico. Folk Catholicism assumed an increasing importance and included local religious art, hymns and prayers, religious dramas or plays such as *Los Pastores* and *Las Posadas*, and pious associations of which the most famous was the Penitentes (the Confraternity of Our Lord and Father Jesus the Nazarene). Bishops of Durango had the greatest success in training a native clergy for New Mexico in the first half of the nineteenth century. These priests, such as Antonio José Martínez of the pueblo of Taos, served their parishes devotedly and supported the republican ideals of the Mexican nation.

Subsequent to conquest by the United States, Jean Baptiste Lamy arrived as the first vicar apostolic of Santa Fe in 1851 and commenced a half-century of French clerical reform of New Mexican Catholicism. Lamy recruited in his native France for priests and sisters, as well as for finances. Under his guidance, Santa Fe developed into an archdiocese with church-run schools, hospitals, and orphanages, and religious who included the Sisters of Loretto, Sisters of Charity of Cincinnati, Christian Brothers, and Jesuits. Lamy and his vicar, Joseph P. Machebeuf, clashed with Padre Martínez and the native-born clergy over a variety of the changes, particularly Lamy's insistence on collecting tithes from an impoverished laity. In his determination to assert his authority and to make the changes he deemed necessary, Lamy suspended several of these clerics and excommunicated Martínez.

Lamy's responsibilities also included the territory of Arizona, to which in 1866 he dispatched a trusted French priest, Jean Baptiste Salpointe, who established himself in Tucson, the largest Catholic settlement. The Holy See created Arizona as a vicariate apostolic in 1868, and Salpointe was the first of three French clerics who served as ordinaries until 1922. Salpointe recruited priests from France, established parishes, opened schools with the aid of the Sisters of St. Joseph of Carondelet, and succeeded Lamy as archbishop of Santa Fe. Upon his retirement in 1891, he returned to Tucson and wrote his valuable history of the church in the Southwest, *Soldiers of the Cross,* which appeared only days before his death in 1898.

As in New Mexico and Arizona, the faith of Spanish-speaking Catholicism in Texas relied upon a handful of priests and on vibrant popular religious devotions of a committed laity. Few Mexican priests were available to serve the Tejanos in settlements, particularly after Texas achieved independence in 1836. Though the Holy See named John Timon, C.M., as prefect apostolic in 1840, he remained in Missouri, and his assistant or vice prefect, Jean-Marie Odin, C.M., attended to Texas for the next twenty-one years, during which time he supported the deeply rooted Hispanic Catholicism. The vicariate evolved into the Diocese of Galveston in 1847, with Odin as first bishop, though he lost the services of his fellow Vincentians that same year.

Like Lamy and Salpointe, Odin recruited priests and religious from Europe and elsewhere to serve the Tejano Catholics, as well as immigrants attracted to the developing colonies in the fertile valleys of south Texas. Odin supervised the expansion of Catholic churches and schools among Poles, Belgians, Germans, French, Swiss, Czechs, Spaniards, and Irish in settlements such as New Braunfels, Fredericksburg, San Patricio de Hibernia, and Panna Maria, the first Polish community in the United States. The Oblates of Mary Immaculate from Montreal successfully established themselves in the diocese in 1852, and their most famed member was Pierre-Fourrier Parisot, author of *Reminiscences of a Texas Missionary.* Ursuline Sisters from New Orleans and Sisters of the Incarnate Word responded to Odin's appeals, as did Marianists, Jesuits, Franciscans, Benedictines, Cistercians, and others.

When Odin was named archbishop of New Orleans, his successor, Claude Marie Dubuis, assumed leadership of a diocese which encompassed approximately 100,000 to 125,000 Catholics served by forty-six priests. Odin had supervised the establishment of schools, academies, a seminary, and a college, as well as brought the total number of parishes to forty-five. Continued Catholic growth necessitated the creation in 1874 of the See of San Antonio and the Vicariates of Brownsville and Corpus Christi, and in 1890 the Diocese of Dallas. Nicholas A. Gallagher replaced Dubuis in Galveston, first as administrator and later as bishop. During his tenure, 1882–1918, Gallagher steadily asserted English-speaking leadership in place of the French priests and religious. In 1910, however, revolution south of the border forced thousands of Mexicans to enter Texas, and they vastly increased the Spanish-speaking Catholic population. Not until 1970, however, was a Tejano ordained to the episcopacy, when Patricio K. Flores became an auxiliary bishop of San Antonio. Since then he was named bishop of El Paso in 1978, and the following year he was promoted to the archbishopric of San Antonio.

Hispanic Traditions

82. Tejanos Celebrate the Feast of Our Lady of Guadalupe, 1841

In his travels across Texas in the 1840s, Jean-Marie Odin, C.M., reported sympathetically to his superiors in Paris on the piety of Mexican Catholics. In this letter, Odin notes with appreciation the festivities commemorating the feast of Our Lady of Guadalupe in San Antonio in 1841.

On the 12th of December, the feast of Our Lady of Guadaloupe [*sic*], the patroness of Mexico, and of all the Spanish Colonies, the inhabitants of San Antonio, who, in more prosperous times, solemnized this day with great rejoicings, felt their ancient zeal for the veneration of Mary revived in seeing their church restored. A good old man, together with some of his friends, wished to bear the principal part of the expenses of the feast; they purchased a hundred and fifty pounds of powder, borrowed all the pieces of cloth they could procure, whilst the women, on their part, lent with emulation their most valuable ornaments for the decoration of their temple.

The image of Our Lady, loaded with all the necklaces and jewellery [*sic*] of the town, was placed upon a bier elegantly adorned. At three o'clock in the afternoon the cannons and bells were heard: this was the hour of the first vespers. A numerous procession was immediately in motion: young girls dressed in white, with torches or *bouquets* of flowers in their hands, surrounded the banner of the Queen of virgins; then came the statue of Mary, raised upon a bier borne by four young persons, and in their train followed the women and men of the city. Sixty of the militia escorted the procession with their arms, which they discharged continually. At eight o'clock in the evening all the town was illuminated; enormous bonfires lighted the two great squares in the middle of which the church of San Antonio rises. We then came forth again from the sanctuary, to the sound of the bells and cannon, with the cross, the banner, and the image of Our Lady of Guadaloupe, and made the circuit of the squares, reciting the rosary, and singing canticles in honor of the mother

Wedding Procession at San Jose, New Mexico, circa 1885.

Credit: The Huntington Library, San Marino, Calif. Reproduced by permission.

of God. It was ten o'clock when we re-entered the church. Perfect order prevailed, and I confess that I have seen few processions more edifying. Besides the inhabitants of the town, we had at the ceremony all the Mexicans that reside along the river, together with a considerable number of Americans, that had come from Austin and from other different countries.

Jean-Marie Odin to Jean-Baptiste Étienne, 7 February 1842, in *United States Catholic Magazine and Monthly Review* 3 (October 1844): 729.

83. Padre Antonio Martínez of Taos Preaches on the Fourth of July, 1860

While better remembered for his conflict with Bishop Jean B. Lamy, Padre Antonio José Martínez (1793–1867) was an avid patriot of Mexico and, after the conquest in 1846, of the United States. The republican ideals of both governments attracted the praise of the long-time pastor of Taos, New Mexico.

This text from the Book of Proverbs [8:16], my brothers, my fellow Taoseños, my listeners, offers a topic for our celebration of the anniversary of the glorious independence of the United States of North America, for on the Fourth of July in the year of the Lord 1776, they became independent of Great Britain. The exalted wisdom of God, universal cause of all that exists, preserver and absolute ruler, inspires legislators and rulers to do what will be effective in decreeing justice, effective in declaring with certitude the form of government in which his rational creatures may choose for themselves for the purpose of attaining the honorable goals of society. [Those goals] are to live tranquilly in peace and quiet, to love, help, and protect one another, and to walk together some steps along the pathway of justice. From these traits indeed derives the happiness of all people in general and of each people in particular.

This it was that stood as principle on that aforementioned day, the Fourth of July in North America, for the Hero of Independence, the great Washington, a man worthy of eternal remembrance. This hero, whose wisdom serves as a standard...which in imitation of the United States achieved her independence, liberating herself from Spain, though she never consolidated herself due to the lack of an outstanding genius like our hero in [North] America. But what am I saying? This triumph was meant not only for our Republic and the Mexican Republic but for all the societies in the world, for wherever they might be, to serve as an example; they long for this beloved liberty, many of them have tried to throw off the yoke of the monarchies, and some successfully have thrown it off.

Yes, my fellow citizens of the District [of Taos] and my beloved fellow-countrymen: the Fourth of July of the Year of the Lord 1776, that remarkable moment, just eighty-four years ago today, there dawned in this America of the North the triumphant, happy day, full of rejoicing for the population because they heard the proud cry of liberty, of independence, and of union...

From the same constitution has come spiritual prosperity, since one of the fundamental bases of the constitution is the acknowledgment of freedom of thought, of speech, of writing, and of communicating one's notions to the public so that communities can study and adopt a religion according to the dictates of their own consciences. Do you suppose this achievement does not amount to much? Indeed, it is of utmost importance not only to our North American republic but also to the other nations of the globe that have followed the example of this government and established tolerance of religions since they have calmed those disastrous wars that fanaticism creates, wars that have drowned societies and battlefields in blood. So as to cause humankind even greater terror, in those dark and shadowy times the tribunal of the Holy Office of the Inquisition arose, along with some volunteer armies called crusaders, incited by the cruelest and most rigid fanaticism. But after this hydra, this destroyer of humanity, had sacrificed millions of inhabitants in the whole of Europe, the most cultured part of the world, their rulers took the idea of liberty [of religion] from us and have established it all over the world, making it the very wellspring [of freedom]. All these triumphs, my brothers of the audience, are the outcomes of liberty and tolerance: such an idea doubtless our great hero Washington deduced from the sacred scriptures, which preach tolerance of cults in various places...

This supreme policy concerning religious toleration, my brothers in the audience, this supreme policy, I repeat, caused by the emigration of foreigners to populate those vast stretches, formerly deserted, in such numbers that with them and the natural population increase, from the thirteen states of the union of the original era, at this date there are upwards of thirty quite populous states as well as several territories. For the love of liberty and religious toleration brings peace with it along with other benefits that logically ensue when they are animated by the philosophical spirit. Industry and the cultivation of the fields through agriculture and other labors, as well as the new advances in mechanical and liberal arts, give day by day new growth to the prosperity of the nation, to its greatness and its wealth.

The liberality and justice of our government has put an end to the cruel and tyrannical laws which prevailed in former times and are perhaps even now characteristic in certain monarchical governments, laws that decreed that some crimes were all-embracing. But in our system of government, those laws are done away with, laws whereby the crimes of the forebears and degrading penalties punish even the children and other descendants. In our government, by contrast, as is right, [only] the perpetrators are responsible for their crimes, and no penalty descends from the person who commits the crime...

The little I have said, kind listeners, about the triumph of our liberty, independence, and union, will please the good attitude of this illustrious gathering that has celebrated this holiday; and let me conclude by saying that in the republic of North America, we are its happy citizens for having a supreme government that is just, wise, liberal, and generous. We are happy because of its judges and writers, who fulfill the duties of justice fairly, giving to all what is due them; happy because of the industry of all classes of workmen, so that we can live in abundant prosperity; happy because we live in peace, harmony, and mutual cooperation in our contractual obligations and in our other ordered relationships. For all this, long live our hero, the immortal Washintong [*sic*]! Long live the great government of the United States, sustaining the happiness of its peoples! And long live God, who receives the homage of adoration of these citizens in every appropriate and honorable manner in which they offer it.

Reverend Antonio José Martínez, Fourth of July 1860 sermon, quoted in *New Mexican Spanish Religious Oratory*, ed. Thomas J. Steele, S.J. (Albuquerque: University of New Mexico Press, 1997), 81, 83, 85, 87. Translated from the Spanish. Printed by permission.

84. Missionaries Visit Tucson and Mission San Xavier del Bac, 1864

The chronic shortage of priests and religious marked the frontier era of the church, as revealed in this description of the 1864 visit to Tucson of two Jesuits, Reverends Aloysius Bosco and Charles Messea, S.J. The response of the Indians to the arrival of the priests reveals the persistence of religious practice despite the absence of clergy.

Tucson is a pretty large town, inhabited by Mexicans with a few companies of United States' soldiers and a few American traders. There is a large Catholic church under construction, commenced by an Italian Priest now absent. We expect the Bishop in a few days.

San Xavier del Bac is a beautiful place, on high ground. The church is a magnificent building in all its proportions, in the form of a Latin cross, of bricks and cement, surmounted by a cupola of masonry. The roof is not of frame, but a vault plastered over with coarse cement. The interior is decorated with statues in good preservation. The five altars all gilt stucco-work. The pavement is a kind of Venetian pavement; the architecture is beautiful, in the style of Moorish barocco [*sic*]. Our Fathers attended the mission up to the time of the suppression. The last Father was Fr. Ignatius Espinola, as appears from the baptismal record. The convent is in ruins. But all the damage done to the church and house was done not by Indians, but by Whites, in the time of the war between the Americans and Mexicans. The church was formerly exceedingly rich. Now there remain only two silver candlesticks, two pixes, three chalices, and a few other trifles. A few yards from the church there is a field of seven acres belonging to the mission, well irrigated.

At the arrival of the Fathers, the Indians, Catholics and even Protestants, were evidently delighted. As soon as the Papagos Indians saw us coming, they ran to the two towers of the church, and set to ringing the seven bells with all their might, as if the village was on fire. We went to the church to thank God, and recited the Rosary with the Indians. The next day we sang the *Te Deum*, and gave Benediction. A good number of the Indians come to Mass every day, and sing canticles in Spanish.

The Papagos number from 10- to 14,000, though not all Christians. The Pimas Indians are Gentiles, with a few exceptions: they number 6,000. The Maricopas are about 2,000. You see that the field is great. These Indians are good, industrious and docile, and treat us with cordial kindness. If the Bishop gives us Tucson, two Fathers and a Brother can live very well.

Extract of a letter of Rev. Burchard Villiger, S.J., to Rev. Felix Sopranis, S.J., in "Journey of Fathers Messea and Bosco," *Letters and Notices* 2 (April 1864): 144–45.

85. Journey of the Sisters of St. Joseph of Carondelet to Tucson, 1870

The contrasts between urban life in St. Louis and frontier conditions in Arizona emerge in this journal kept to document the trip of seven Sisters of St. Joseph of Carondelet in 1870. Sister Monica Corrigan, C.S.J., reveals the religious beliefs that sustained these women and enabled them to undertake a school in Tucson, which was then a largely Spanish-speaking town.

Before leaving Carondelet, I promised to write a "Journal" of our trip to Arizona. It seems to me that the fulfillment of this promise is almost out of date. You know, we had scarcely time to brush the dust off our habits before opening school, consequently I was obliged to defer writing the events of our trip until vacation...

Saturday, May 7, 1870, Leaving San Diego

The carriage was too small for all to ride inside, consequently one was obliged to ride outside with the driver. Sister Ambrosia volunteered to make the great act of mortification and humility. It is beyond description what she suffered in riding 200 miles in a country like this, without protection from the rays of a tropical sun. Yet, poor sister did this.

About 10 o'clock we passed a white post that marks the southwest boundary of the United States. We dropped a few tears at the sight of it, then entered Lower California. At noon we halted and took lunch in a stable 12 miles from San Diego. Sister Maximus and I went in search of gold; seeing quantities of it, we proposed getting a sack and filling it. Just think, a sack of gold! — but we soon learned from experience that "all is not gold that glitters."

We camped after sunset, at the foot of a mountain; made some tea, and took our supper off a rock. All were cheerful. We wished Reverend Mother could see us at supper. After offering thanks to the Giver of all good, we retired to rest — Mother, Sister Euphrasia and Martha under the wagon, others inside where there was room for only two to lie down.

Sister Euphrasia and I sat in a corner and tried to sleep. We had scarcely closed our eyes when the wolves began to howl about us. We feared they would consume our little store of provisions and thus let us perish in the wilderness; but driver told us not to fear. During the night Sister Euphrasia was startled from her sleep by one of the horses licking her face. She screamed fearfully, and we concluded she was a prey to the wolves.

Next morning, May 8th, feast of the Patronage of our Holy Father St. Joseph, we were determined to celebrate it the best way we could. After offering up our prayers, we formed a procession, going in advance of the wagon — Mother walking in front, bearing a Spanish lily in her hand. We followed in solemn order and imagined ourselves in Egypt with St. Joseph as leader.

Sister Euphrasia Marin, C.S.J., with Pima students from the fancy-work class. Note the contrasting student work: blankets from Native American culture and lace work from Euro-American culture. Saint John the Baptist Indian School, Komatke, Arizona Territory, circa 1910.

Credit: Guadalupe Cota Collection, Archives of the Los Angeles Province, Carondelet Center, Sisters of Saint Joseph of Carondelet, Los Angeles. Reproduced by permission.

Ranchers Propose Marriage

At noon we came to a cool, shady place in which we rested. The ranch-man (a person who keeps refreshments, stable feed, etc. on the western plains), invited us to dinner. He offered us a good meal of all we could desire. There were several ranch-men there from neighboring stations, but no women. There are few women in this country. After dinner they became very sociable. We retired to the stable where our driver and only protector was, and they followed. Some of them proposed marriage to us, saying we would do better by accepting the offer than by going to Tucson, for we would be all massacred by the Indians. The simplicity and earnestness with which they spoke put indignation out of the question, as it was evident that they meant no insult, but our good. They were all native Americans. For that afternoon we had amusement enough.

We then resumed our journey. That evening we camped in a very damp place, made some tea, the only beverage we had. We then offered up our evening prayers and retired to rest. Mother, Sister Ambrosia, Maximus and

I mounted a rock; the others went to the wagon. The night was very cold. I think there was frost.

We had only one blanket among the seven of us. Sister Martha and I had only summer shawls; the others were fortunate enough to have brought their winter ones along. Yet, we all kept up good spirits, being convinced that we were doing the Divine Will. We were much fatigued and though hard the bed and cold the night, we soon fell asleep...

May 26, 1870

When having passed unharmed through the most dangerous portion of our route, we returned fervent, heartfelt thanks to our good God for our preservation. After refreshing ourselves with a cup of coffee, we continued until within 15 miles of Tucson, when we stopped for a short rest.

The citizens desired us to remain there all night, as they wished us to enter Tucson in daylight, where a grand reception was in preparation. You see, they were very proud of us! After considerable reasoning, they became very enthusiastic over the matter; but Father finally succeeded in obtaining their consent for us to enter that night. Four men went in advance with the joyful tidings of our arrival. We were expected about six o'clock p.m.; and were afterwards informed that the ladies and children had stationed themselves on the housetops, being too modest to mix in the crowd with men.

At about three miles from the town we were met by the procession, which was headed by four priests on horseback; but as we came in sight, they dismounted and ran rather than walked to meet us; the crowd, in the meantime was discharging firearms.

Before we reached the city, their number had increased to about 3,000; some discharging firearms, others bearing lighted torches; all walking in order and heads uncovered. The city was illuminated — fireworks in full display. Balls of combustible matter were thrown in the street through which we passed; at each explosion, Sister Euphrasia made the sign of the cross.

All the bells in the city were pealing forth their merriest strains. On reaching the convent we found our good Bishop [Salpointe] in company of several ladies and gentlemen awaiting our arrival. The crowd then fired a farewell salute and dispersed.

We feel truly grateful to these good people for their kind reception, as it is a convincing testimony of their reverence of our holy Faith. The Bishop conducted us to our dormitory; one of the priests brought us some water, and, after arranging our toilet, the ladies ushered us into the refectory, where a nice supper had been prepared for us. They waited on us at supper, and endeavored to make everything as pleasant as possible...

Sister Monica Corrigan, C.S.J., "Journal," 20 April 1870 to 26 May 1870, Archives, Los Angeles Province, Carondelet Center, Sisters of Saint Joseph of Carondelet, Los Angeles. Printed by permission.

86. Changes in Celebrating the Feast of St. Augustine, Patron of Tucson, 1881–82

These descriptions of the feast of Saint Augustine, in Tucson, reveal changing Anglo-American reactions in Arizona against Hispanic customs associated with public religious celebrations. Such antipathy was also found earlier in California and in Texas and led to the gradual elimination of these folk traditions once popular on the Hispanic frontier.

It was the custom of the early Spanish settlers of this country to name each mission which they established after some Saint in the Catholic calendar; and accordingly when Tucson was first established in 1648 it was named the Mission of San Agustin. As this patron Saint died on the 28th of August the celebration of that day has been regularly held here during two hundred and thirty-two years. In early days the celebration was solely a secular ceremony within the church, but as years flew on it began to grow into a general festival lasting ten days or two weeks, among the Indian and Mexican population.

Since the American occupation it has still augmented in importance until now it is the annual attraction for both Christians and sinners throughout Southern Arizona.

Up to three years ago the celebration always took place in the Court plaza of the city, near the church edifice of San Agustin, and the town received from $300 to $700 annually for ground rent from the owners of booths and gambling places. But as many scenes of drunkenness and ruffianism occurred which were considered beyond the pale of decency, the authorities finally decided that it should no longer be held within the corporation limits. Since then the festivities have been held just back of Levin's Park, which, although just beyond the city limits, is close to the business part of town.

Arizona Daily Star, 1 September 1881.

•

The commemoration is celebrated in the churches here by the usual prayers at mass and vespers, with perhaps a little more pomp than marks ordinary occasions. The profane feast consists of some public amusement, in this city principally gaming. In former years it was held within the city limits, at Military Plaza, the property being rented by the city fathers for such purposes...

The difference between the celebration here and in Sonora is great. In the different cities of that state the religious and profane feasts are in a measure but one, the latter being, however, subordinated, but not disowned by the church. Thousands upon thousands of people from neighboring cities and the surrounding country make this a sort of pilgrimage to the shrine of their saint, whose image is brought out in the cathedral and worshiped by his devotees. The cities wear a holiday appearance and are profusely decked and ornamented with flags and bunting. The throngs come to spend their savings and accumulations of the year and the merchants reap a rich harvest.

The latter was formerly also the case in Tucson, and many citizens of Mexico made this an especial time to visit Tucson to make their purchases. A large sum of money was thus brought to the city and times were lively and flush...

It has grown to be a licensed public exhibition of gambling, and possesses no attraction beyond the excitement from engaging in such sport. While the church celebration will always continue as a fitting mark of homage to the life and services of a great, able and good man,...the tendency to prohibit the profane feast will grow stronger and stronger each year...

> *Arizona Daily Star*, 28 August 1882, as quoted in George W. Chambers and C. L. Sonnichsen, *San Agustin: First Cathedral Church in Arizona* (Tucson: Arizona Historical Society, 1974), 22.

87. Yuma Indians Bury Their Dead, Yuma, Arizona, 1894

Women religious who served on the frontier frequently encountered resistance to certain western European cultural traditions and religious customs. In her journal entry, Sister Mary Thomas Lavine, C.S.J., narrated the conflict between the Catholic sisters and the Yuma Indians centering on death, dying, and the accompanying rituals at the Indian School at Fort Yuma, Arizona.

(1894) On the feast of Saint Augustine [28 August], Sister saw her first cremation. A man had died on the reservation after having been baptized. The Indians cremated their dead, and it was little use to interfere for they would dig up a body after an indefinite period. It had been customary to burn all a man's possessions even his animals, until the government issued an order forbidding their latter practice. When an Indian was near death, his relatives and friends began preparing for the cremation that all might be in readiness immediately after death. A deep trench was dug and beams laid cross-wise in its depths to form a lattice-work. On this the carefully dressed body was placed. All the while, the Indians kept up an incessant howling which began with death and continued for hours after. One man was appointed to converse with the departed Spirit. The sight of one cremation left a lasting impression, for few (sisters) cared to attend another...John had been the sister's right-hand man for many years. He liked best of all to drive the horse and buggy, feeling the importance of such a position. But now John was dying, his one wish to be buried in the mission cemetery...Knowing the Indians would steal his body he was loath to be left alone. A bed was fixed near the sister's quarters and Sister promised to watch by the dying man. By Good Friday night, Sister was tired from her vigil of two days. Sitting in the chair, she wondered about the long night. Hearing the Indians in the camp around, her only thought was to keep awake. But John was taking no chances...for his relatives plagued him about accepting the religion of the white man. How would he feel in

Funeral at Isleta Pueblo, New Mexico, ca. 1890.

Credit: The Huntington Library, San Marino, Calif. Reproduced by permission.

Heaven where all were Americans?...Realizing that she had dozed off, feeble as he was, he crept out of bed to her chair. Awake with a start she found the old man bending over her pulling her eyelids to arouse the sleeper...Mother Ambrosia insisted on watching for the remainder of the night (but she too fell asleep). With morning, she learned that John was gone, and in spite of every effort, (he) had been disposed of in the traditional fashion of his ancestors.

> Sister Mary Thomas Lavine, C.S.J., "Journal," 1893 to 1894 (collection no. 400-208.7); Archives, Los Angeles Province, Carondelet Center, Sisters of Saint Joseph of Carondelet, Los Angeles. Printed by permission.

88. Death of a Convert at St. Michael's Mission, Arizona, 1914

Native Americans developed spiritual expectations in their associations with mission schools, even as they retained their own concepts of spirituality. As Sister Mary Loyola wrote in her 1914 letter to the motherhouse in Pennsylvania, both whites and Indians recognized the validity of blended cultures.

This morning shortly after Father Egbert finished his breakfast, an Indian woman, the mother of Katharine Besh-la-que, came here looking for him. She said her old grandmother was dying and had asked them to go get the priest to give her baptism. Father hurried to get ready what he needed to administer Baptism, Holy Eucharist, Extreme Unction and took Gertrude Lynch with him to interpret and went off in our little cart. Katharine went home also, but she sat back of her mother on the horse [on] which she had come for Father. When the priest reached there the poor old woman was so far gone she could not receive Holy Communion. Father administered Baptism and Extreme Unction and after imparting the last blessing to this blessed soul, he came home for dinner. This afternoon a grandson of the old Indian woman came and said she had died and they wanted us to bury her in our ceme-tery. Two of the boys have now driven over to get the body and she will be buried as a Catholic tomorrow morning. Out of this old Indian's numerous children, grandchildren, and great-grandchildren only two — the girls we have at school — are baptized. They are all well disposed and surely this privileged soul will plead for them all when she enters into the Home which Baptism has given her a right to.

Friday morning — I started this letter yesterday afternoon and I had to leave it so often I gave up trying to get it finished. The last interruption came when one of the Sisters said the boys had returned with the body of the old Indian. I went down to look at her in [the] wagon to see how the Indians had arranged her before the boys would lift her into the coffin we had prepared for her. She looked so small wrapped in her blankets that you would think she was a little child about eight or nine years. We unrolled the covering, and there was the little old woman, lying on her side as if asleep. Her knees were drawn up and the Indians had tied them this way. This was what made her appear so short. Her dark and very much wrinkled face bore a very peaceful expression in spite of the daubs of paint on her chin, cheeks, and eyes. She had a wine colored velvet waist and a new very full dark satin skirt on. Her limbs up to above her knees were wrapped in kidskin and she had very pretty deerskin moccasins on. She had very expensive beads around her neck and the Indians had wrapped three new blankets around her body. She was placed in the coffin just as the Indians had arrayed her. The chaplain was here hearing confessions and he proposed burying her at once; so we had the funeral about 5 P.M. The body was taken to the chapel. Father performed the absolution. The Sisters sang as the boys carried the body out and up to the little graveyard on the hill. Father and the altar boys followed the body to the grave. Some of the Sisters and the children went also. This old grandmother was a person of note in her own family but true to their Indian custom of not looking at the dead, not one except Katharine, of her own family was at the funeral...

Your daughter in the Blessed Sacrament,
Sister M. Loyola

Sister M. Loyola, S.B.S., to Rev. Mother M. Katharine [Drexel], 24 April 1914, Records of St. Michael's, Ariz., Archives of the Sisters of the Blessed Sacrament, Bensalem, Pa. Printed by permission.

89. Vincentians Begin Ministry in Dallas among Exiles of the Mexican Revolution, 1914

In some areas of the West, Catholics of diverse cultural backgrounds melded together from the earliest contacts. As seen in this account from Dallas, international borders meant little in the pursuit of religious expression within one's cultural heritage.

Last Sunday morning at nine o'clock the first Mass was said in the newly organized Mexican church, with a large attendance of Mexicans. During the past week this mission was started by the exiled priests of Chihuahua, Mexico; many families were visited and a building on the corner of Griffin and McKinley Streets was rented for a chapel under the patronage of Our Lady of Guadalupe.

There are about three hundred and fifty Mexican families in Dallas and two Spanish Vincentian Fathers, Rev. Juan Litra and Rev. Manual Francisco, will administer to the spiritual wants of the Mexicans. These Fathers will live at the University of Dallas and every Sunday at nine o'clock there will be Mass in the chapel, and in the evening Rosary and sermon.

These Fathers were formerly in charge of the seminary and college in Chihuahua, until Gen. Francisco Villa expelled them after confiscating their church and convent. Ten of the Fathers sought refuge with their confreres in Dallas; two will remain in the city to tend to the Mexicans. In the near future the Fathers hope to open a school for the children, to be taught by Sisters from Mexico.

Entirely without means and trusting to Divine Providence and the generosity of others the Fathers have started this good work and are endeavoring to preserve and increase in the Mexicans the faith of their fathers.

Southern Messenger 22 (8 January 1914): 48.

Conflicts

90. Ending Hispanic Religious Traditions at Santa Clara College, California, 1851–52

Described through the eyes of the last survivor of Santa Clara College's first faculty, the following reminiscence reveals the conflicts at the first institution of higher learning west of the Rockies. The changes the Jesuits implemented in the 1850s provide examples of the cultural clash between the arriving Euro-American culture and the established culture of Mexican Californians.

When I went to the college in December, 1851, the studies and most of the recitations were conducted in a part of the old adobe building that flanked the church on the South side. Later, in order to enable the mechanics employed

by Father [John] Nobili to improve the condition of the school room inter-
nally, the school was removed temporarily to a detached building rented from
J. Alexander Forbes, who occupied and owned, under some kind of title, the
southern half of that old building and the lawn in front, as well as the garden
and vineyard in the rear. All the buildings and their appurtenant grounds of
course belonged originally to the Mission; but how, in the course of time, the
title to any part of them became vested in private hands, and whether so held
validly or not, I never knew, and did not busy myself to find out, as I might
have done had I been then what I afterwards became, a lawyer. Later we got
back into the first school room; but in the progress of the material improvements carried on constantly and vigorously by Father Nobili, the chief study
room was changed again more than once. The principal improvements that I
recall, not only in the school rooms and dormitories, but throughout all the
buildings that came into Fr. Nobili's possession and control, were new floors,
doors and windows, hard white-coat plaster on walls and ceilings, and new
furniture. These improvements were progressive, from room to room, as the
means, material and mechanical help at hand permitted. And as fast as made
they presented to the eyes of all residents a great transformation. The rooms
in the old building were dark and dingy, blackened by the smoke and obscured
by the dust and cobwebs of half a century. Many of them had earthen floors
and some of them had been used as stables. In one sense, therefore, Father
Nobili was another Hercules, as one of his grandest works was the conversion
of those old adobe Augean stables into clean and bright and beautiful school
rooms, parlors, and dormitories…

Early in the morning I had occasion to call at Father Nobili's room in
the front part of the building, next [to] the church, and from which there
was a view of the street and plaza in front. Looking out of the window I noticed and called his attention to a singular object immediately in front of the
church. Mounted on a common wagon, and lashed to an upright pole attached
to the wagon bed, stood a *stuffed Judas,* and native Californians, with tasseled
sombreros and gay calzineros, were engaged in the religious duty of thrust-
ing at him with swords and smiting him with clubs as they rode up on their
dashing chargers. Such a spectacle naturally attracted the villagers and passers
by, and a crowd soon began to gather. Father Nobili was indignant and went
out to order the removal of the effigy, but no one seemed willing to obey his
orders. In vain he remonstrated in vigorous Spanish, with vigorous gesticula-
tions. The Californians were bent on having their ancient customs observed,
and in equally vigorous Castilian, with equally expressive gesticulation, they
responded — "Es nuestro costumbre! Es nuestro costumbre!" [It's our custom!]
Finding no one willing to remove the effigy, he seized it himself and gave it a
violent jerk, which partially loosened the fastenings, and poor Judas fell over
on the head and shoulders of his liberator, to the merriment of the boys in
the crowd. This did not tend to mollify the indignant Father, and straight-

ening himself up, with very positive tones and gestures he commanded the actors to remove the wagon and its contents at once, *or the church would be closed and would not be open for Easter Sunday!* This threat brought the hidalgos to their sense, and they proceeded to wheel the effigy away some distance from the church. Meantime, three of the caballeros had lassoed a wild bull, and bringing him a prisoner to the spot, they lashed the unfortunate Judas upright astride of the bull, and set the latter free. The result can be imagined. The infuriated animal dashed wildly across the plain, his rider gradually slipping under his belly, but being still held there by the lashings, he was soon trampled to pieces, — and so, retributive justice having at length overtaken the traitor, the hidalgos were satisfied. That I believe, was the last time they undertook to practice their Holy Saturday "Costumbre" at Santa Clara.

And here it may not be inappropriate to refer to the last miracle play ever performed in the Mission Church of Santa Clara. It preceded by only a few weeks the transfer of the Mission property to the Jesuit Fathers. I arrived at Santa Clara just before New Year 1851. The old friar, Padre José Refugio Real, O.S.F., was then parish priest in possession of the church and what was left of the Mission property. A week later, on the night of Epiphany, — "el día de Reyes, — " there was to be a miracle play in the old church, and I went to witness it. I had heard of the miracle plays that in earlier times had been performed under the supervision of the missionary fathers to interest and instruct their half tutored neophytes, the indians, and I expected to be interested and edified; but I was disappointed. What the plot was and who the characters (except one) were, I have entirely forgotten. That one I well remember was Satan, who, it seemed to me, did not sustain his role with due solemnity. The audience instead of being simple minded indians gathered there to imbibe scriptural knowledge from object lessons and parables, was composed in good part of the newly arrived race — the Americanos — who came to laugh at the incongruous burlesque — and it was nothing else — except that to me it seemed a desecration; and I am glad to know that it was the last of its line.

B. J. Reid, "Early Reminiscences of Santa Clara College" (1901), 3–4, 6–8; Reid Papers, Santa Clara University, Archives, Santa Clara, Calif. Printed by permission.

91. A French Bishop and His Vicar Conflict with a New Mexican Priest, 1854

This 1854 account by Father Joseph P. Machebeuf (later bishop of Denver) reflects the hostility that erupted when European clergy came to have oversight for Hispanic churches during the mid-1800s. What Machebeuf and his bishop, Jean Baptiste Lamy, saw as reform, indigenous Catholics perceived as an assault on their own clergy and traditions.

My position was sufficiently delicate and difficult, for he [Rev. José Manuel Gallegos] was very popular with his set. I took advantage of his temporary absence in Old Mexico to take possession of the church and to announce from the pulpit the sentence of the Bishop, suspending him from the exercise of any priestly function.

Some time later, when I was visiting some Indian parishes in the mountains, about seventy-five miles from Albuquerque, I heard that the Padre had returned and was going to dispute the possession of the church with me the next Sunday. This did not alarm me, but I thought it best to be prepared, so I sent a messenger in haste to the Bishop to get a confirmation in writing of the sentence pronounced upon the Padre, and my authorization in clear terms to administer the affairs of the parish.

I returned to Albuquerque on Saturday night, and on Sunday morning I went to church an hour earlier than usual in order to be on the ground and ready for anything that might happen. What was my astonishment upon arriving here to find the Padre in the pulpit and the church filled with people whom I knew to be his particular friends. These he had quietly gathered together, and now he was exciting them to revolt, or at least to resistance. I tried to enter the church through the sacristy, but this communicated with the presbytery, which he still occupied, and I found the doors locked. Going then to the main door of the church, I entered, and assuming an air of boldness, I commanded the crowd to stand aside and make room for me to pass. Then, as one having authority, I forced my way through the crowd and passed up by the pulpit just as the Padre pronounced the Bishop's name and mine in connection with the most atrocious accusations and insulting reflections.

I went on until I reached the highest step of the sanctuary, and then turning I stood listening quietly till he had finished. Then all the people turned to me as if expecting an answer. I replied, and in the clearest manner refuted all his accusations, and I showed, moreover, that he was guilty of the scandals which had brought on his punishment. I then took from my pocket the letter which my courier had brought me from the bishop, and I read it in a loud voice. To finish, I called upon him to justify himself, or at least to answer, if he had any reply to make. But, not a word; he went out as crestfallen as a trapped fox and left me in peaceful possession of the church. I sang the high mass as usual, and preached on the Gospel of the day without making the least allusion to the scene which had just taken place.

A few days later, to repair his humiliating defeat, he went to the neighboring villages and used every means to arouse the people, and he succeeded in getting together twenty-five or thirty of the most influential and the richest, with some of his intimate friends from Santa Fé. These, profiting by the absence of the Prefect, who was an intimate friend of mine, came to me in a body, and, with an air of insolence and bravado, ordered me to leave the parish, adding that they did not want any of my administration, and if I did not go they would have recourse to other measures.

At that moment the good God must have given me patience and strength that were more than natural, for I answered them with firmness that I had come to take possession of the parish by order of the highest ecclesiastical authority, and that I would receive no orders except from that same authority. I told them that they might take such measures as they saw fit, but, like the sentinel on guard, I would not quit my post, and as the shepherd of the flock I was ready to die for my sheep rather than abandon them.

This short and forcible answer disconcerted them; they did not have a word to say in reply, but returned to the Padre to apprize him of the little success of their mission. They did not know that I was an Auvergnat. *"Latsin pas."* Never give up!

Hardly had they left me when the Prefect, whom some one had notified of the affair, came up in a fury. He had already given orders for their arrest and appearance in court, but I reasoned with him and finally persuaded him to drop the matter, for I was sure that such a course would be the best in the end. This, in effect, was the case for a reaction took place in my favor and several deputations waited upon me to offer their services and protect me if necessary. I thanked all of them for their good will, but I declined any protection, as I did not fear any trouble. This scene took place on Saturday, and on Sunday morning I went to the church unattended by anyone except by the sacristan, and the only change I noticed was that everyone I met saluted me with apparently greater respect than ever. There were only three men from Albuquerque who took part in the rebellion; all the rest were from the Ranchos, or villages on the land of the rich proprietors.

From that moment the Padre lost all hope of driving me away, and, abandoning the Church, he went into politics. There was no doubt about his talents, and he used them to good effect in his new field, for through them he worked every kind of scheme until he succeeded in getting himself elected to the Congress of the United States as Delegate from the Territory of New Mexico ...

> Joseph P. Machebeuf to his sister, Sister Philomène Machebeuf, quoted in W. J. Howlett, *Life of Bishop Machebeuf* (Pueblo, Colo.: Franklin Press, 1908), 192–94.

92. Padre Antonio Martínez of Taos Protests Bishop Jean Lamy's Tithes, 1856

In challenging Bishop Jean B. Lamy's policy on tithing and stole fees, Rev. Antonio José Martínez (1793–1867) protested the reintroduction of customs he had fought to eliminate in his native New Mexico. He later retracted his resignation as pastor of Taos to oppose what he considered to be Lamy's authoritarian and un-American actions.

Beloved Parishioners: In the year 1826 I began to serve you in spiritual things as Minister in charge, and as your Canonical Rector ... I was always generous and liberal with the people, and never made the full charges appointed by the ecclesiastical tariff, though, as they stand are as low as can be considered sufficient for the decent support of the Clergy. But seeing the unwillingness of the people to pay these charges I did not make them pay in full...

I have now to announce to you that, for the reasons that follow, I have been constrained to resign my Cure, and therefore to take my leave of you my beloved people. I do this with great sorrow for my inability to continue to serve you...

The first reason which leads me to resign is my advanced age of nearly sixty four years, and the bodily infirmities which I feel and which do not permit me to perform my duties as they ought to be performed. You will have observed that I have no longer strength to preach even a short sermon of a half hour or a little more, as I have usually done.

The second reason is that by a Pastoral letter and certain circulars the Parochial clergy are deprived of the faculty to administer the Sacraments and give ecclesiastical burial to the heads of families who do not pay tithes of crops, fruits, and increase of animals, with the strictness required by the canons; and that when such persons or any of their families ask for the administration of any of the offices of the ministry, they shall be charged three times the amount appointed by the tariff, half of which is to be paid to the bishopric. It appears to me there are two difficulties here: first, that the Parochial Clergy being prohibited to administer the Sacraments to such persons, even if they are at the point of death (in articulo mortis) they fall under the canonical censure pronounced against the priest who thus violates the interdiction; and it is the same if they give ecclesiastical burial; for such is the canonical rigor of this edict of our Superior. The second difficulty is in regard to the collection of three times the amount of the tariff [stole] fees from these persons, if they refuse to pay it. One must pay it out of one's own pocket, unless he exacts it against his conscience. I have already paid some of these fees, and the parties have not reimbursed me...

The last reason is, that the people refuse to assist in the repairs upon the church and cemeteries, leaving me to bear the cost of keeping the roofs in order, to provide wine and wax [candles], and other necessary articles for which there are no funds. This I cannot do...

On the 22nd of April I wrote to Bishop Lamy, asking him to send a Priest to take charge of this Parish, laying before him the first reason above mentioned — my advanced age and my physical infirmity. I did not then resign, but I told the Bishop that when he should send the Priest, I would send in my formal resignation. He has not yet replied, but I suppose he consents...

Taos
May 4, 1856

(signed) A. José Martínez

La Gaceta de Santa Fe/ Santa Fe Weekly Gazette, 24 May 1856. Translated from the Spanish.

93. Bishop Jean Lamy's Regulations for the Penitente Brotherhood in New Mexico, 1856

The popular religious culture of New Mexico in the nineteenth century included religious art (santos), passion plays, hymns about the passion (alabados), and the penitential Brotherhood of Our Father Jesus the Nazarene (the Penitentes). The response of the first bishop of Santa Fe, Jean B. Lamy, appeared in these "Twelve Rules for the Brotherhood of Penance" (27 October 1856), rules meant to curb superstitious customs which received occasional ridicule from non-Catholics.

Rule 1st

No individual, can be admitted to this brotherhood who does not profess the religion of the Catholic, Apostolic and Roman Church.

Rule 2nd

Every person, who desires to enter into the confraternity shall present his application to the President (Hermano Mayor) for his consideration and who after mature examination will determine the acceptance or non-acceptance of the candidate. In case of his acceptance he shall deputize certain brothers to confidentially collect information regarding the conduct of the pretender and if nothing infamous results against such a postulant, he may be admitted and delivered to the master of novices who during the year within which he is under his charge shall attentively and conscientiously watch his inclinations and in case he should discover some grave faults, which might be incorrigible he shall be obliged to inform the President (Hermano Mayor) the councellors and other officers of the brotherhood, so that they themselves may observe the conduct of the novice, and if being satisfied that all is according to the report of the master of novices, he shall now be allowed to form a part of the brotherhood.

Rule 3rd

All brothers must keep secret all matters that may be transacted at the meetings to be had and the President (Hermano Mayor) shall himself or through another notify the parish Priest in order that he may attend and be present at all meetings, if he so desires. If any one of the brothers should break the secrets he shall be severely reprimanded according to the disposition of the President (Hermano Mayor) and councellors and if he after being admonished should insist, he shall be expelled from the brotherhood.

Rule 4th

The individuals composing the brotherhood have to be moral and virtuous men in order that by their good example and virtues and obedience may induce others to a good life. But if some brother gives scandal, regarding the sixth, seventh, and second commandments, he shall be severely punished by the President (Hermano Mayor) and Councellors and should he insist he shall be expelled from the brotherhood.

Rule 5th

All brothers, who formerly formed a part of the brotherhood and who were not, due to some crime, excluded from it, or who are not actually in compliance with the foregoing rules may if they desire return to form a part of the brotherhood.

Rule 6th

If any of those who shall in the future be expelled ask to again become duly incorporated into the brotherhood, and when it has been proved after prudent investigation that they have mended their ways, these may be re-admitted into the brotherhood. But if they again should happen to offend, they shall be forever excluded from the brotherhood.

Rule 7th

The President (Hermano Mayor), Councellors and Aides are empowered to take part and know all matters and questions that may come up between the brothers concerning the good order and compliance by the brothers with their obligations. The First Assistant shall be the marshal, and in all matters which may seem difficult to him or where it is necessary to pronounce some sentence the Parish Priest, must be notified and given a concise, clear, faithful and conscientious statement of the facts and circumstances available.

Rule 8th

All and every one of the components of the confraternity must frequent the Holy Sacraments of Penance and Holy Eucharist particularly during the holy season of Lent, and if any one shall fail in this sacred obligation he shall be expelled from the confraternity forever and without being entitled to being again admitted.

Rule 9th

All and every one of the individuals of the Brotherhood shall obey and respect the legitimate Supreme Pastor of this territory, His Grace, the Most Reverend Catholic Bishop, Don Juan Lamy, and his successors in all matters which he may be pleased to ordain, whether it be this or any other matter and likewise in the same manner the parish priest, whom he may be pleased to place in this or any other point of his diocese without complaint or grumbling regarding the dispositions of these matters which the prelate may be pleased to ordain and anyone who having been duly advised should insist in so doing he shall be expelled from the brotherhood as unworthy of being a member of a Catholic congregation, the fundamental basis of which is obedience and charity.

Rule 10th

As in the foregoing rule, obedience and respect to the parish priest is prescribed and as the pastor is directly responsible to his prelate for anything
which might occur within the brotherhood regarding such abuses which
might be committed by some of the components of the brotherhood. It shall
be the duty of the president (Hermano Mayor) to deliver to the parish priest a
list of all the persons who may belong to the brotherhood so that he may be
at all times able to answer as to the conduct of each of the individuals and thus
foresee the slander that may be committed by some ill intentioned members
in the name of the brotherhood.

[Rule 11th]

Each president (Hermano Mayor) shall keep an original copy of these rules
duly signed by the parish priest under the strict responsibility not to permit
any copies thereof to be made so as to avoid in this manner the changing
of their originals either through malice or due to a bad scribe. In the same
manner they shall also receive their corresponding titles duly signed by the
parish priest.

Rule 12th

All these rules must be shown to all the individuals for their knowledge and
in order that they may not be forgotten they must be read from time to time,
it not being possible for anyone to interpret them at his will but they must
be understood literally. In case of doubt they must be referred to the parish
priest that he may determine the controversy after due consultation with his
prelate. The same method must be taken in case that any rule may have to be
added or eliminated according to circumstances.

The greatest and best method of preserving a brotherhood consists in the
good selection of its superiors. The angelic St. Thomas of Acquin used to say:
"Give me a superior who to his sanctity has added the virtue of prudence and
such a community will be well conducted." We must bear in mind also that
all nature tends to unity. The Divine Nature itself is admirable and undivided
in three persons. The Superior (Hermano Mayor) must always have before
him the examples of Our Lord Jesus Christ who humbled Himself even unto
death giving His life for the salvation of souls.

For the management of the brotherhood there shall be named as has been
customary all the officers with their same faculties and privileges endeavoring
at all times that said individuals be men of good behaviour, probity and above
all of good morals.

All the prayers which the Brotherhood of Penance has used having been
examined with all due care and attention and nothing having been found contrary to the Catholic faith the president and the others may continue the use
of same for their services and pious practices; but they shall not have the

Corpus Christi Procession around the plaza of Albuquerque, New Mexico, ca. 1875. Church of San Felipe Neri in center.

Credit: Reproduced by permission of the Huntington Library, San Marino, Calif.

power to add to or to subtract from any of them under the pretext of zeal, devotion or for any other reason without first consulting the parish priest and submitting them for his revision.

> Santa Fe New Mexico Sentinel, 2 February 1938, 12, and 9 February 1938, 16, quoted in Marta Weigle, *Brothers of Light, Brothers of Blood* (Albuquerque: University of New Mexico Press, 1976), 201–4. Translated from the Spanish.

94. A New Mexican Layman Explains the Role of Catholicism for Hispanics, 1878

While seeking tax-exempt status for their College of Las Vegas, Jesuits in New Mexico clashed with the territorial governor in 1878. One legislator, Princeton-educated Rafael Romero (1850–1919) of Mora County, articulated a native New Mexican's understanding of the relationship of Catholicism and American citizenship.

A great number of those who are here present are the descendants of those valiant and daring men of the proud blood of Spain, the oldest settlers of United States. Our settlements not very far from here are the most ancient over which the grand American flag flies. Our ancestors penetrated into these deserted and dangerous regions many years before the Mayflower floated over the dancing waves that washed Plymouth Rock. Some of the settlers came here resplendent in the gorgeous rich clothing of sixteenth-century *hidalgos*, soldiers of the crown, while certain other persons arrived quite simply dressed.

[They were] the noble and intrepid [Franciscan] soldiers of the Cross, whose more recent colleagues [the Jesuit fathers] give us in our own day proof of their commitment to and solicitude for the education of youth. The emigrants who disembarked at Plymouth Rock came under the flag of England. Our forebears arrived under royal pennon of heroic Spain. New England was colonized by men of a daring, valiant, energetic, unbending spirit — but in imitation of the false "standard-bearer of enlightenment," they committed the sin of pride and were cursed with the loss of their faith. New Spain, or what we call today New Mexico, was settled by equally fearless and forceful men who joined their pride to a wonderful courtliness. They were noble, friendly, and loyal, but they were at the same time endowed with a loftier concept of the Creator and possessed of a more refined love of their fellow men, and they rejoiced to acknowledge the supreme authority of God (*Applause*). Catholics settled New Mexico, people filled with respect for any group concerned with the culture and growth of Catholic faith and doctrine (*Applause*). And it is the most pleasant recompense for being true descendants of the ancient explorers of New Mexico that in the midst of all the troubles and changes of this world they have preserved the faith and doctrines of their ancestors, holding them all in the greatest reverence and considering them the object of their most sincere and obsequious submission. Besides the doctrines of the Catholic faith and on a human level, they honor the teachers of these sublime lessons by means of which man comes to disdain the delights of this earth and aspire to the glories of heaven. And among the expositors of these doctrines, as you are surely aware, the Jesuit Fathers do not occupy the last place . . .

The Savior God was tormented by a provincial governor, and we are not without a governor who has been playing a worse part even than Pilate (*Applause*). The Pilate of old failed by not protecting the innocent; our new one devotes himself to persecution (*Thunderous Applause*). And should I then put a muzzle over my mouth? Why should I fail to speak in my own home? Am I not a Catholic citizen of a Catholic land, New Mexico? And have I not, as a New Mexican Catholic, been grossly insulted by a pathetic public official? What does it mean when a man sent to be the governor of a Catholic land, in an official message directed to Catholic legislators and to our Catholic people, piles insult upon insult against a religious order of the Catholic Church? That man does this, and am I supposed to refrain from stigmatizing his language, on an appropriate occasion, attacking it as it deserves? Does he suppose that the sons of Spanish *hidalgos* need lectures on morality from those who style themselves "ex-Mormon bishops" and official vagabonds from "Western Reserve" [University]? I care nothing about the vociferation of the gang whose mouthpiece our present Pilate is, nor would I care to reply to them. All that I want is to let our foreign brethren [the Jesuits] know that we do not forget who we are and that as long as we keep our eyes on the enemy, we laugh at their attacks (*Applause*).

It is a beautiful cardinal principle of our creed that we distinguish between the individual and his deeds. We can reprove and totally execrate a man's bad deeds without asserting that the man himself is bad. In my ears always echo those terrible words "Judge not lest you be judged." So I denounce the evil deeds, but to the man himself I extend the cloak of charity and apply to him the consoling prayer of the Divine Master, "Father forgive him, for he knows not what he does" (*Prolonged Applause*).

Rafael Romero, Commencement Speech at Las Vegas College, 16 August 1878, quoted in Thomas J. Steele, S.J., *New Mexican Spanish Religious Oratory* (Albuquerque: University of New Mexico Press, 1997), 153, 155, 157. Printed by permission.

95. A *Morada* of the Penitentes Described by a Sister of the Blessed Sacrament, 1906

The cultural contacts among Roman Catholics in the Southwest often focused on religious practices dating from the Spanish era that Euro-Americans did not readily appreciate. The Pennsylvania-based Sisters of the Blessed Sacrament from St. Catherine's School in Santa Fe visited Abiquiu and viewed a morada of the Confraternity of Our Father Jesus Christ the Nazarene, the Penitente brotherhood, famed for its penitential practices.

We had not come to Abiquiu to view the scenery, but at the invitation of the pastor who had called on Mother Gabriel and asked her to send some Sisters out there that they might see for themselves how "Indian" these people were and so she might be persuaded to accept more of the children at St. Catherine's. Father seemed particularly anxious for us to get the children of the Penententes [*sic*] as these, he said needed to be well instructed in Catholic doctrine so that they would not fall into the errors of their fathers when they grew up. I think you heard about these Penententes. They are a society of men who call themselves "The Penitent Brothers." They have processions during Lent and especially on Good Friday in which some carry immense crosses, others have bundles of cactus tied to their naked backs while others discipline themselves to blood with disciplines made of a certain kind of cactus...

Miss Chavez took us to the house of one of the chief Penententes and asked for the key of the Morado [*sic*]... The first morado is built on a level space at the top of the hill. It is a one story adobe building with four rooms in a straight row, all facing the big black mountain at the back of the pueblo. Coming out from this house one could not see the pueblo at all but would have to walk around the back of the place to see it. The cleanliness of this place was remarkable, even the little plain outside the door seemed to be swept clean. The first room we entered looked like a chapel, there was a large wooden altar at one end of the room and on the wall back of it was a very large crucifix. The figure was all covered but we raised the cover and O! such a sight! The face of the image was awful and the whole figure was covered with daubs of red paint which made a very realistic representation of blood. Right beneath the cross was a statue of our Mother of Sorrows. The statue had a very woe-be-gone face and was dressed in black with a black lace veil over the head and the hands were clasped under a white apron. Any number of ugly little statues were hanging on the wall but the gem of the whole collection was the statue or skeleton which represented "death." It stood on the floor in the corner at the left hand side of the altar. It was a plaster figure made in a very good like-ness to a skeleton. The head or skull especially was so real that I believe it must have been a human skull which they plastered over. I believe we all, that is the Sisters were just a little frightened when we first spied this thing. The room was in semi-darkness as the only light we had was admitted through the open door at one end of the room. The whole figure of this wonderful thing was enveloped in a black cloak which was drawn up over the head and face leaving only the horrible jaw and the eyeless sockets visible. Strange as it was those very sockets seemed to glare in spite of their being eyeless. Instead of the proverbial scythe which "Death" carries this one had a bow and arrow set ready to shoot. After your first glance at this thing you instinctively step out of the way. The position of the figure and the poise of the arrow would make you feel sure you were the target. Sister Immaculate felt the thing was going to move and after a little gazing she conquered her timidity and went up to it and touched it to make sure it was neither human nor superhuman. Unlike other Mexican houses, the four rooms of the Morado [*sic*] opened into each other and we walked from one room to another without going outside... The fourth room was darker even than the first in which the chapel was and here in this room were all the penetentes crosses and instruments of penance. I do not think any of us would have believed that these crosses were what they really are if we had not seen them...

Letter, 1906, Sister Loyola, S.B.S., *Annals of the Sisters of the Blessed Sacrament* (1906–7), 9:34, 38–41, Archives of the Sisters of the Blessed Sacrament, Bensalem, Pa. Printed by permission.

96. Intermingling of Religious Customs at Cochiti Pueblo, New Mexico, ca. 1895

Memoirs of those who lived at mission houses often reveal rich insight into the relationship that existed between Native Americans and missionaries. This account, almost sixty years after the events, by Sister Mary Liguori, S.B.S., shows both the happy and the fractious encounters that grew out of personal commitments to religious identity.

On another occasion, Sister M. Philip and I were sent to Cochiti, New Mex-ico. This, too, was a midnight excursion. We went by train and as we alighted we found one of our large boys awaiting us with his team. It was about one o'clock when we reached his house where we were to pass the night. In those early days only a few Indians had a door on their house. To enter one had to climb a ladder to the roof and descend by means of another ladder indoors. The boy saw us safe in the room and then disappeared. This one roof in the abode contained an old table a few rickety chairs but no bed. It was late or rather early in the morning, and we were tired so we stretched ourselves on the floor and slept the sleep of the just. There was a nice little church but not a resident priest so there was no Mass or Holy Communion that morning. We always had a number of boys and girls at St. Catherine's from this Pueblo. These we visited and really had an enjoyable day with them. One of these girls learned to play the organ very well. In fact she learned so fast that soon she was able to play the High Mass on their Feast Day. This pleased the Indians very much. Every year on the 14th of July, the Feast of St. Bonaventure and patron saint of the pueblo of Cochiti, Mother would hire a team to convey several of the Sisters to help celebrate the great day. We really had to start on the day before as the roads were bad to travel, especially the Lavajado Road which was mountainous and at places, very steep. Often we feared we would fall over the precipice, wagon and all. On arriving at the pueblo, we had to cross the Rio Grande to get to Father's house at Pena Blanca where we lodged during that night.

The tom tom was heard at a great distance; the women went attired in their finest Indian costumes. The men and dancers, wore bright feathers on their heads. It was quite picturesque. On the arrival of the priests the church bells rang for Mass. Rosaria, the little organist, with her brother (who had met us at the station mentioned above) and several other boys who belonged to our choir at St. Catherine's had good voices and were there ready to sing their best at Mass. During the elevation at the Mass, three shots were fired in front of the church to announce the solemnity of the moment. After Mass it is customary to have a procession in honor of the patron saint. The statue of the saint stands on an improvised altar. Loaves of bread are offered to the saint and place[d] on the altar. During the procession the litany of the Blessed Virgin is sung. Several shots are fired at the altar of the statue. At the conclusion of these ceremonies, the signal is given for the Indian dance. It may be the Snake Dance, Eagle Dance, or Rain Dance — all performed in perfect order and rhythm. This kept up for hours at a time and the poor things never seem to tire of it, no matter how hot the weather. Thousands of white people attend these Indian feasts ... I must not forget to note a very edifying story about our little Rosaria, the organist. After she was married a few years she contracted tuberculosis and very soon succumbed. It is said that on her deathbed on seeing the Sacred Host raised before her she tried to get on her knees saying she was not worthy that our Lord should come to her. She had kept Faith in spite of the many bad examples of superstitious practices so common among the Pueblo Indians.

Another girl of this pueblo named Doroita Trujillo wrote me a letter one

summer telling of the conflicts she was having with her mother for not adoring the little gods she had on hand. As well as I can remember this is what she
said, "Sister, I was sitting in a room looking over a paper. I noticed my mother
getting her little gods ready and in order not to be asked to worship them, I
went into the back room. Very soon I heard her call, 'Doroita, come here and
adore these gods with me.' I told her I could not because it would be a sin for
me. My mother got very angry with me and would not speak to me." I think
she too remained faithful. Our Lord took her while she was quite young.

Here is another example of the heroism of one of our Indian boys. His
name is Juan de la Cruz Padilla, a native of Tesuque. He, too, refused to join
the superstitious practices of the Indians . . . Some of us went to the pueblo to
see the Indians but Juan was not at home at the time. We met his mother who
had since become blind and his brother who had also been at St. Catherine's
years ago. It was a real joy to see them. Juan de la Cruz felt so disappointed
at not seeing his old teacher that he begged a friend of his to bring him to
St. Catherine's to have a little talk with us before we left for our return trip
to Marty. I forgot to say that the poor boy, or rather, man, was blind . . . When
asked how he had been all these long years, he answered, "Well, Sister, I have
been blind for thirty years; but it's all right, it's God's will. You see, Sister,
when I refused to be initiated or to take part in the superstitious practices
they got very angry and made me suffer much. They it was who made me
blind, but I get along all right. I gather sticks for fuel and do other odd jobs. I
often talk to Indians and tell them they ought to give up their pagan religions
and practice the Faith they learned at St. Catherine's. But they won't listen
to me. You see, my house don't face other adobes, just because I won't follow
them. They go to Mass on Sunday mornings when the priest and Sisters come
but at night they are real pagans." I asked him if they really worship the devil
to which he replied, "Yes, Sister, they really worship the devil. Oh, Sister, I
am so thankful to God that I had the chance to go to St. Catherine's where
I learned to know the true God and all about the Catholic religion." I could
not help but admire his sincerity; and thank the good God that saints may
be found even among the Indians in spite of the terrible temptations and very
sinful examples to which they are exposed . . .

Memoirs of Sister M. Liguori, S.B.S., 1895–1952, written at the request of Sister
Mary of Lourdes, S.B.S., Records of St. Catherine's, Santa Fe, N.M., Archives of
the Sisters of the Blessed Sacrament, Bensalem, Pa. Printed by permission.

AFTERWORD

Thomas W. Spalding, C.F.X.

When, on 12 May 1893, Frederick Jackson Turner dropped his historiographical bombshell entitled "The Significance of the Frontier on American History," he turned a cautious statement of the superintendent of the 1890 census, that "there can hardly be said to be a frontier line," into an obituary of that three-hundred-year-old phenomenon in the nation's history — the wilderness frontier.[1] Prospective settlers knew better; nothing changed after 1890. Homesteaders continued to people the arid, empty regions on both sides of the Rockies and the vast Columbia Plateau in the same way as before. More Americans, in fact, took up land between 1900 and 1920 under the Homestead Act of 1862 than between its passage and 1900.[2] Even today frontier conditions exist in Alaska.

Homesteading was the most persistent and productive of the economies that carried the Catholic Church westward and planted it in parts of the nation where, after some ecological adjustments, small farmers throve. The Homestead Act of 1862 simply reinvigorated a movement in the Catholic Church that began with the Maryland Catholic diaspora: the small farmer's quest for a better life "out there." During the decades that the church in the East was overwhelmed by a transplanted peasantry turned proletariat, the church "out there" built a permanent demographic base of yeomen farmers. By 1900 farm families constituted nearly a fifth of the Catholic population in the United States (some 2,653,000 of 14,210,755).[3] But for the nation as a whole farming families in 1900 constituted almost three-fifths.

The heartland of rural Catholicism in 1900 was an expanse of twelve states of the upper Middle West stretching from Ohio to North Dakota. There approximately 1,140,000 of the estimated 2,653,000 rural Catholics were to be found. The Southwest, however, with only four states — Texas, New Mexico,

---

1. For a description of the "Turner Thesis" and the literature it provoked, see Ray Allen Billington, *Westward Expansion: A History of the American Frontier*, 4th ed. (New York: Macmillan, 1974), 1–11, 665–70.

2. Richard White, *"It's Your Misfortune and None of My Own": A History of the American West* (Norman: University of Oklahoma Press, 1991), 433.

3. These and the following numbers are taken from David S. Bovee, "The Church and the Land: The National Catholic Rural Life Conference and American Society, 1923–1985" (Ph.D. dissertation, University of Chicago, 1985), 28–32, tables 1–3. While only approximations for the rural populations, they are perhaps the best that can be calculated from available data.

Arizona, and California — counted roughly 381,000 farming Catholics, the next largest region in its rural count. Of the 335,000 estimated for the twelve states of the South, the state of Louisiana alone counted some 300,000. Louisiana, in fact, was the state with the largest number of rural Catholics. Over the next four decades, as the population grew, the percentage of Catholic farmers remained about the same. The religious census for 1936 revealed about the same proportion of urban to rural Catholics: 16,041,764 to 3,873,173, or 19.5 percent. This was a remarkable achievement in the light of the fact that the rural population of the United States had dropped to about one-fourth of the total population.

In 1900 a large percentage of Catholic farmers were first- or second-generation immigrants: 1,938,000 of the 2,653,000 total, or 73 percent. The other 27 percent would include old stock (many of Maryland descent), Hispano, Cajun, and third- or fourth-generation German and Irish farming families. But many of these products of the backwoods, the bayous, and the scrublands of the Southwest had worked the same farms from the opening decades of the nation.

Rural America is the twentieth century's residual frontier. To the extent that semblances of frontier life still exist today they are to be found in rural and small-town settings, where old ways persist the longest. "German can still be heard on the streets of New Leipzig, North Dakota," Kathleen Norris observed in *Dakota*, "where only a radical nonconformist would hang out laundry on any day but Monday."[4] Among central Kentucky families of Maryland descent and southern Indiana households of German ancestry the moral lessons and devotional practices inculcated by pastors Stephen Badin, Charles Nerinckx, and Joseph Kundek are still in evidence. Bishop Aloisius Muench of Fargo, North Dakota, argued in 1939 that only in the countryside could be found "initiative, prudence, thrift, courage, and other priceless virtues" that made for "the promotion of simple but wholesome and rugged living."[5] Turner redivivus!

The two most important legacies of the frontier, according to Turner, were genuine democracy and rugged individualism. With Catholic farmers today there is still little compulsion to be other than the small farmers their parents and grandparents had been, certainly egalitarian in all its implications. A rugged individualism is evidenced by a self-reliance born of subsistence farming. For many even today a visit once a week to the small town that came into existence to serve the simple needs of a limited rural hinterland is sufficient.

Other characteristics of Turner's frontier were simplicity, industry, hospitality, and sociability. Whether in central Kentucky or central Kansas one

---

4. Kathleen Norris, *Dakota: A Spiritual Geography* (New York: Ticknor and Fields, 1993), 126–27.

5. Aloisius Muench, introduction to *Manifesto on Rural Life* (Milwaukee, 1939), vi.

Many Catholic farming communities in the West continued to raise crosses on hills as their ancestors had done in the pioneering periods of the nineteenth century.

Credit: National Catholic Rural Life Conference photo collection, Archives of Marquette University, Milwaukee. Reproduced by permission.

finds in the Catholic farming community a simple lifestyle, less fastidious, less cumbered by the trophies of the consumer society that characterizes, by comparison, their suburban coreligionists. With simplicity comes a tradition of hard work. The physical endurance needed to domesticate the frontier can still be found among a people for whom minimum wage and maximum hours have little meaning. Of geographic isolation was also born a trusting hospitality at variance with the wariness of urban denizens and a need for such social interaction as country fairs, outdoor picnics, and barn dances, which still have their Catholic expressions at the parish level.

Weekly liturgies are simpler and more communal, piety less dependent on the variety of devotional practices still found in cities. Liturgical reform came out of an American heartland center: St. John's Abbey, Collegeville, Minnesota. Socializing before and after Mass, countryside processions on Corpus Christi and Rogation Days, blessings of the fields, cross raisings on knolls, all symbolize today an outdoor brand of Catholicism not far removed from frontier practices.

Rural Catholicism represented a distinctive way of life that was increasingly threatened in the twentieth century, a threat that gave birth to the Catholic rural life movement. Even in the nineteenth century, however, a back-to-the-land movement on the part of rural-minded bishops, especially in the colonization ventures of Bishop John Lancaster Spalding of Peoria and Archbishop John Ireland of St. Paul, served notice of the need to preserve and extend a way of life.[6] They first articulated what would become a popular theme of the Catholic rural life movement: rural virtue as opposed to urban vice and

---

6. John Lancaster Spalding, *The Religious Mission of the Irish People and Catholic Colonization* (New York: Catholic Publication Society, 1880); James P. Shannon, *Catholic Colonization on the Western Frontier* (New Haven: Yale University Press, 1957); Marvin R. O'Connell, *John Ireland and the American Catholic Church* (St. Paul: Minnesota Historical Society Press, 1988), chap. 7.

a belief that the small farmer was the quintessential American. The "agrarian myth" of Thomas Jefferson would remain a staple in the manifestos of Catholic agrarians.

The organization of rural Catholicism in the twentieth century began with the founding of the Extension Society in 1905 by Francis Clement Kelley, a rural pastor who wished to draw attention to the neglected rural church. By 1924, when Kelley was named bishop of Oklahoma City, Extension was estimated to have funded half of the churches built in the United States since the society's beginning.[7]

In 1923 the National Catholic Rural Life Conference (NCRLC) was founded by Reverend Edwin Vincent O'Hara (1881–1956).[8] From a rural parish in Oregon he was picked in 1921 to head the Rural Life Bureau of the newly created National Catholic Welfare Conference. From this base he called in 1923 a meeting at St. Louis that gave birth to the NCRLC.[9] Until his appointment as bishop of Great Falls, Montana, in 1930, O'Hara would remain the guiding spirit and theologian of the NCRLC. For O'Hara, Catholic farm life was sacred, even sacramental. Prolific farming families had a God-given mission to save the church in America from demographic extinction, a contention shared by his successors until the baby boom of the 1950s and new waves of immigration belied their often dire predictions.[10]

A worthy successor to O'Hara was Reverend W. Howard Bishop (1885–1953), pastor of a rural parish in Maryland.[11] President of the NCRLC from 1928 to 1934, Bishop was spokesman for rural Catholicism during the crucial years of the Great Depression. A critic of capitalist exploitation, he was a strong advocate of another back-to-the-land movement. In 1939 Bishop would found the Glenmary Home Missioners for the establishment of Catholic parishes in priestless parts of rural America, especially in the South. In the Depression years, meanwhile, the annual conventions of the NCRLC drew tens of thousands of anxious participants.

In 1940 Reverend Luigi G. Ligutti (1895–1984) became, as it turned out, the first full-time executive secretary of the NCRLC.[12] He had come into

---

7. Francis C. Kelley, *The Story of Extension* (Chicago: Extension, 1922); James P. Gaffey, *Francis Clement Kelley and the American Dream*, 2 vols. (Bensenville, Ill.: Heritage Foundation, 1980).

8. Timothy M. Dolan, *Some Seed Fell on Good Ground* (Washington, D.C.: Catholic University of America Press, 1992); J. G. Shaw, *Edwin Vincent O'Hara, American Prelate: A Biography* (New York: Farrar, Straus and Cudahy, 1957).

9. Bovee, "The Church and the Land," chap. 2; Raymond Philip Witte, *Twenty-Five Years of Crusading: A History of the National Catholic Rural Life Conference* (Des Moines: National Catholic Rural Life Conference, 1948).

10. Timothy M. Dolan, "The Rural Ideology of Edwin O'Hara: Analyze, Publicize, Organize," *U.S. Catholic Historian* 8 (fall 1989): 117–29.

11. Christopher J. Kauffman, *Mission to America: The Story of W. Howard Bishop, Founder of Glenmary* (New York: Paulist Press, 1991).

12. Vincent Yzermans, *The People I Love: A Biography of Luigi G. Ligutti* (Collegeville, Minn.:

prominence with his homesteads project in Granger, Iowa, in the Depression years. He would move the NCRLC headquarters to nearby Des Moines, Iowa, where it would remain until the present day. A towering figure, Ligutti became a familiar voice for Catholic rural America. As did the United States, the NCRLC under Ligutti went global, the conference tackling such problems as the refugee crisis and world hunger. Ligutti, a friend of popes, became the Vatican representative to the Food and Agriculture Organization of the United Nations.

One of the great contributions of these three charismatic figures — O'Hara, Bishop, and Ligutti — was to instill that measure of self-esteem badly needed by a segment of the Catholic population often dismissed or belittled by urban Catholics. This they did in great part by advancing a rationale for the moral superiority of rural life. All three were true believers in the Jeffersonian "myth" that such virtues as integrity, thrift, individualism, stability, piety, and family unity flourished on family farms.[13] They conveyed an antiurban bias that perceived the countryside as fertile, the city as sterile, especially in its acceptance of birth control, divorce, and other urban vices. Their rural theology elaborated the belief of Virgil Michel, Benedictine liturgist and ruralist, that Catholic life should be close to nature, "for the supernatural in the dispensation of God builds on the natural-rural life restores the natural basis of Christian living."[14]

Buoyed by such confidence, the NCRLC in the postwar years addressed such issues as poverty, hunger, and the exploitation of American minorities. Issues of social justice continued to dominate the meetings and publications of the conference in years of the power movements and War on Poverty. But changing patterns in American agriculture in the 1970s and 1980s redirected the energies of the conference to constituency service once more. Its principal concern became the survival of the Catholic family farm itself.

In 1980 the collaborative efforts of the forty-four dioceses of the heartland brought forth a major statement of concern, titled *Strangers and Guests,* signed by seventy-two bishops. "We are witnessing profound and disturbing changes in rural America," they declared. Agricultural production was being heavily industrialized and concentrated in fewer and fewer hands. "On much of the rural landscape now we see deserted and dilapidated farm buildings, dying communities, eroding soil, urban sprawl, and mining scars."[15] They were describing a trend that would reduce the number of farmers in America from

Liturgical Press, 1976); David S. Bovee, "Catholic Rural Life Leader: Luigi G. Ligutti," *U.S. Catholic Historian* 8 (1989): 143–61.

13. For the Jeffersonian "myth" as expressed in their time, see Richard Hofstadter, *The Age of Reform, from Bryan to FDR* (New York: Knopf, 1955); and Leo Marx, *Machine in the Garden: Technology and the Pastoral Ideal in America* (New York: Oxford University Press, 1964).

14. Dolan, "Rural Ideology," 120.

15. *Strangers and Guests: Toward Community in the Heartland* (Sioux Falls, S.D.: Heartland Project, 1980), 1.

25 percent of the population in 1945 to 2 percent in 1992. The number of Catholic farmers declined in about the same proportion.[16] As with other small farmers, many Catholic owners went into bankruptcy.

The villains were agribusiness, or the "factory farm," and the government policies of the 1980s that favored corporate farming. As the champions of agribusiness justified their expansion in the name of efficiency, spokesmen of the NCRLC countered with the argument that the small farm was not simply a business but a way of life and that the national character was diminished to the extent that small farmers disappeared from the land. This was the contention of the first of the two documents that follow (documents 97 and 98, below).

The heartland bishops demonstrated an equal concern for the environment, calling attention to a statement Pope John Paul II addressed to the farmers of the heartland when he visited Des Moines in 1979: "The land must be conserved... You are the stewards of some of the most important resources God has given the world."[17] It was a papal confirmation of the belief that the small farmer was the natural guardian of the planet. Increasingly thereafter NCRLC spokespersons inveighed against the destructive and polluting practices of agribusiness.[18]

As rural Catholic communities shriveled, the priest shortage exacerbated their plight. An increasing number of small and isolated parishes were forced to close, to the great sorrow of their parishioners, as document 98, below, poignantly demonstrates. Consolidation and personnel problems, especially the declining number of sisters, also led to the closing of rural parochial and Catholic high schools and to the curtailment of health care and other social services in a drastically altered economy that could no longer support them. Frontier conditions encroached again.

Yet Catholic agrarians remained hopeful. The good fight is still being fought. To commemorate the seventy-fifth anniversary of its founding, the NCRLC launched in 1998, as part of a larger movement, the Green Ribbon Campaign to lend moral support to family producers and to promote a cleaner environment. For Catholic ruralists it was a time for remembering: the hopeful planting in new lands; the hard and often strife-ridden beginnings; the gratifying advance of Catholic populations and institutions often in unexpected parts of the nation; the ever-strengthening identification of diverse Catholic populations with a church that responded well to their changing needs.

---

16. As estimated by the National Catholic Rural Life Conference.

17. See *Strangers and Guests*, 16.

18. See David Andrews, C.S.C. (executive director of the NCRLC), "Big Food Bad News for the Little Guy," *National Catholic Reporter*, 8 May 1998, 24.

97. A National Catholic Rural Life Conference Testimony before Congress, 1984

Bishop Maurice J. Dingman of Des Moines, Iowa, past president of the NCRLC (1976–79) and in its name, voices his concern at a congressional hearing for the plight of the family farm as a result of a government policy in the 1980s that favored the growth of corporate agriculture to the detriment of the family farm.

It would be very difficult to overstate the gravity of the situation facing our farmers today. Simply put, the family farm system of agriculture — upon which so much of our history and tradition were built — is in imminent danger.

Without immediate federal action, upwards of one-quarter of the farmers in the Heartland of our nation will be out of farming by the end of this year!

The fate of our family farmers is not an abstract concern. What happens to them will determine whether or not a land-owning elite will increasingly control our food, and the price of that food.

Family-farm agriculture is, we believe, the most sustainable, efficient, and community-supportive system yet devised to provide quality food to the larger community, and at an affordable price.

America's present course, supported and in many instances fostered by government policy, is destroying our family farms, ruining our resource base, and producing food which is increasingly raised with and adulterated by chemicals.

Our present course will result in ever more concentrated patterns of land ownership, with dire consequences for the survival of our rural communities and for the future of a functioning democracy.

Even though the NCRLC has been among the early voices attempting to alert the wider community to the dangers inherent in the present system of agriculture — a system that is as destructive to its human resources as to its natural ones — we are astounded at the rapidly escalating nature of the crisis...

Our rural communities are dying now — are we to anticipate the creation of a new wasteland of barren countryside with a "regional trading center" every 50 miles or so the only human communities left?

Since our nation's birth — and most immortally in the words of our great President, Thomas Jefferson — family-owned and operated farms have been a foundation-stone for the independent-minded citizenry. Economically self-sufficient, with strong family and community ties and responsibilities, such citizens provided key leadership and inspiration for the creation and development of a free republic...

In the Catholic tradition we have a noble role for government. Government represents for us the highest human organization for achieving the common good. In fact, a just government is that which most seeks to achieve the greatest good for the greatest number, all the while taking special care to nurture and protect the weak and the powerless.

We also believe that the wisest government, and the most just, seeks to act proportionately to the situation. The situation facing our family farmers is extremely serious. Without help, tens of thousands of them will no longer farm the land they love, nor produce the food we all consume.

Are not our food producers as important as the defense budget? Is not internal security and solidarity as crucial to a nation as its defense budget?

Are not our family farmers as good a risk, with as much long-term benefit to society, as the Lockheed and Chrysler corporations [which had been voted generous loans by Congress]?

Or is, indeed, our dream as a free and equal people dead?

If that is so, there will be no more fitting interment ceremony than bankruptcy for our farmers, and no more fitting gravestone for our family farmers than the windswept desolation of deserted farmsteads where once the pride of an independent people thrived.

"Testimony to Congress Presented for NCRLC by Bishop Maurice Dingman, 1984," *Catholic Rural Life* 41 (fall 1998): 35–36 (reprint).

98. The Demise of a Country Parish, 1997

Windthorst, Kansas, in what is today the Diocese of Dodge City, was founded in 1878 by the Aurora Colonization Society of Cincinnati for German Catholics. Although the parish was able to raise an imposing church, its fate was the same as many other small rural missions in isolated parts of the Great Plains.

It can't be separated. Faith and heritage are one and the same in this community that is centered on Immaculate Heart of Mary Church. And it's been that way for 119 years. The railroad didn't run through here; no businesses were established, no town developed, but that did not lessen the resolve of several generations of farm families. The church was always the center, providing a unifying element in their lives.

Immaculate Heart of Mary celebrated its faith and heritage with a Mass of Thanksgiving on June 8. The 350-seat church was filled with people who came to support the 48 households who today make up the parish. The church will be closed at the end of June as part of the diocesan restructuring process that addresses the current priest shortage.

The significance of this Mass was not lost on anyone. It was apparent in the songs sung before the Mass by the choir: "We Must Say Goodbye," "Wherever You Go," "Friends," and "The Church on the Prairie." Father Ted Skalsky, a 1964 graduate of Windthorst High School, [celebrated the Mass]...

In his homily Father Ted spoke of "exciting times" in the parish. When the parish built this their third church "to see the building rise...to see it tower over pastures and wheat fields. The excitement of the first Mass here, the many first Holy Communions, the baptisms and weddings. Those were exciting times on this hill in this community. It was a time when there were at least four families on every section of land.

"We come together on this sad and painful occasion in a very different time. The families are largely gone, because they couldn't make a living here. These are different economic times. And they are different times for our Church that has depended on priests from different lands...first German priests and later priests from Ireland. We as a diocese have never been able to meet our own need for priests."

Father Ted spoke...about the decision to close the church. "I do not criticize it, nor do I praise it...[L]et us accept it. We may not know what was God's will until we reach eternity. We must accept the things we cannot change. We must move on from where we are. It will not be easy, but don't let pain and hurt lead to anger and bitterness..."

At the conclusion of the Mass, [a parishioner] read "A Tribute to Windthorst Heritage" [that ended:] "Times are passing us by. Rural America is dying as are its churches. However, we hope that our cathedral on the prairie will stand forever as a symbol of another time, another way of life."

Southwest Kansas Register, 22 June 1997, 5 (written by Timothy F. Wenze).

ADDITIONAL SUGGESTED READINGS

Bagley, Clarence B., ed. *Early Catholic Missions in Old Oregon.* 2 vols. Seattle: Lowman and Hanford, 1932.

Baudier, Roger. *The Catholic Church in Louisiana.* New Orleans: Chancery Office, 1939.

Baumgarten, Nikola. "Education and Democracy in Frontier St. Louis: The Society of the Sacred Heart." *History of Education Quarterly* 34, no. 2 (summer 1994): 171–92.

Bayard, Ralph, C.M. *Lone-Star Vanguard: The Catholic Reoccupation of Texas, 1838–1848.* St. Louis: Vincentian Press, 1945.

Blanchard, Charles. *History of the Catholic Church in Indiana.* 2 vols. Logansport, Ind.: A. W. Bowen, 1898.

Bridgers, Lynn. *Death's Deceiver: The Life of Joseph P. Machebeuf.* Albuquerque: University of New Mexico Press, 1997.

Burns, Jeffrey M. "Building the Best: A History of Catholic Parish Life in the Pacific States." In *The American Catholic Parish: A History from 1850 to the Present,* edited by Jay Dolan, 7–135. Vol. 2. Mahwah, N.J.: Paulist Press, 1987.

Butler, Anne M. "Mission in the Mountains: The Daughters of Charity in Virginia City." In *Comstock Women: The Making of a Mining Community,* edited by Ronald B. James and Elizabeth Raymond, 142–64. Reno: University of Nevada Press, 1997.

———. "Mother Katharine Drexel: Spiritual Visionary for the West." In *By Grit and Grace: Eleven Women Who Shaped the American West,* edited by Glenda Riley and Richard W. Etulain, 198–220. Golden, Colo.: Fulcrum, 1997.

Cantwell, Margaret. *North to Share.* Victoria, Canada: Sisters of St. Ann, 1992.

Carriker, Robert C. *Father Peter John De Smet: Jesuit in the West.* Norman: University of Oklahoma Press, 1995.

Castañeda, Carlos Eduardo. *Our Catholic Heritage in Texas, 1519–1936, Supplement, 1936–1950.* 7 vols. Austin, Tex.: Von Boeckmann-Jones, 1936–59.

Chavez, Fray Angelico, O.F.M. *My Penitente Land.* Albuquerque: University of New Mexico Press, 1974.

Chittenden, Hiram Martin. *The American Fur Trade of the Far West.* 2 vols. Reprint. Lincoln: University of Nebraska Press, 1986.

Coburn, Carol K., and Martha Smith. *Spirited Lives: How Nuns Shaped Catholic Culture and American Life, 1836–1920.* Chapel Hill: University of North Carolina Press, 1998.

Crews, Clyde F. *An American Holy Land: A History of the Archdiocese of Louisville.* Wilmington, Del.: Michael Glazier, 1987.

Duffy, Consuela Marie, S.B.S. *Katharine Drexel: A Biography*. Bensalem, Pa.: Mother Katharine Drexel Guild, 1966.

Dwyer, John. *Condemned to the Mines: The Life of Eugene O'Connell*. New York: Vantage Press, 1976.

Engh, Michael E., S.J. *Frontier Faiths: Church, Temple, and Synagogue in Los Angeles, 1846–1888*. Albuquerque: University of New Mexico Press, 1992.

Garraghan, Gilbert J., S.J. *The Jesuits of the Middle United States*. 3 vols. New York: America Press, 1938.

Hoffmann, Mathias M. *The Church Founders of the Northwest; Loras and Cretin and Other Captains of Christ*. Milwaukee: Bruce Publishing, 1937.

Horgan, Paul. *Lamy of Santa Fe: His Life and Times*. New York: Farrar, Straus and Giroux, 1975.

Kelly, Mary Gilbert, O.P. *Catholic Immigrant Colonization Projects in the United States, 1815–1860*. New York: United States Catholic Historical Society, 1939.

Killoren, John J. *"Come, Blackrobe": De Smet and the Indian Tragedy*. Norman: University of Oklahoma Press, 1994.

Lamott, John H. *History of the Archdiocese of Cincinnati, 1821–1921*. New York: Frederick Pustet, 1921.

Llorente, Segundo, S.J. *Jesuits in Alaska*. Portland, Oreg.: Service Office Supply, 1969.

Louder, Dean R., and Eric Waddell, eds. *French America: Mobility, Identity, and Minority Experience across the Continent*. Baton Rouge: Louisiana State University Press, 1983.

Lyons, Letitia Mary. *Francis Norbert Blanchet and the Founding of the Oregon Missions, 1838–1848*. Washington, D.C.: Catholic University of America Press, 1940.

Mattingly, Mary Ramona, S.C.N. *The Catholic Church on the Kentucky Frontier, 1785–1812*. Washington, D.C.: Catholic University of America Press, 1936.

McAvoy, Thomas T., C.S.C. *The Catholic Church in Indiana, 1789–1834*. New York: Columbia University Press, 1940.

McGloin, John, S.J. *California's First Archbishop: The Life of Joseph Sadoc Alemany*. New York: Herder and Herder, 1966.

Miller, Randall M., and Jon L. Wakelyn, eds. *Catholics in the Old South: Essays on Church and Culture*. Macon, Ga.: Mercer University Press, 1983.

Moore, James Talamadge. *Through Fire and Flood: The Catholic Church in Frontier Texas, 1838–1900*. College Station: Texas A&M University Press, 1992.

Neri, Michael. *Hispanic Catholicism in Transitional California: The Life of José González Rubio, O.F.M., 1804–1875*. Berkeley, Calif.: Academy of American Franciscan History, 1997.

Norton, Mary Aquinas. *Catholic Missionary Activities in the Northwest, 1818–1864*. Washington, D.C.: Catholic University of America Press, 1930.

Oates, Mary J., C.S.J. "Catholic Female Academies on the Frontier." *U.S. Catholic Historian* 12, no. 4 (fall 1994): 121–36.

O'Connell, Marvin R. *John Ireland and the American Catholic Church*. St. Paul: Minnesota Historical Society Press, 1988.

Palladino, L. B., S.J. *Indian and White in the Northwest: Or a History of Catholicity in Montana*. Baltimore: John Murphy, 1894.

Paré, George. *The Catholic Church in Detroit, 1701–1888*. Detroit: Gabriel Richard, 1951.

Peterson, Jacqueline. "Sacred Encounters in the Northwest: A Persistent Dialogue." *U.S. Catholic Historian* 12, no. 4 (fall 1994): 37–48.

Peterson, Susan C., and Courtney Ann Vaughn-Roberson. *Women with Vision: The Presentation Sisters of South Dakota, 1800–1985.* Urbana: University of Illinois Press, 1988.

Pillar, James J., O.M.I. *The Catholic Church in Mississippi, 1837–1865.* New Orleans: Hauser Press, 1964.

Rohrbough, Malcolm J. *The Trans-Appalachian Frontier: People, Societies, and Institutions, 1775–1850.* Belmont, Calif.: Wadsworth, 1990.

Rothensteiner, John. *History of the Archdiocese of St. Louis.* 2 vols. St. Louis: privately printed, 1928.

Rummel, Leo, O.Praem. *History of the Catholic Church in Wisconsin.* Madison: Wisconsin State Council, Knights of Columbus, 1976.

Salpointe, Jean Baptiste. *Soldiers of the Cross: Notes on the Ecclesiastical History of New Mexico, Arizona, and Colorado.* Banning, Calif.: St. Boniface's Industrial School, 1898.

Schauinger, J. Herman. *Cathedrals in the Wilderness.* Milwaukee: Bruce Publishing, 1952.

Schoenberg, Wilfred P., S.J. *A History of the Catholic Church in the Pacific Northwest, 1743–1983.* Washington, D.C.: Pastoral Press, 1987.

Schoofs, Robert. *Pioneers of the Faith.* Revised by Fay Wren Midkiff, edited by Louis Boeynaems. Honolulu: Sturgis Printing, 1978.

Shannon, James P. *Catholic Colonization on the Western Frontier.* New Haven: Yale University Press, 1957.

Stritch, Thomas. *The Catholic Church in Tennessee.* Nashville: Catholic Center, 1987.

Szasz, Ferenc M., and Margaret Connell Szasz. "Religion and Spirituality." In *The Oxford History of the American West,* edited by Clyde A. Milner II, Carol A. O'Connor, and Martha A. Sandweiss, 359–91. New York: Oxford University Press, 1994.

Walsh, Henry L., S.J. *Hallowed Were the Gold Dust Trails: The Story of the Pioneer Priests of Northern California.* Santa Clara: University of Santa Clara Press, 1946.

Webb, Ben J. *The Centenary of Catholicity in Kentucky.* Louisville: Charles A. Rogers, 1884.

Weber, Francis J. *Century of Fulfillment: The Roman Catholic Church in Southern California, 1840–1947.* Mission Hills, Calif.: Archival Center, 1990.

Wright, Robert E., O.M.I. "Pioneer Religious Congregations of Men in Texas before 1900." *Journal of Texas Catholic History and Culture* 5 (1994): 65–90.

Yzendoorn, Reginald. *History of the Catholic Mission in the Hawaiian Islands.* Honolulu: Honolulu Star-Bulletin, 1927.